Theodore Roosevelt's
Naval Diplomacy

Henry J. Hendrix

Theodore Roosevelt's Naval Diplomacy

The U.S. NAVY and the
BIRTH of the
AMERICAN CENTURY

NAVAL INSTITUTE PRESS
Annapolis, Maryland

Naval Institute Press
291 Wood Road
Annapolis, MD 21402

Library of Congress Cataloging-in-Publication Data
Hendrix, Henry J.

  Theodore Roosevelt's naval diplomacy : the U.S. Navy and the birth of the American century / Henry J. Hendrix.
    p. cm.
  Includes bibliographical references and index.
  ISBN 978-1-59114-363-5 (acid-free paper) 1. United States—Foreign relations—1901–1909. 2. Roosevelt, Theodore, 1858-1919. 3. United States—History, Naval—20th century. 4. United States. Navy—History—20th century. 5. United States. Navy—Cruise, 1907-1909. 6. National security—United States—History—20th century. I. Title.

  E756.H46 2009

  973.91'1092—dc22

                                     2009009085

Printed in the United States of America on acid-free paper

14 13 12 11 10 09   9 8 7 6 5 4 3 2
First printing

Book design: David Alcorn, Alcorn Publication Design

Contents

	Acknowledgments	ix
	Prologue: The Sailing of the Great White Fleet	xiii
chapter one	Roosevelt, Navalism, and the Monroe Doctrine	1
chapter two	Overwhelming Force and the Venezuelan Crisis of 1902–1903	25
chapter three	Scalable Response in Defense of the Panamanian Revolution	54
chapter four	Morocco and the Limits of Naval Power	82
chapter five	The Unlikely Location: Making Peace at the Portsmouth Navy Yard	104
chapter six	T. R., Technology, and Transformation	132
chapter seven	The Great White Fleet and the Birth of the American Century	155
	Notes	177
	Bibliography	205
	Index	221

Acknowledgments

I am forty-two years old as I write these words and complete this book. Forty-two is an odd time in life to become an author, especially with my "day job" as an action officer in the Office of the Secretary of Defense. Suffice to say that I have arrived at this point in my life only because of the support of a multitude of people. As a proper American individualist who hails from the cornfields of Indiana, I am usually repulsed by the popular notion that "it takes a village," but in this case it has been all too true. My life and this book have been greatly aided by a series of teachers, organizations, and family members who have supported me in my intellectual odyssey over the past thirteen years.

Mrs. Melva Eddy was my English teacher in high school, and her challenge to me within the classroom was so exacting that when I arrived at Purdue University the only subject that I did not have trouble with was English. She made me believe that I could write something that someone else would want to read. She left a huge hole in my hometown when cancer took her in 2004. Dr. Claude A. Buss was my lead thesis adviser at the Naval Postgraduate School. A career foreign service officer whose commission was signed by Herbert Hoover, Dr. Buss encouraged me in my passion for history and refined my writing skills. I keep a tattered copy of his *Who's Who* entry in my wallet to remind me what a real life of accomplishment looks like. Dr. David Rosenberg, a superb historian and a Naval Reserve officer to boot, guided me toward my eventual method of utilizing operational history to examine diplomatic incidents. He continues to mentor me to this day.

Organizations have also had their impact upon me. I joined the Theodore Roosevelt Association in 1994 shortly after I became a member of the USS *Theodore Roosevelt*'s crew. The association's longtime executive director, Dr. John A. Gable, quickly took me under his wing, not only encouraging me in my writing and research, but also making an effort to introduce me to other Roosevelt historians. Sadly, he passed away before I could complete my doctoral research, but I still feel his presence in my life. When John left us, Professor William Tilchin stepped in to fill his shoes as the editor of the

Theodore Roosevelt Association Journal, and as my sounding board and friend. Other leading members of the Theodore Roosevelt Association as well as members of the Roosevelt family have each taken their turn in providing me with guidance, and I am deeply grateful.

No scholar of U.S. naval history could succeed without the assistance of the Naval History Center at the Washington Navy Yard. Its library and archives have become a home away from home for me, and I love nothing better than to be ensconced in a study carrel there with my laptop open, surrounded by books, letters, and journals. My education and research were supported financially by the center, which twice honored me with its Samuel Eliot Morison scholarship as well as its Rear Adm. John D. Hayes Predoctoral Fellowship. I extend special gratitude to Dr. Edward Marolda, until recently the center's Senior Historian, who befriended me in 1997 and invited me to present a paper at a conference on the topic of the Spanish-American War. Since then, he has read nearly every word I have written, including my doctoral thesis. He is truly a scholar and a gentleman.

Dr. Marolda may have read everything I have written, but it is by the editorial efforts of the staff at the U.S. Naval Institute at Annapolis that these words have made their way to you. The two Freds—Fred Rainbow and Fred Schultz—longtime editors of the Naval Institute's *Proceedings* and *Naval History Magazine,* refined my early efforts and actively helped me to become a better writer. Many of the facts contained in this book made their first appearance in articles published in these two journals. With their assistance, I became a member of the institute's editorial board and board of directors, which introduced me to the rest of the dedicated staff of this great organization, including Adam Kane. Adam and my copy editor, Mindy Conner, worked hard to overcome my awful habit of speaking in a historical, passive voice, as well as dealing with the inconsistent nature of my personal and professional schedule. I am deeply honored by my association with these individuals and the entire staff of the Naval Institute.

In August 2003 I was fortunate to be assigned as a Federal Executive Fellow to the Weatherhead Center for International Affairs at Harvard University. While there, I interacted with twenty-one of the most interesting individuals I have ever met. Our daily discussions covered all manner of topics on diplomacy and international security. Our shepherd along the way was Dr. Kathleen Molony, the fellows' program director, who served up interesting speakers and events for our consumption. While at Harvard, I had the opportunity to take a degree under the direction of two distinguished diplomatic historians, Professor Akira Iriye and Professor Ernest May. Exposure to the individuals at the Weatherhead Center and to Professors Iriye and May convinced me that it was time to take the step toward a Ph.D., literally the turning point of my adult professional life.

This decision led me to the War Studies Department at Kings College, London. I was blessed to work there with Dr. Alan James and Professor Andrew Lambert in the development of my doctoral thesis. Andrew Lambert, a distinguished naval historian in every sense of the phrase, made a special effort to shepherd me through the ensuing process, working closely with me, mostly at extreme distances, over the three years that followed. As I wrote most of my dissertation while at sea, Andrew would review each chapter quickly and mail his comments back to me via British airmail. It was quite an experience. The fact that I can claim the title "Doctor" today is largely owing to Professor Lambert.

I have also been mentored by three senior officers of the U.S. Navy. Adm. Frank Pandolfe, Adm. Patrick Walsh, and Adm. James Stavridis, each a Ph.D. and each a brilliant operational commander, took the time to guide me as I pursued both my professional and educational goals. Their example served to inspire me, letting me believe that a serving line officer of the U.S. Navy could manage a squadron, his family life, and a doctoral dissertation simultaneously. Admiral Stavridis, author of several books and the current Combatant Commander of the Southern Command in Miami, Florida, was particularly attentive to my progression. He was instrumental in bringing me to the attention of the Naval Institute, and when it came time to pursue orders, he was there to guide me again.

No acknowledgment could be complete without mentioning my parents, Jerry Hendrix and Roger and Carol Cannon. I am a product of all three of their personalities, dreams, and aspirations. They provided me with a solid moral base, a sense of dedication, and a belief in myself. They taught me how to work hard, to be honorable, and to seek justice for others. I am where I am in life because of their example. A farm is a wonderful place to grow up, and to dream.

I have two daughters, Amanda and Michaela, who served as sources of constant, joyful interruptions in the development of this book. They are gorgeous, athletic, and intelligent young ladies who inspire me to be a better man. Their births answered for me the age-old question of "who am I?" When I look at them, I know that military rank, education, and job aside, I am Amanda and Michaela's daddy, and that is somehow enough for me.

Finally, there is my wife, Penny. I have known her all of my life, and there is nothing about me that she does not intrinsically understand. She is my frequent literary critic, emotional backstop, and best friend. Twenty years ago I asked for her hand, and to this day, walking down the street, I still find simple joy in holding it within my own. With all that is going on in my life, she makes our family's activities run on time. It is because of to her constant and abiding love that my dreams have migrated from travel to foreign lands to thoughts of being ever at her side, and forsaking the selfish sea.

Prologue: The Sailing of the Great White Fleet

A man-of-war is the best Ambassador.
OLIVER CROMWELL

On 16 December 1907 Theodore Roosevelt stood on the windswept quarterdeck of the presidential yacht *Mayflower* grinning large white teeth as he tipped his hat to each of the sixteen Atlantic Fleet battleships whose guns blazed in presidential salute as they steamed past. "Did you ever see such a fleet and such a day?" Roosevelt asked in boyish wonder as the fleet disappeared from view and his own yacht turned back toward Washington, D.C. Slowly the signal flags that had flown from the *Mayflower*'s halyards throughout the ceremony were brought down. The message the flags spelled out, "Proceed on your assigned duty," was insufficient to convey the full importance of the fleet's mission.[1]

One man who did understand the implications of Roosevelt's interrelated military and diplomatic policies was Rear Adm. Robley Evans, a Civil War and Spanish-American War veteran on the last assignment of a remarkable career. Evans' sixteen battleships were the most modern units in the American Navy. The hull of the USS *Connecticut* had been in the water less than a year, while the oldest of the ships, the USS *Kearsarge,* had not yet reached the age of eight.[2] Each burned coal for fuel, carried no less than a 12-inch main battery, and displaced between 11,500 and 16,000 tons.[3] The ships represented a naval wall of steel that Roosevelt had worked arduously his entire adult life to build, bringing the U.S. Navy from a seventh-place ranking up to the third (and soon to be second) largest fleet in the world. The ships were intended to shield the United States from its enemies, and now they sailed toward the Pacific Ocean at the behest of their patron, denuding the Atlantic of an effective combat force.

Described in the press as a "practice cruise," the fleet's movement was in fact a blunt signal of coercive diplomacy to the Japanese, who were engaging in a bit of saber rattling after U.S. immigration policies restricted the freedom of Japanese citizens to immigrate to the United States.[4] Roosevelt, writing to a fellow Harvard alum who was Japanese, remarked, "Nothing during my Presidency has given me more concern than these troubles."[5]

Asians, mostly Chinese, had been providing a reliable pool of cheap labor on the western coast of the United States for some time. Following Japan's victory in the Russo-Japanese War, its citizens joined the movement and soon made up the largest percentage of newly arrived immigrants in California. Although European Americans welcomed them as laborers, they did not consider Asians their equals. San Francisco's school board in 1906 passed a law requiring Japanese children to attend a segregated school that had been built for the children of Chinese and Korean immigrants.[6] Roosevelt worked out a gentleman's agreement in which the United States would not pass segregationist immigration policies and Japan would voluntarily restrict the movement of its citizens to the United States; but that did not put the matter to rest.[7] Later in May 1907 racial tensions burst into full-scale riots in San Francisco and other large cities where Japanese had settled.[8] Populist press outlets fanned the flames of unrest, drumming up fears of a yellow menace from the East and the possibility of war with recently victorious Japan.[9]

Americans were not the only ones being led toward conflict. Japan, having defeated a white Great Power, was in no mood to accept second-class status behind any other race or nation.[10] The island nation had struggled for fifty years to reverse the unequal treaties that had been forced on it when it was involuntarily "opened," and treatment of Japanese as one of the "lesser races" was an insult Japan would not tolerate.[11] The Japanese press began talking of war.[12] Concerns arose about the safety of the new U.S. possessions in Hawaii and the Philippines, and Roosevelt moved quickly to demonstrate his resolve to defend the new territories. He had a plan in mind to remind Japan that the United States was not a nation at whom one could rattle sabers without consequences. A letter to his son at the onset of the crisis summed up the scope of this plan: "I tell you I feel mighty glad to think of all these battleships, now that there is friction with Japan."[13]

Theodore Roosevelt had foreseen growing tensions with Japan and had tasked the Navy's General Board, a loose-knit planning committee comprising active and retired officers such as Admiral of the Navy George Dewey and renowned strategist Capt. Alfred T. Mahan, to compose a response.[14] The General Board lay at the center of Roosevelt's expanding naval engagement strategy. At his direction, its members had formulated a series of exercises and war games that inexorably pressed the influence of the American Navy outward, first dominating the Western Hemisphere, then moving into the

Mediterranean and the waters around Africa. Now Roosevelt instructed the board to confront the broad expanse of the Pacific theater and the rising Japanese threat.

On 18 June 1907 Admiral Dewey submitted the board's suggestions in a letter to the president. While Dewey's letter included a wide range of recommendations, the board's preeminent advice was that "the battle fleet be assembled and dispatched to the Orient as soon as practicable." Other naval leaders, however, were quick to point out that such a movement came with inherent challenges. There were not enough bases or dry docks on the West Coast to service the battle fleet, and there would be even less support should a mechanical failure occur after the fleet left American waters. Additionally, each day the battle fleet consumed a tremendous amount of supplies, including coal, which was not abundant in most Pacific ports. Any movement of the fleet into Asian waters would require a series of long-lead preparations to ensure a smooth operation. In particular, the board recommended that a large supply of coal be laid up at Subic Bay in the Philippines.[15]

Fortunately, the General Board had spent the better part of two years drafting a training exercise whose central aim was to sail the Atlantic Fleet into the Pacific. The board's effort would provide the basis for more detailed decisions once Roosevelt's full intentions were known. On 27 June 1907 a delegation comprising the secretary of the Navy, an admiral, and an Army general arrived at Sagamore Hill, the president's home at Oyster Bay, New York, to present options to the commander in chief and receive his orders. Immediately after the meeting, orders were issued to begin moving coal and defensive guns to the naval anchorage at Subic Bay and to recall the Asiatic Fleet's cruiser squadron from Hong Kong to the West Coast. Roosevelt also endorsed Dewey's recommendation to move the battle fleet into the Pacific, ostensibly to visit ports in California, Oregon, and Washington.

Probably the most important question raised during the hour-and-a-half-long meeting was how many battleships to send. Earlier in the year Captain Mahan, who was by now retired, had read that Roosevelt was considering sending battleships into the Pacific in response to aggressive statements from Japan. Mahan's strategic paradigm allowed no division of the battleship fleet, and he wrote to enjoin Roosevelt from considering any plan to apportion the Navy between the two oceans. The president, no minor naval strategist himself, responded somewhat curtly, "Don't you know me well enough to believe that I am quite incapable of such an act of utter folly as dividing our fighting fleet?"[16] Hence, when the delegation at Sagamore Hill asked the president how many battleships he wanted to send, the notes of the meeting recorded that he said, "If the Navy has fourteen ready, he wanted fourteen to go; if sixteen, eighteen, or twenty, he wanted them all to go."[17]

Preparations for the move to the Pacific soon began in earnest. Following an early June naval review as part of the Jamestown Exposition organized to celebrate the 300th anniversary of the settlement at Jamestown, the fleet cruised off Cape Cod conducting gunnery exercises. After six days of fleet maneuvers in September, the ships all returned to their homeports for final maintenance and resupply before reassembling in Hampton Roads, Virginia, in December.

On 31 August 1907 the State Department had issued a circular to embassies and legations throughout Central and South America informing them of the fleet's itinerary and its refueling requirements. The crews would receive liberty in Rio de Janeiro and Callao. Rear Admiral Evans expected to confer with port authorities on his arrival.[18] The American representatives in residence in the various Latin American locales immediately set about determining how to leverage the impending display of overwhelming naval power to forward the nation's foreign policy. It would not be a difficult process. Having served Theodore Roosevelt's administration for nearly seven years, these diplomats had grown comfortable with his tendency to promote American interests with naval power.

The association of Theodore Roosevelt with the U.S. Navy that persisted throughout the twentieth century is certainly no accident. Even at the dawn of the twenty-first century, American sailors regard him as the Navy's patron. The date set aside as Navy Day, 27 October, is in fact his birthday. The reasons for Roosevelt's stature are many. At the time of his entry into public life, the United States was a third-rate power with a fifth-rate navy. When he left the presidency in March 1909, the United States sat firmly in the first tier of Great Powers, and almost by shear force of will Roosevelt had created the second most powerful navy on earth. Linking his success with the Great White Fleet and his bellicose claims that he "took Panama" is too simplistic, though. Of the men whom historians rank as "great" American presidents, Roosevelt stands alone as a man who achieved his status in the absence of war or major domestic disturbance. His fame stands as a testament to his deft handling of diplomacy and his constant preparation for conflict.

If "Speak softly and carry a big stick and you will go far" is the expression most often associated with Theodore Roosevelt, certainly the voyage of the "Great White Fleet" best epitomizes the "big stick" aspect of his diplomacy.

The perception of Roosevelt as a martial figure, however, stands in stark contrast to the underlying fact that his presidency was unblemished by a war or major conflict. The evolving narratives of both diplomatic and military (naval) historians do not adequately explain Roosevelt's success in this regard. Diplomatic historians, focusing on archival records of the State Department and various foreign ministries, have questioned Roosevelt's role and effectiveness in some of the major international events of his day.[19] Naval historians have focused either at the microlevel, on events that occurred within the span of Roosevelt's service as president, or have taken a top-down, macrolevel look at his efforts to build up the Navy. Both approaches fall short in that they fail to fully discern the interrelated nature of Roosevelt's foreign and military policies—the fact that Roosevelt could speak softly because he had a "big stick."

This book seeks to explain how Theodore Roosevelt utilized naval power to support a foreign policy that fundamentally altered the trajectory of the United States from inward development to outward participation in the dialogue of nations. He is a curious character, so multifaceted that a complete understanding of his policies and motivations eludes modern scholars, yet his voice still rings out in strident, somewhat high-pitched, clipped tones. It speaks to Americans of peace and preparedness, of imperial power and civil reform, of ceremonial tradition and technological innovation, and of national honor and personal integrity—issues that have not lost their relevance with the passage of time. Even today, preoccupied as we are with global terrorism and crumbling international institutions, Theodore Roosevelt has something to say to us, if we will only take the time to listen.

chapter one

Roosevelt, Navalism, and the Monroe Doctrine

We're dining out in twenty minutes,
and Teddy's drawing little ships!
ALICE LEE ROOSEVELT, 1880

Roosevelt's Great White Fleet was not created in a moment of epiphany. It was an expression of his origins, his physical and intellectual evolution, and his own concept of where he stood in the world. The historian Henry Adams, a grandson and great-grandson of American presidents as well as a contemporary and friend of Theodore Roosevelt, fixed on him "the quality that medieval theology assigned to God—he was pure act."[1] Certainly Roosevelt's adherence to "the strenuous life," a phrase he coined, did come to characterize his public persona. He remade the weak body of his youth at his father's insistence and later joined in the rough-and-tumble life of Dakota cowboys. He played tennis, boxed (until he lost his sight in one eye during sparring), became a formidable judo expert, and was an enthusiastic point-to-point hiker. But it would be a grave mistake to define him merely as an embodiment of physical fitness.

By any measure, Theodore Roosevelt was also one of the great intellects of his age. He was conversant in three languages and able to read a fourth.[2] A speed-reader who could devour three books a night and then recall whole passages verbatim years later, he was a sponge for information.[3] He was a naturalist who could properly claim expertise as an ornithologist, paleontologist, zoologist, and taxidermist. The staff of the National Museum of Natural History consulted him on the setting and display of wildlife exhibits. An able historian and social commentator, Roosevelt wrote more than thirty-five books and was elected president of the American Historical Association.[4] In 2001 C-SPAN, a private nonprofit company created in 1979 by the American cable television industry as a public service, named him one of the twentieth century's most influential writers, highlighting his book *The Naval War of 1812* and his multivolume effort *The Winning of the West* as standouts in American historical literature.⁵ While serving as president, his cultured and sophisticated White House took social events to new levels and brought Old World protocol to the executive mansion of the New World.

All of these interests and abilities aside, Theodore Roosevelt arrived in official Washington in his late thirties with one striking claim that allowed him to stand out in the intellectual milieu that characterized the town. He was one of only a handful of men in the United States who could claim a preeminent reputation as an expert in naval and foreign policy. Where did this combination of interests find their origin in Roosevelt's background, and how did they mature over time? Specifically, how did a socialite from one of New York City's most elite families make the transition from a Harvard University freshman whose goal was to become a naturalist to one of America's first national security experts?

Early Influences

Born just prior to the Civil War, Theodore Roosevelt descended on his father's side from a line of well-to-do Dutch merchants who had lived on Manhattan for seven generations.⁶ Glassmakers by profession, the Roosevelts were among the elite in attitude, dress, and the society they kept.

The Rebel gray and the sea salt in his mother's bloodline directed the destiny of young "Teedie," as he was known within his family, in a dramatically different direction. Martha "Mittie" Bulloch Roosevelt epitomized the southern belle. Married to Theodore Roosevelt Sr. in 1853, she left a plantation home in Roswell, Georgia, to reside with him in New York but never abandoned her culture or her sympathies.⁷ Her children would later remember Mittie lying immobile on her couch during the Civil War, a physical symbol of the agony racking the nation. Theodore Sr., perhaps out of sympathy for his wife, or perhaps because it was what rich businessmen of the day did, paid a substitute to take his place in the Union Army. Regardless of his reasoning, he certainly knew that if he enlisted, his fragile wife would bear the awful burden of knowing that her husband was fighting against her brothers.⁸ While his son never voiced any criticism of that action, many historians would later attribute T. R.'s enthusiasm for war and his desire to prove himself in combat to an ambition to offset his father's lack of martial involvement in the Civil War.⁹ The elder Roosevelt's sympathies were never in question, however; he traveled between New York and Washington, D.C., raising funds for Union charities.

Theodore's maternal uncles, James and Irvine Bulloch, served with distinction in the Confederate navy. James, after early successes as a blockade-runner, masterminded the construction and launch of the famed southern commerce raider CSS *Alabama* and ultimately attained the rank of rear admiral.[10] His younger brother, Irvine, served in the *Alabama* as a midshipman and gained distinction as the man who "fired the last gun discharged from her batteries in the fight with the *Kearsarge*."[11] In the days following Robert E. Lee's surrender, both men visited the Roosevelts' New York home incognito prior to taking up residence in England, where, as unreconstructed Rebels, they spent the rest of their lives in exile.[12]

Young Theodore's loyalties during the Civil War mirrored his father's (he often prayed loudly in the presence of his mother for the ruination of the rebellious South), but he nevertheless held his maternal uncles in high esteem.[13] While the war was never mentioned (mother and father, for the sake of the marriage, had agreed to disagree), the children knew that when their father was out of the house, Mittie prepared baskets of supplies to be shipped first to Bermuda and then on to blockade-runners that would sneak them into the South.[14] Mrs. Roosevelt spoke glowingly to her children of her brothers' adventures, telling Teedie tales "about ships, ships, ships, and fighting of ships till they sank into the depths of my soul."[15]

Young Theodore met the subjects of these tales twice during his adolescence. His father, in an effort to improve the overall health and education of his brood, took the family on yearlong tours of Europe, Africa, and points of interest in between when Theodore was ten and again when he was fourteen. Each trip began and ended in England to allow Mittie to visit her brothers. An awed Teedie sat at the feet of the mythological heroes of his bedtime stories, absorbing firsthand the salt of their briny tales.[16] Their accounts ignited his imagination.

Restricted as he was by childhood asthma, books became natural companions for young Teedie and the sustaining fuel for his early interest in the sea. A prominent example of this influence was the nineteenth-century book by Capt. Frederick Marryatt (RN), *Mr. Midshipman Easy*. Cited numerous times in Roosevelt's *Autobiography*, it is a tale of a young officer torn between the freedoms of childhood and the harsh discipline of the British navy in the age of sail. Roosevelt "reveled" in such popular tales, and they sustained his appreciation of the age of sail throughout his young adulthood.[17]

3

The Naval War of 1812 and Other Works

One hundred years after it appeared, Theodore Roosevelt's first book, *The Naval War of 1812*, remains a mainstay of the historical literature surrounding the subject, for a number of reasons.[18] First, it is good literature, faultless in its sentence structure and grammar. Second, it reflects the first attempt by an American to conduct serious archival research and write an honest account of the war. The strength of Roosevelt's research has allowed his effort to hold up well against the challenges of time, despite new sources and 130 years of additional effort. The aim of every serious historian, this achievement is rendered all the more impressive by the fact that Roosevelt was only twenty-four when the book appeared.[19] Third, in this, his first attempt at serious history, Roosevelt demonstrated a characteristic that would become a standard of his later contributions: He wrote with an agenda in mind.

Invited to write an honors thesis as a prerequisite to graduating with distinction from Harvard, Roosevelt bypassed traditional subjects (and the chance for "distinction") and instead addressed the subject that had fascinated him since childhood: the sea and its impact on national power. Drawing heavily on primary source materials in the Library of Congress, the Navy Department, and the British National Archives in London, Roosevelt soon found himself so overwhelmed by the sheer mass of the material that he began to question his ability to complete his effort in a readable form. "I have plenty of information now," he wrote to his sister Anna, "but I can't get it into words; I am afraid it is too big a task for me."[20] A pilgrimage during his European honeymoon to visit his uncle James Bulloch in England bucked up the young writer's confidence. He sorted out his materials and overcame his concerns.[21]

The Naval War of 1812 is an operational history of the naval aspects of the conflict between the United States and its former colonial master. Although the book begins with two chapters that are, in the author's own words, "so dry that they . . . made a dictionary light reading,"[22] the succeeding chapters treat readers to a blow-by-blow recounting of great sea battles, with vivid descriptions of the personalities involved and penetrating observations about actions that either ensured victory or foreshadowed defeat. Tactical considerations surrounding fleet actions, one-on-one ship duels, and commerce raiding are spelled out in excruciating detail. That a civilian barely out of college (or still in college, in the case of the early chapters) grasped the technicalities of these great clashes still amazes readers. His mastery of detail did not come without hard work. A friend later remembered arriving at the Roosevelt home for a night out in society to find the young historian standing before his mantle with deck logs, models of ships, and cannon strewn before him, lost in the visualization of battles long past.[23]

While a fine achievement, the tactical accounts alone did not guarantee Roosevelt's place in the pantheon of naval theorists; it was his strategic insights that brought the book into the spotlight of international naval discourse. Not satisfied to simply recount the frigate and sloop conflicts of "Mr. Madison's War," Roosevelt extracted historical lessons and applied them to contemporary events. Insights into the strategic lessons of the day woven into *The Naval War*'s layers of operational analysis demonstrate the author's instinctive grasp of sea power years before Capt. Alfred T. Mahan even reported to the Naval War College. In fact, many of Mahan's "elements of sea power" appeared first in some form within Roosevelt's masterpiece.

Roosevelt's effort had the benefit of historical timing, appearing as it did on the upswell of an expansionist movement in the United States. Among the forces at work in the murky undercurrents of American political culture was the renewed interest in a messianic spreading of republican democracy—and its attendant attribute, individual liberty—throughout the world. Other groups in the United States, not satisfied with the continent under their control, sought additional territory as a path to more wealth.[24] Social Darwinism, which held that nations, like species, had to battle to survive, was another factor in the expansionism of the age. Failure to expand was failure to compete.[25] The post–Civil War industrialization of the economy required new outlets for American products. Market leaders, feeling that their industrial production would soon outrace Americans' desire to buy, sought additional outlets to bring under their control.[26] Regardless of the underlying reason for the growing wave of expansionist sentiment, Roosevelt rode its swell.

The Naval War of 1812 was published while Roosevelt was serving in New York's state legislature and was well received. The *New York Times* called it "excellent . . . in every respect," and the *Army and Navy Journal* praised Roosevelt's "easy command of material . . . broad reasoning . . . [and] excellent historical perspective." The *Philadelphia Bulletin* lauded *The Naval War of 1812* as "a rich contribution to our national history," while Great Britain's *Saturday Review* praised it for having "very little disposition to national self-laudation . . . none whatever to abuse or depreciate the enemy."[27] Other individuals more critical to Roosevelt's future also took note of the new work.

"Your work must be our textbook," wrote Rear Adm. Stephen B. Luce, president of the Naval War College in Newport, Rhode Island.[28] Luce had founded the institution in 1884, housing it in a former home for the poor on an island within sight of the ostentatious summer mansions of the nation's wealthy elite.²⁹ Stephen Luce was the leader of a growing group of insurgents within the Navy's commissioned ranks who were urging modernization and reform for the fleet. He felt that modern naval officers could no longer learn everything necessary for success in modern warfare on the quarterdeck of a ship. The Naval War College was a postgraduate school dedicated to the study of conflict.³⁰ Luce's letter to Roosevelt included an invitation to come to Newport and deliver a lecture.³¹ Roosevelt gladly accepted. His topic, "True Conditions of the War of 1812," allowed him ample room to sound the trumpet of preparedness. The visit itself came after Rear Admiral Luce had returned to sea duty, but it gave the young author the opportunity to meet the War College's new president, Capt. Alfred T. Mahan. Within four years of its publication, American naval regulations required every ship in the U.S. Navy to carry a copy of *The Naval War of 1812* in its library.³²

Roosevelt's expertise and the evolution of his personal thought did not stop at the publication of *The Naval War of 1812*. In two biographies written in seclusion at his ranch in the Dakota Badlands following the tragic death of his first wife, Alice—*Thomas Hart Benton* (1887) and *Gouverneur Morris* (1888)—Roosevelt used the careers of early second-tier statesmen as a platform to expound on the failings of the early Congress vis-à-vis sea power.

Gouverneur Morris served the United States in the Continental Congress during the revolution against British colonial rule, as minister to France during the period of confederation, and as a Federalist senator in the young U.S. Senate. Of this early statesman Roosevelt opined, "He never showed greater wisdom than in his views about our navy; and his party, the Federalists, started to give us one; but it had hardly begun before the Jeffersonians came into power, and, with singular foolishness, stopped the work."³³ Here Roosevelt was suggesting a future propensity for federal activism, especially in the case of the executive branch.

By the time Thomas Hart Benton of Missouri took his seat in the Senate in 1821, the Federalist Party had faded from the American political landscape, surrendering to the Democratic-Republican steamroller that arrived with Jefferson, grew under Andrew Jackson, and dominated the nation in the decades that followed. A devoted disciple of Andrew Jackson, Benton espoused the philosophy of "manifest destiny" that would underlie and direct U.S. foreign policy for most of the nineteenth century. Benton sought to align the resources of the government toward western expansion and thought the

Navy had limited utility in this regard.[34] Roosevelt wrote, somewhat unfairly, that "Benton's opposition to [the Navy's] increase seems to have proceeded partly from bitter partisanship, partly from sheer ignorance, and partly from the doctrinaire dread of any kind of standing military or naval force, which he had inherited, with a good many similar ideas, from Jeffersonians."[35] Memories of the power of Britain's strong central government would haunt the new republic for years to come.

Roosevelt's strong views concerning Thomas Jefferson are evident in all that he wrote during this period. The third president's passive naval policy of avoiding confrontation on the high seas by building gunboats that could operate only in coastal waters was anathema to the nation's twenty-sixth president. While acknowledging Jefferson as "a man whose views and theories had a profound influence upon our national life," Roosevelt cast him as "perhaps the most incapable executive that ever filled the presidential chair." James Madison, Jefferson's apprentice and political heir, fares only slightly better: "The [Madison] administration thus drifted into a war which it had neither the wisdom to avoid nor the forethought to prepare for."[36] Roosevelt viewed early American government as unworthy of its populace and damaging to the nation's influence on the sea. Even as a young man he demonstrated a nuanced appreciation of the position of naval power as a subset of military power and the importance of military power within the spectrum of international relations.

Prophet of Preparedness

Had Theodore Roosevelt written *The Naval War of 1812* and stopped there, he would soon have faded into obscurity. His prominence in U.S. history reflects his ability to overcome setbacks, articulate a vision, and realize a focused ambition. As a junior state assemblyman in New York, Roosevelt possessed a well-developed and rounded personal philosophy rare in men in their early twenties. His books and correspondence reveal a driven man possessed by a destiny yet to be realized—a destiny intertwined with public service. His earlier decisions not to pursue his childhood ambition of becoming a naturalist or to join the family's lucrative glassworks business came about as he began to focus on government as a career. Certainly, his early works undergird much of his future political philosophy.

A persistent central theme runs through Roosevelt's writings: The United States needed a modern fleet if it were to take its place among the world's

Great Powers, and needed to be prepared to use it. In January 1888 Roosevelt accepted an invitation to speak before the Union League Club of New York. His presentation combined concepts of global mercantilism and the need for a strong Navy into a powerful, coherent argument. Seeking to raise an alarm among the leading members of the New York merchant class sitting before him, Roosevelt said, "It is a disgrace to us as a nation that we should have no warships worthy of the name, and that our rich sea-board cities should lie at the mercy of a tenth rate power like Chili [sic]."[37] Thus, by 1890, well before the noted naval strategist Alfred Thayer Mahan burst on the scene, Theodore Roosevelt was well established within elite intellectual circles as a leading contributor to strategic discussion within the United States.

Mahan's contribution to this discourse should not be minimized, of course. Mahan was born into a military intellectual tradition. His father was an instructor at West Point, and Alfred earned entry into the Naval Academy when he was sixteen. His thirty-four-year naval career was undistinguished, and his intellectual powers still unrecognized when he was posted to the Naval War College in 1885.[38] Mahan experienced an epiphany while reading about the importance of sea power in warfare in a history of the Roman Empire.[39] With orders to Newport in hand, he closeted himself in New York's Astor Library to prepare the lectures he intended to deliver to his new students. These presentations and the resultant professional articles came together in 1890 in Mahan's landmark book *The Influence of Sea Power upon History: 1660–1783*.[40]

Casting about for a reviewer for this new book on sea power, the *Atlantic Monthly* landed the leading voice on the subject, Theodore Roosevelt. He had already read the book and was an enthusiastic fan. In a letter to its author Roosevelt gushed: "During the last two days I have spent half my time, busy as I am, in reading your book. . . . I can say with perfect sincerity that I think it very much the clearest and most instructive general work of the kind with which I am acquainted. . . . I am greatly in error if it does not become a naval classic."[41] Roosevelt's review was equally generous.

Mahan's thesis can be summarized as follows: Trade is the source of national power, but stable trade requires a navy to protect ports and patrol the sea lines of communication; hence, a strong navy is essential to achieving national greatness. Years later, a British admiral would comment, "I can remember no event in my time in the Navy so epoch-making as the publication of Mahan's first books."[42] Roosevelt continued to advocate a larger U.S. Navy throughout the 1890s, even as he began to collaborate with, and champion the ideas of, Captain Mahan.[43]

During those years Roosevelt found a friend in historian Henry Cabot Lodge, a rising political power from Massachusetts. Lodge represented the joining of the Cabots, one of the oldest European families in Massachusetts, with the Lodges, a relatively new family of wealth that had made its name in shipping. Raised among some of the leading historians in America, Lodge went to Harvard and studied history as well as English literature. Extensive travels during his youth gave Lodge a sophisticated appreciation of the world, especially Europe, with its nuanced approaches to international relations. Returning to Harvard, he combined his interests in a doctoral dissertation that took a comprehensive look at the historical development of Anglo-Saxon law and launched himself into a career as a writer, editor, and educator. Lodge taught for a number of years at Harvard, but finding no fulfillment there, turned to politics.[44]

Henry Cabot Lodge became a member of the U.S. House of Representatives in 1887 and served in the American legislature's lower house until 1893 when he was elevated to the Senate.[45] Lodge and Roosevelt met at the 1884 Republican National Convention in Chicago, where both served as delegates from their respective home states. One of Roosevelt's biographers would later note that "at first sight the two men seemed an unlikely pair."[46] Unlikely they were—one exuberant and extroverted, the other so constrained by his Puritan upbringing as to appear pained by the simplest human contact. Yet a pair they became. Roosevelt would later say that Lodge "was my closest friend, personally, politically, and in every other way, and occupied toward me a relation that no other man has ever occupied or ever will occupy."[47] It was a friendship built upon trust, loyalty, mutual interest, and an intense intellectual collaboration.

The two men began corresponding and ultimately started joint writing projects that drew on their mutual love of American history. Together they began to shape a comprehensive diplomatic-military initiative that they referred to as the "Large Policy." Anchored on one side by a broad interpretation of the Monroe Doctrine, and on the other by a great and powerful Navy, the Large Policy sought no less a goal than to establish the United States as the dominant power in the Western Hemisphere.[48] On 2 March 1895 Henry Cabot Lodge made his "Large Policy" speech on the floor of the Senate. Framing the controversy surrounding the proposed annexation of Hawaii within strategic and commercial contexts, Lodge concluded that the United States needed at least three more battleships and nine torpedo boats to guarantee the success of its interests around the world.[49] Roosevelt, for his part, knew that the Large Policy had to draw some basis from a traditional American foreign policy standard if Americans were to view it as legitimate. He found that precedent in the doctrine of James Monroe.

For Theodore Roosevelt, the Monroe Doctrine represented not only a long-standing tradition of American foreign policy but also a path to the nation's future as an influential power within the international system. As early as 1893, he wrote: "I believe in ultimately driving every European power off this continent, and I don't want to see our flag hauled down where it has been hauled up."[50] Returning to the topic in 1896 in a letter to the editor of the *Harvard Crimson,* Roosevelt took exception to the efforts of certain Harvard professors to lobby against U.S. policies with regard to South America. Britain was attempting to intimidate Venezuela into repaying loans on which it had recently defaulted. The United States took the step of warning Great Britain against any move to acquire territory in the Western Hemisphere. Roosevelt, after placing the question in the context of American "honor and dignity," went on to state,

> The Monroe Doctrine forbids us to acquiesce in any territorial aggrandizement by a European power on American soil at the expense of an American state. . . . If we permit a European nation in each case itself to decide whether or not the territory which it wishes to seize is its own, then the Monroe Doctrine has no real existence. . . . If Harvard men wish peace with honor they will . . . demand that our representatives insist upon the strictest application of the Monroe Doctrine; and will farther demand that immediate preparation be made to build a first-class Navy.[51]

His letter created such a stir among Harvard's academic and alumni communities that Roosevelt, then serving as police commissioner in New York, wrote an extended article for publication in *Bachelor of Arts* magazine defending his interpretation of the doctrine. The *Arts* article traces the principles within Monroe's 1823 annual message to Congress to precedents set in the earliest days of the republic, citing France's early efforts to acquire territory from Spain. "Our statesmen at once announced," Roosevelt observed, "that they would consider as hostile to America the transfer of the territory in question from a weak to a strong European power."[52] Roosevelt was certainly aware that such a policy would require a Navy comparable to Britain's in size and strength to uphold. Indeed, for nearly half a century the Monroe Doctrine had quietly depended on the naval power of Great Britain to dissuade other colonial powers from moving into the Western Hemisphere.

His ideas, framed against the backdrop of nineteenth-century diplomacy, clearly suggest that Roosevelt believed in a muscular interpretation of President Monroe's doctrine and saw it as a key to establishing the United States as a Great Power. Yet he knew that the Great Powers of Europe would not welcome this expansion.[53] To make the interpretation effective, the United States needed to back the Monroe Doctrine with credible combat power, and needed to be prepared for war in order to avoid it.

It was this understanding of preparedness and deterrence that allowed Roosevelt to surpass Alfred T. Mahan in influence and marked him to as one of those rare men who combine thought and action. Roosevelt's writings throughout the 1880s and 1890s consistently frame the debates of his own time within the lessons of the past, beginning with his masterpiece, *The Naval War of 1812,* which makes an emphatic call for preparedness while comparing the naval policies of the Jeffersonian Democrats and contemporary Republicans:

> Our navy in 1812 was the exact reverse of what our navy is now, in 1882. . . . [W]e now have a large number of worthless vessels, standing very low down in their respective classes, we then possessed a few vessels, each unsurpassed by any foreign ship of her class. To bring up our navy to the condition in which it stood in 1812 it would not be necessary (although in reality both very wise and very economical) to spend any more money than at present; only instead of using it to patch up a hundred antiquated hulks, it should be employed in building half a dozen ships on the most effective model.[54]

Roosevelt went on to conclude, "It is too much to hope that our political short-sightedness will ever enable us to have a navy that is first-class in point of size; but there certainly seems no reason why what ships we have should not be of the very best quality."[55] Words such as these earned him an invitation to serve as assistant secretary of the Navy.

The Fulcrum of Greatness

During the presidential election campaign of 1896 Theodore Roosevelt dedicated himself to the success of the Republican ticket. An oddity among New York's social elite, he had immersed himself in partisan politics after graduating from Harvard in 1880. After paying his dues to the Republican Party while serving on the Federal Civil Service Commission and as New York City police commissioner,[56] in 1896 found Roosevelt actively sought a position of real influence in Washington. William McKinley's triumph gave him hope that the opportunity he sought was at the door. A mutual friend of Roosevelt and McKinley later related, "When . . . we were walking home, Mr. Roosevelt said: 'There is one thing I would like to have, but there is no chance of my getting it—McKinley will never give it to me. I should like to be Assistant Secretary of the Navy.' He said he did not think that Mr. McKinley liked him (which I knew was true enough, but, of course, I did not tell him so)."[57]

In late November Senator Henry Cabot Lodge traveled to Canton, Ohio, to speak with the president-elect at his home. During the conversation, Lodge urged McKinley to grant Roosevelt's wish and appoint him to the influential post. McKinley seemed hesitant about Roosevelt from the beginning. He appreciated Roosevelt's energy, loyalty, and intellect, but told Lodge, "I hope he has no preconceived plans which he would wish to drive through the moment he got in." Lodge assured him that Roosevelt did not.[58] McKinley was not immediately convinced. "I want peace," he informed one of Roosevelt's friends, "and I am told that your friend Theodore . . . is always getting into rows with everybody. I am afraid he is too pugnacious."[59] The decision took awhile. The New York magazine *Review of Reviews* reported late in the spring that "there has been no great haste in making the official changes at Washington, but such places as the assistant secretaryships are now filled. The Hon. Theodore Roosevelt has . . . become Assistant Secretary of the Navy."[60] Roosevelt sensed that the professional politicians of New York would be happy to see him move to Washington. He confided to a friend, "The machine people here evidently have it in their heads that I am to be made Assistant Secretary of the Navy."[61] The posting could not have been more appropriate.

On 19 April 1897, at age thirty-eight, Theodore Roosevelt assumed his duties as the second-ranking civilian in the Department of the Navy. He remarked to his friend Capt. Bowman McCalla, "I have assumed my new duties today, and although I am as yet unfamiliar with the details, I believe that my surroundings here will be most pleasant. As you know, I have always taken a great interest in the Navy, and I sincerely hope that my connection with the service will be as beneficial to it as will certainly be to me."[62]

As assistant secretary of the Navy, he reported to John D. Long, a former congressman and governor of Massachusetts. Long began his professional relationship with Roosevelt with great misgivings. He counted himself philosophically among those who believed that the ongoing arms race among the several Great Powers would end disastrously either in bankruptcy or in war.[63] Roosevelt's views could not have been further from this outlook, but Long quickly grew to appreciate the young man's energy as a natural complement to his own lethargy. Following their first meeting, Long recorded in his diary that Roosevelt was the "best man for the place [the Navy Department]."[64] Roosevelt, for his part, considered the older man "a perfect dear."[65] Long quickly moved to define his assistant's role. In an internal memorandum establishing administrative duties within the Navy Department, Long directed Roosevelt to "at all times when the Secretary of the Navy shall be absent from the Department, whether such absence shall continue during the whole or any part of an official day, perform the duties of the Secretary of the Navy and sign all orders and other papers appertaining to such duties."[66]

Roosevelt returned to Oyster Bay to spend time with his growing family the following weekend, but in a combination of a sense of duty and lost opportunity, he promised Long that he would never leave Washington again unless specifically ordered. In typical Rooseveltian fashion, he justified his devotion to duty: "I don't wish again to be away when there is the slightest chance that anything may turn up."[67]

Less than two months after being sworn in, on 7 June 1897, Roosevelt delivered an explosive policy statement at the Naval War College. *Harper's Weekly* reported that "the address recently delivered before the Naval War College at Newport by our new Assistant Secretary of the Navy, Mr. Theodore Roosevelt, has deservedly attracted much attention. It was a very eloquent and forcible defense of the proposition that this republic must have a great navy in order to be well prepared for war, and that being prepared for war is the surest means of preserving peace."[68]

Roosevelt used the occasion to criticize the slothfulness of the American middle and upper classes and to endorse a return to the warrior spirit of the past with an accompanying rapid buildup of the U.S. Navy. In his speech, titled "Washington's Forgotten Maxim," Roosevelt utilized the founding father's dictum that "to be prepared for war is the most effectual means to promote the peace" to sound the tocsin of personal and national preparedness. The speech represented the outward expression of his internal philosophy. If it seems overly bellicose, even for the age in which it was written, it was.

Insisting that "preparation for war is the surest guaranty for peace," Roosevelt complained that American society was in danger of losing its competitive edge in the world, an edge that could be honed only in war or warlike professions. Drawing on his extensive knowledge of the War of 1812,

Roosevelt exhorted the naval officers assembled before him to take pride in their profession.

> Popular sentiment is just when it selects as popular heroes the men who have led in the struggle against malice domestic or foreign levy. No triumph of peace is quite so great as the supreme triumphs of war. The courage of the soldier, the courage of the statesman who has to meet storms which can be quelled only by soldierly qualities—this stands higher than any quality called out merely in time of peace. It is by no means necessary that we should have war to develop soldierly attributes and soldierly qualities; but if the peace we enjoy is of such kind that it causes their loss, then it is far too dearly purchased, no matter what may be its attendant benefits. It may be that some time in the dim future of the race the need for war will vanish; but that time is yet ages distant. As yet no nation can hold its place in the world, or can do any work really worth doing, unless it stands ready to guard its rights with an armed hand. That orderly liberty which is both the foundation and the capstone of our civilization can be gained and kept only by men who are willing to fight for an ideal; who hold high the love of honor, love of faith, love of flag, and love of country.

Roosevelt finished his exhortation by calling for a rapid increase in the size of the Navy, tying it to a defense of the Monroe Doctrine.[69]

The warlike tone of his presentation did not go unnoticed. The speech appeared in most of the nation's large newspapers. Many editors commented on its unapologetic tone with regard to the role of the United States in the world. For many Americans, Roosevelt's pronouncements at Newport repre-sented the culmination of nearly two decades of developing expansionist thought.[70] Some, however, found fault with Roosevelt's logic. If peace begat a weakening of a nation's moral timber, social commentator Carl Schurz argued, and war strengthened it, then the prevention of war by a buildup of naval forces would ultimately result in national "effeminacy." At least one of Roosevelt's biographers thought that the Newport speech had but one target. With Hawaii and Cuba square in the sights of policy makers in Washington, Edmund Morris believed Roosevelt's words were intended "to create, rather than just influence, national foreign policy." President William McKinley, of course, also read Roosevelt's unauthorized words. "I suspect Roosevelt is right," he said to a member of his staff, "and the only difference between him and me is that mine is the greater responsibility."[71] In the Navy Department Theodore Roosevelt had found his fulcrum, and he soon discovered that with it he could move things.

The hot and humid Washington summer provided the assistant secretary of the Navy with the opportunity to exert his considerable energies. Long returned to his Massachusetts farm to avoid the unpleasant weather, leaving Roosevelt in charge. The younger man did not hesitate to act. Replying to a formal request from a member of Congress, he joyfully stated, "At last . . . I am in sole command, and your request goes through. . . . I am not certain that my conduct will be approved, but I made up my mind."[72] To his credit, Roosevelt dedicated himself completely to work for which Long had neither the interest nor the energy. Comfortable with the broader questions of naval strategy, he immersed himself in the study of the technical, administrative, and logistical challenges facing the U.S. Navy.[73] His confidence grew as he chaired numerous exploratory committees covering the spectrum of naval activities. During this period he deliberately finalized decisions that Long had avoided for various technical and political reasons.[74] Roosevelt, never one to avoid controversy, had the time of his life. He recounted his time as the "hot weather Secretary" in letters to his friends. "The Secretary is away," he wrote to one, "and I am having immense fun running the Navy. I am absorbed in my work. It is delightful to be dealing with matters of real moment and of great interest."[75]

Theodore Roosevelt had entered the Navy Department with a coherent philosophy regarding the Navy and the nation. Following the appearance of *The Naval War of 1812,* he consistently promoted a big Navy and an enlarged role for the United States in world affairs. Now positioned on the fringe of power in Washington, he took on the challenge of convincing his seniors—the secretary and ultimately the president—of the correctness of his ideas. Initially, however, he needed to establish an actionable plan that fit within the budgetary and philosophical constraints imposed by the White House.

In May 1897 Roosevelt wrote to Captain Mahan regarding the need for naval expansion and a robust fleet-support infrastructure in the Pacific and Atlantic oceans. Mahan and Roosevelt had by now communicated for years on similar subjects, but Roosevelt's letters became increasingly specific after he took office as he actively sought Mahan's advice. Painting with a broad strategic brush, the subcabinet functionary boldly stated to the Navy's preeminent strategist,

If I had my way we would annex those islands (Hawaiian) tomorrow. If that is impossible I would establish a protectorate over them. I believe we should build the Nicaraguan canal at once, and in the meantime that we should build a dozen new battleships, half of them on the Pacific Coast. . . . I would send the Oregon, and, if necessary, also the Monterey (either with a deck load of coal or accompanied by a coaling ship) to Hawaii. . . . But there are big problems in the West Indies also. Until we definitely turn Spain out of those islands (and if I had my way that would be done tomorrow), we will always be menaced by trouble there.[76]

Within days, perhaps at Mahan's request, the assistant secretary had received copies of war plans dealing with Pacific and Atlantic contingencies.[77] Created under the guiding hand of the director of the new Office of Naval Intelligence, Lt. Cdr. William W. Kimball, a pioneer in ordnance and submarine power who went on to lead the Torpedo Flotilla Squadron during the Spanish-American War, the plans represented detailed preparations and execution orders covering a wide spectrum of contingencies. Kimball served the fleet for forty years (1870–1910) and ultimately achieved the rank of rear admiral. Throughout his service he bore a reputation for tactical innovation and strategic brilliance.[78] Now, with Kimball's plan in hand, Roosevelt began to flesh out his strategic skeleton.

Despite his exertions, Roosevelt had yet to overcome the innate resistance of John D. Long, who remained skeptical of the need for a larger American fleet, particularly battleships. The secretary, uncomfortable with the constantly evolving nature of European ship construction, feared that any ship laid down in American shipyards would be obsolete before it ever touched water. In particular, he questioned the utility of battleships within the context of the American naval strategy. If the U.S. Navy remained a coastal defense force, smaller, cheaper armored cruisers might fit the bill. Battleships bespoke a transoceanic offensive strategy not in keeping with long-standing American policies.

Roosevelt began working behind the scenes, turning again to Mahan for assistance. In a letter dated 9 June 1897 he told Mahan "in strict confidence . . . that Secretary Long is only luke-warm about building up our Navy, at any rate as regards battleships. Indeed, he is against adding to our battleships. This is, to me, a matter of profound concern. I feel that you ought to write to him—not immediately, but sometime not far in the future—at some length, explaining to him the vital need of more battleships now."[79] Ultimately, Roosevelt recognized that he needed more than just Mahan's assistance to overcome the reluctance of the American people.[80]

Convinced that the United States faced conflict with either Japan or Spain in the near future, Roosevelt looked for ways to enlarge the fleet. On 29 September 1897 he set the stage by asking the secretary to meet with him to discuss a major change in naval policy.[81] Roosevelt presented a detailed memorandum to Long the next morning. Drawing heavily on the Kimball war plans, he framed his proposal against the background of the United States' imminent annexation of Hawaii and the ongoing challenge of upholding the Monroe Doctrine in the Western Hemisphere against increasing pressures from European colonial powers. Reminding his superior that warships serve the dual purpose of preserving the peace and winning wars, he characterized battleships as "the cheapest kind of insurance." Roosevelt followed with specific needs. "I believe that Congress should at once give us six (6) new battleships, two (2) to be built on the Pacific and four (4) on the Atlantic; six (6) large cruisers, of the size of the *Brooklyn,* etc." Demonstrating a sophisticated grasp of the complex issues underlying a buildup of naval forces, he drew Long's attention to the need for new dry docks and the expansion of existing repair facilities. Additionally, Roosevelt pressed for the rapid replacement of obsolete guns with the new rapid-fire weapons rolling out of the Navy's factory at the Washington Navy Yard. Finally, he recommended the purchase of a reserve supply of projectiles.[82]

Long began to wear down under the force of Roosevelt's arguments and the strength of his personality. The secretary's diary suggests that he began to acquiesce out of mental and physical exhaustion. On 13 January 1898, for example, he wrote in his journal, "Busy morning. Mr. Roosevelt came in, shut the door, and began in his usual emphatic and dead-in-earnest manner. . . . He bores me with plans of naval and military movement, and the necessity of having some scheme of attack arranged for instant execution in case of an emergency. By tomorrow morning, he will have got half a dozen heads of bureaus together and have spoiled twenty pages of good writing paper, and lain awake half the night."[83] It is clear from his tone that John D. Long knew of nothing at the Navy Department worth staying up half a night for. Papers containing Rooseveltian ideas yet bearing John D. Long's signature began to emerge from the Navy Department.

Confident of the "righteousness" of his cause and of its ultimate success, Roosevelt turned his attention to the operational fleet. Then as now, day-to-day management of the fleet was a jealously guarded prerogative of its uniformed leaders. Roosevelt needed the assistance of someone of considerable influence to adequately prepare the ships currently at sea, and he needed it quickly. Tensions with Spain were rising rapidly, but the Navy remained woefully unprepared. Utilizing arguments honed by months of careful thought and challenging written and verbal dialogues with Mahan and Lodge, Roosevelt brought his powers of persuasion to bear on the individual who ultimately held the reins of command: the commander in chief, William McKinley.

Since taking office, Roosevelt had sought to engage the president's interest in the Navy through a systematic, step-by-step process.[84] Leading off with an analysis of the capabilities of every ship class in the fleet, followed by a detailed overview of fleet tactics and strategy, and finishing up with assessments of the character and capabilities of senior commanders, Roosevelt ultimately requested that ships be positioned near Cuba and the Philippines in preparation for the outbreak of hostilities.[85] McKinley, a private soldier who rose to the rank of brevet major during the Civil War, remained politely noncommittal about the future of the Navy. Of the looming threat of Spain or Japan he remained entirely unconvinced. Roosevelt, frustrated by McKinley's lack of enthusiasm for such an important topic, nevertheless promised the president that "the Department would be in the best possible shape that our means would permit when war began."[86] His interpretation of McKinley's indifference as passive assent allowed Roosevelt to proceed as if tasked.

Preparations for War

Roosevelt set about readying the U.S. Navy for a war with Spain with his typical relentless enthusiasm. Equipped with a Mahanian philosophy of power projection and the details of Kimball's war plan, he promoted the formation and exercising of cohesive battle groups from the loose squadrons that currently patrolled the American coasts or foreign waters. In June 1897, as acting secretary in Long's absence, he wrote an addendum to an order authorizing an August exercise. "I am especially anxious to see you try our seven seagoing armor-clads in squadron," he wrote, "for although they include three 1st-class battleships, two 2nd-class battleships and two armored cruisers, yet they are sufficiently alike in type to make it possible to manoeuvre with them, and I suppose they will all be used in the line if we have a naval war." He then invited himself along to view gunnery drills.[87]

Having ordered American ships to maneuver as a cohesive force, Roosevelt turned his attention to the question of just where these forces might be most effective. Months prior to the sinking of the USS *Maine* in Havana Harbor, Roosevelt confided to Mahan that he was promoting a strategy of positioning the bulk of the Atlantic Fleet off Key West, with the remainder being directed to the coast of Spain to harass commercial shipping and selected Spanish ports. In the Pacific, Roosevelt felt that "our Asiatic squadron should blockade, and if possible take, Manila."[88] The assistant secretary warned that all American actions must be swift lest they invite the attention of powerful European imperialist poachers.

On 14 January 1898 Theodore Roosevelt urgently lobbied Secretary Long to prepare the ships at sea for war. Warning that a descent into combat without adequate preparation courted disaster, he specifically he requested a "radical" alteration of the disposition of the fleet. Referring to the Kimball war plan, he again suggested that the Atlantic Fleet be immediately moved to Key West and that the newly installed Asiatic Squadron's commander, Commo. George Dewey, be directed to prepare his forces for actions in the Philippines.[89] Long considered his assistant's suggestions and did nothing while Theodore Roosevelt's rapid-fire mind continued to churn.

Just as nineteenth-century armies traveled on their stomachs, turn-of-the-century naval vessels depended on a steady diet of coal. Every blue-water navy needed overseas bases to service its ships, or at least a significant number of support vessels to provide underway replenishment. For years, Roosevelt, Lodge, and Mahan had advocated the acquisition of both. While the annexation of Hawaii promised to provide a central hub for U.S. operations in the Pacific, building the necessary infrastructure would take years—years that the assistant secretary of the Navy felt the nation did not have. Roosevelt envisioned a Navy operating independently in three regions. While Cuba presented the advantage of relative proximity, the Spanish coast and the Philippines did not. To enable the American fleets to operate for extended periods outside American waters, Roosevelt lobbied his superiors to procure strategic reserves of coal and transport ships (colliers to accompany and resupply the warships) and to enhance the capabilities of forward maintenance facilities.

As winter settled over Washington in late 1897 and Spanish-American relations grew ever tenser, Roosevelt's increasingly strident letters to Lodge, Long, and McKinley consistently urged the importance of maintaining coal supplies for the battleships at maximum capacity.[90] Roosevelt boldly urged

Long to order the Atlantic Fleet to be "filled with coal in readiness for action" and advised in particular "an ample supply of colliers" for every vessel.[91]

Roosevelt's efforts to obtain new guns and accompanying ammunition for the Navy were even more vigorous. Months of study and participation in various naval planning boards and committees had educated him on the vast differences in capabilities and effectiveness of various gun systems. Indigenous American naval gun development had been stunted by years of neglect and disinterest, but Roosevelt's investigations made him aware of the newly emerging technologies.[92] Unfortunately, many of these new weapons were placed on aging ships while the newer, faster vessels were equipped with older guns. Writing in June 1897 to a Navy engineer, Roosevelt stated,

> We need to replace our old slow-fire guns on the battleships, and cruisers with modern rapid-fire guns. A battery of rapid-fire guns has been provided by law for the *Hartford,* where they are of no earthly use; at least as compared with the use they would be if put upon the *Philadelphia* or *San Francisco.* I am very anxious to consult with you to find out if there is not some way by which we can put this battery on one of these two ships where it will be of real service.[93]

His letters written throughout the following summer continued to mention the need to match the most capable ships with the most capable weapons.[94] Referring to an order to substitute a more rapid-firing 6-inch gun for an older 8-inch gun throughout an entire class of battleships, he wrote, "I personally rather regret that the 8-inch gun was taken off these battleships. It is to a certain extent an armor piercer, and the 6-inch gun is not."[95] As the threat of war loomed ever closer, Roosevelt directed that new guns emerging from the Navy's gun factory be installed "as rapidly as possible."[96]

Roosevelt also connected the dots and realized that the new guns required new ammunition. For years, ammunition had been in short supply in the Navy. Austere budgets forced naval leaders to restrict the firing of guns. The situation became so acute that commanding officers had to account for every shell and faced the possibility of having to pay for overexpenditures. During his service in the Navy Department Roosevelt sought to relieve the pressures on the captains and to encourage frequent live-fire exercises to improve gunnery accuracy.[97] He put to sea with the ships of the Atlantic Fleet to watch gunnery drills and came away with a tremendous respect for the new weapons. In the event of multiple exchanges between fleets, however, he doubted that current stockpiles would last the duration of the conflict. Forecasting expenditures, he wrote, "We should provide a reasonable reserve supply of projectiles (about nine thousand in all) so as to permit a complete refill of all the ships."[98] In letters to Long he characterized the requirement for more ammunition as an "urgent need."[99]

Roosevelt's correspondence during this period consistently refers to the need for all available ships to maintain a high state of readiness, a direction consistent with his personal philosophy, which trumpeted preparedness. As 1897 gave way to 1898, his attention transitioned from the ships at sea to those under repair in dock facilities.[100] In his eagerness to bring the largest force possible to bear against the enemy, Roosevelt overlooked no ship.[101] Everything from battleships to post–Civil War monitors had a place in his plans. Speed was of the essence. Reinforcing Henry Adams' characterization, Roosevelt required constant action from those around him. A representative letter from this period is sprinkled with the phrases "immediate and prompt" and "as quickly as possible" along with time limitations such as "within forty-eight hours."[102] Roosevelt's every action at this date proceeded with a sense of urgency.

Theodore Roosevelt perceived himself to be the lone sighted man in a room of the blind, and his letters betrayed an increasing desperation to prepare his country for action. On Friday, 25 February 1898, John D. Long came into the office tired, nervous, and irritable after a sleepless night. The tragic destruction of the USS *Maine* in Havana's harbor was hastening war and disturbing his rest. He did only minimal work before announcing his intention to return home for the afternoon to rest, leaving the assistant secretary in charge of the department. His perception of Roosevelt had changed now that the war his assistant had warned about and done so much to prepare for was in the offing. He wrote of Roosevelt in his diary that evening: "He is so enthusiastic and loyal that he is, in certain respects, invaluable, yet I lack confidence in his good judgment and discretion. He goes off very impulsively and, if I have a good night tonight, I shall feel that I ought to go back in the Department rather than take a day's vacation."[103]

Long's misgivings were well founded. After his departure, Theodore Roosevelt closed his own door and began to dictate the first of a series of messages to the fleet: "Cablegram. Dewey, Hong Kong: Order the squadron, except for the *Monocacy*, to Hong Kong. Keep full of coal. In the event of declaration of war Spain, your duty will be to see that the Spanish squadron does not leave the Asiatic coast and then offensive operations in Philippine Islands. Keep Olympia until further orders."[104]

CHAPTER ONE

Aftermath

When Secretary of the Navy John D. Long returned the following morning, he was shocked to discover that in his absence, his assistant had initiated a series of actions that had the potential to shift the basic mission of the U.S. Navy from coastal defense to power projection. In a flurry of activity covering five hours, the assistant secretary of the Navy had ordered warships in the Atlantic and Pacific to forward positions, directed the purchase of additional stores of coal and ammunition, moved state-of-the-art guns from the Washington Navy Yard to battleships based in New York, and placed docked ships on alert for immediate movement.[105] In doing so, he—and the Navy Department—acted without the sanction or direction of the president, which is not a good thing to do in American politics. John Long, stunned by the magnitude of his subordinate's actions, remarked in his diary, "The very devil seemed to possess him yesterday afternoon."[106]

That Theodore Roosevelt acted without the authorization of his superiors cannot be argued. Neither the president nor the secretary of the Navy would have approved Roosevelt's plans that day. But they had been briefed on them; they knew the details and had declined to act. For months he had laid before them the requirements of a wartime Navy, and they—out of philosophy, political economy, or ignorance—had ignored him. It is also true that despite the strong negative reaction to Roosevelt's activities (he was never left in charge again), a review of the Navy letter books reveals that not one of Roosevelt's messages, requests, or orders was subsequently rescinded.

Roosevelt's actions on 25 February 1898 satisfied his friends Mahan and Lodge; he had fulfilled their strategic vision. Roosevelt, for his part, was not satisfied. Having expended all of his influence in the Navy Department in one desperate act, he realized even before Long returned to the office the next morning that he had no future there. His final letter on 25 February went to Gen. C. Whitney Tillinghast, commanding general of the National Guard in his home state of New York, warning him that he should begin preparing his units for actions in the coming conflict. In exchange for this valuable information, Roosevelt made one simple request: "Pray remember that in some shape I want to go."[107] T. R. soon left his position in the Navy Department. Never again would his life be confined to Washington, D.C., or even to the United States. He had become an active participant in the world at large, with all of its attendant complexities.

Theodore Roosevelt resigned from his post as assistant secretary of the Navy in May 1898 to assume the post of second in command of the 1st U.S. Volunteer Regiment, which later gained fame as the "Rough Riders."[108] He soon found himself promoted to the rank of colonel and assumed command of the regiment prior to leading them in an audacious charge up Kettle Hill in the San Juan Heights area of Cuba. His commanding officer nominated him for a Congressional Medal of Honor for his actions, but the secretary of the Army, Roosevelt's political rival, blocked the nomination. (The medal was awarded to his family 103 years after the fact.) Nevertheless, Roosevelt's bravery on the field made him a national hero, and he returned home to New York to make a successful run for governor of the state.

The governor's office in Albany, New York, was insufficient to contain Roosevelt, who continued to try to influence national and international issues. In February 1900 Secretary of State John Hay signed a treaty with Britain's ambassador that ceded to the United States the sole right to build a canal linking the Atlantic and Pacific.[109] Roosevelt came out strongly against the treaty, actively lobbying, along with his friend Henry Cabot Lodge, against its ratification in the Senate.[110] His actions hurt the feelings of Hay, who had worked hard to ratify the treaty and was also an old friend of Roosevelt's long-deceased father. Writing to give reason for his actions, Roosevelt explained that he opposed the treaty on principle. Hay's treaty would prohibit the canal from being fortified, and Roosevelt felt that the ability to fortify ports was critical to releasing the American fleet to pursue offensive actions. Leaving an asset such as the canal undefended would have the effect of tying the American fleet to it as a defensive force. Second, he felt the treaty left open the question of joint ownership, which would be a violation of the Monroe Doctrine and would invite others to seek territory and other strategic positions in the Caribbean.[111]

Roosevelt's unceasing energy for political reform led New York's political machine to look for an opportunity to remove the young governor from his seat in Albany. His fame on the battlefield seemed to ensure his reelection, but it also made him an eligible candidate for the vice presidency, which had been vacated by the death of Garret Hobart in November 1899.[112] Though McKinley had resisted Roosevelt as a member of the subcabinet in 1897, the brilliance of his political star made the young New Yorker an attractive partner on the 1900 Republican Party ticket. The campaign was a success, but McKinley's life was cut tragically short by an assassin's bullet in September 1901, making Theodore Roosevelt, at age forty-one, the nation's youngest chief executive. Roosevelt's youthful energy was creatively aligned with a coherent national strategy that combined aspects of diplomacy and military power into an effective whole. He also had the advantage of experience operating at the highest levels of the American government and the reputation of proven courage under fire in combat. He was well positioned for success.

chapter two

Overwhelming Force and the Venezuelan Crisis of 1902–1903

But I think I suceeded in impressing on the Kaiser,
quietly and unofficially, and with equal courtesy and emphasis,
that the violation of the Monroe Doctrine by territorial
aggrandizement on his part around the Caribbean meant war,
not ultimately, but immediately, and without delay.
THEODORE ROOSEVELT, 1 NOVEMBER 1905

Few incidents of recent history have remained as clouded as the Venezuelan Crisis of 1902–3. For more than a century historians have disputed the accuracy of Theodore Roosevelt's recollections of the events of the winter of 1902. Many biographers and diplomatic historians have been quick to cite a lack of contemporary evidence to support Roosevelt's accounts. In almost every case, however, these researchers failed to consider the operational record of the military units engaged in supporting Roosevelt's policies. A careful review of the official military records of the military commanders on the scene provides an unmistakable picture of Roosevelt's intentions in the Caribbean during the winter of 1902–3.

The confusion surrounding the Venezuelan Crisis stems from assertions made in Roosevelt's later correspondence. His claim that he actively coerced European blockaders to accept arbitration did not emerge publicly until October 1915, when one of his letters appeared as an appendix to a biography of former secretary of state John Hay.[1] The biography's author, William R. Thayer, included the letter to highlight a previously undisclosed diplomatic crisis in the early days of Roosevelt's administration. Written in early 1915, the letter vividly recalls the events of late 1902 from the president's perspective:

I also became convinced that Germany intended to seize some Venezuelan harbor and turn it into a strongly fortified place of arms . . . with a view to exercising some measure of control over the future Isthmian Canal, and over South American affairs generally. . . .

Germany declined to agree to arbitrate. . . . I finally decided that no useful purpose would be served by further delay, and I took action accordingly. I assembled our battle fleet, under Admiral Dewey, near Porto Rico, for "maneuvres," with instructions that the fleet should be kept in hand and in fighting trim, and should be ready to sail at an hour's notice. . . . I saw the [German] Ambassador, and explained that in view of the presence of the German squadron on the Venezuelan coast I could not permit longer delay in answering my request for an arbitration, and that I could not acquiesce in any seizure of Venezuelan territory. The Ambassador responded that his Government could not agree to arbitrate. . . . I then asked him to inform his Government that if no notification for arbitration came during the next ten days I would be obliged to order Dewey to take his fleet to the Venezuelan coast and see that the German forces did not take possession of any territory. He expressed very grave concern and asked me if I realized the serious consequences that would follow such action. . . . I answered that I had thoroughly counted the cost before I decided on the step, and asked him to look at the map, as a glance would show him that there was no spot in the world where Germany in the event of conflict with the United States would be at a greater disadvantage than in the Caribbean Sea. A week later the Ambassador came to see me, talked pleasantly on several subjects, and rose to go. I asked him if he had any answer to make from his Government to my request, and when he said no, I informed him that in such event it was useless to wait as long as I had intended, and that Dewey would be ordered to sail twenty four hours in advance of the time I had set. He . . . said that his Government would not arbitrate. However, less than twenty four hours before the time I had appointed for calling the order to Dewey, the Ambassador notified me that His Imperial Majesty the German Emperor had directed him to request me to undertake arbitration myself.[2]

This account generated controversy, to say the least. With World War I raging in Europe, many of Roosevelt's critics felt that he was attempting to portray a preexisting animosity toward the kaiser that had not, in fact, existed. He had corresponded regularly with Wilhelm II during his presidency and even journeyed to Germany in 1910 to visit and observe a military exercise as the kaiser's personal guest, exchanging photographs and mementos afterward. Their personalities were similar, and they seemed, to contemporary observers, well disposed to each other.

To his critics' credit, the diplomatic record as it stood at the time did not support Roosevelt's claim, and the politics of World War I and Roosevelt's interest in the 1916 presidential election certainly contributed to the timely appearance of his letter in Thayer's biography. Early Roosevelt biographers such as Henry C. Hill and Henry Pringle followed this line and chose to focus on the inconsistencies between Roosevelt's version of events and the existing diplomatic record. Pringle went so far as to state that Roosevelt's "version of what occurred was romantic to the point of absurdity" and categorized the entire story as "obviously inaccurate."[3]

This characterization appeared most recently in a 1996 paper in *Diplomatic History*. In "The Height of the German Challenge" diplomatic historian Nancy Mitchell dismissed Roosevelt's claims, stating that they had "suck[ed] scholar after scholar into convoluted, circumstantial arguments about the president's credibility: Did he or didn't he?" She clearly believed that he did not issue an ultimatum.[4]

Earlier articles such as Seward Livermore's "Theodore Roosevelt, the American Navy, and the Venezuelan Crisis of 1902–03," published in 1945, encouraged the positive reassessment of Roosevelt's role from that of passive observer to active participant in bringing about a peaceful conclusion.[5] Roosevelt's literary biographer, Edmund Morris, has taken this presumptive approach to a new level of conclusiveness. His research has revealed a number of instances in which the normally voluminous presidential and State Department correspondence dropped off precipitously, suggesting a deliberate attempt to circumvent the historical record. He further explained, "The full extent of the crisis . . . has to be inferred from the existence of an extraordinary void . . . in the archives of three nations: the United States, Germany, and Great Britain."[6] It is Morris' belief that the blank spaces in the historical record, so noticeable against Roosevelt's normal high personal and official postal production, help to define a time period for the events themselves.[7]

All of the modern accounts supporting Roosevelt's role in the Venezuelan Crisis have relied on the argument-from-silence method, drawing attention to the startling lack of entries in the diplomatic records of the United States, Great Britian, and Germany for the period in question, as if there had been a concerted effort not to record events on those days. This is not entirely the case.

The records of the operational units and commanders of the naval forces involved in the "winter exercise" of 1902–3 present a clear picture of the events in the Caribbean. For eleven days, between 8 December and 18 December 1902, the future of U.S., British, German, and Venezuelan relations hung in the balance as Theodore Roosevelt discreetly pursued diplomatic negotiations between Venezuela and the two great European powers. When Germany, intent on nullifying the Monroe Doctrine and gaining a colonial possession in South America, repeatedly ignored the American president's call for arbitration, Roosevelt committed the combined U.S. Atlantic Fleet to the task of establishing the supremacy of American interests in the Western Hemisphere.

Defining Factors

In May 1901 a German warship appeared off Margarita, Venezuela, and began mapping approaches to the harbor. Although Venezuela had maintained its independence for more than seventy-five years, it continued to suffer the common ailments of many Latin American republics: a growing debt to international powers and a corrupt and weak government incapable of paying it off. Venezuela's constitutional structure maintained many of the authoritarian attributes of its colonial past, and the continuing presence and influence of institutions such as the Catholic Church, the military, and an organized landowning class acted to create and support a highly hierarchical social system that was prone to graft and corruption.[8] Five Venezuelan presidents came and went during the 1890s, each alternately playing the role of reformer and strongman, all gaining wealth from commissions received for negotiating loans to their nation on terms very favorable to the European lenders. When Venezuela became so indebted that it could no longer afford to pay the interest on the notes, the European powers moved to collect. In 1895 this resulted in a loss of "disputed" territory to British-held Guiana, but Venezuela warded off outright colonial assimilation.[9] Concern that this surrender of territory might encourage the ambitions of other European powers eager to expand or establish colonial possessions in the area is evident in the strongly worded response and activities of the United States throughout this crisis.[10]

In 1902 the mantle of leadership rested on the shoulders of Gen. Cipriano Castro, who appears from the vantage point of history to be a caricature of the stereotypical Latin American dictator. A career army officer who had spent much of the 1890s exiled in neighboring Colombia, he launched a revolution on 23 May 1899 with the stated intent to create the strong central government he and his supporters felt was necessary to advance the cause of progress in the nation.[11] Castro's military strongman background heavily colored his foreign policy, which was a conglomeration of heavy-handed, aggressive initiatives that lacked sophistication or nuance. The American representative to Venezuela described Castro as "ignorant, obstinate and wilful [*sic*]. He evidently thinks that he is a Power in the World. . . . He has never traveled; he knows nothing of the outside world; he can not realize the force and power of virtue and justice; he believes he is the Child of Fortune, and that he alone is able to govern his country and control its destiny."[12] Castro spent much of 1901 fomenting unrest in Colombia in hopes of overthrowing its government and creating a greater Venezuelan Republic out of Bolivia, Colombia, and Venezuela.[13]

By late 1901 Venezuela's European creditors had become strident in their demands that President Castro pay more attention to his mounting foreign debts. Venezuela had not paid even the interest on its loans in several years, and Germany, Britain, and Italy were increasingly concerned. Castro diverted their requests for economic redress into the Venezuelan court system, whose bench was loaded with Castro supporters who rendered verdicts in Venezuela's favor. Additionally, Castro's navy seized foreign ships and their cargos at sea, and foreign-held homes in Venezuela were raided and looted.[14] When faced with the threat of European armed intervention to collect on debt and address the additional crimes against foreigners, Castro made it clear that he believed that the Monroe Doctrine would effectively shield his country.[15]

The Monroe Doctrine, first enunciated in 1823 by President James Monroe and his secretary of state, John Quincy Adams, forbade the expansion of European colonial efforts in the Western Hemisphere.[16] The combined effects of the Civil War and the abysmal state of the Navy left the United States without the tools to enforce this doctrine for most of the nineteenth century, however, and the responsibility for containing European expansion into the Western Hemisphere actually fell on the shoulders of Great Britain. Britain's colonial and commercial interests in Canada and the Caribbean made it a silent partner in the U.S. strategy, even when the two nations' policies were in conflict in other arenas.[17] The United States was willing to accept the dependent relationship until the final decade of the century, when the burdens of a worldwide empire on Britain, the burgeoning American Navy, and three successive crises (Brazil, 1891; Nicaragua, 1894; and Venezuela, 1895) forced the two nations to reconsider the nature of their relationship.[18] With regard to Venezuela, however, Secretary of State John Hay, a noted anglophile, made it clear that the Monroe Doctrine was never intended to shield a wrongdoing state from justice. A consortium of European powers led by Germany and Great Britain prepared to test the limits of the United States' passivity.

While President William McKinley nominally supported the Europeans by urging Castro to make a good-faith effort to repay the loans, his vice president took a harder line.[19] Vice President Theodore Roosevelt reassured America's southern neighbors that while the doctrine posed no threat to them, it promised certain conflict for any "Old World Power" that sought to permanently acquire territory in the New World.[20] He took the additional step of spelling out his personal interpretation of the Monroe Doctrine directly to the German consul general, who was encouraged to convey it to Ambassador Theodor von Holleben and Kaiser Wilhelm.[21] This conversation must have weighed heavily on the mind of the German ambassador two months later when he called on Roosevelt to express his nation's sympathies to the new president of the United States following William McKinley's assassination.

TABLE I. NAVAL ORDER OF BATTLE, 1901

	Great Britain	France	Germany	USA	Japan
Battleships	28	9	15	10	6
Cruisers	120	37	26	20	31

Source: Navy Yearbook (Washington, D.C.: Government Printing Office, 1909), 655–657.

In the opening days of the first Roosevelt presidency in September 1901, the European powers, with their numerous colonies scattered throughout the Caribbean and their sizable business investments in South America, exercised substantial influence over the Western Hemisphere (Table 1). Roosevelt was well aware that the leading nations of Europe did not welcome his expansive interpretation of the 1823 Monroe Doctrine. If the policy was to be effective, he needed to back it up with credible combat power and convince the imperial powers of Europe that he would use that power.

Naval Coercive Diplomacy

Shortly after entering the White House, Theodore Roosevelt accepted a report prepared for his predecessor by Rear Adm. Robley D. Evans that called into question "the real value of our naval force for fighting purposes." Evans, speaking for the General Board of the Navy—an advisory panel of a dozen or so senior officers created in 1901 to advise the secretary of the Navy on war planning, the disposition of the fleet, the establishment of bases, and so on—went on to detail the effective strength of fighting vessels available to other major naval powers in the event of war.[22] Observing the disparity in naval strength between the United States, the imperial powers of Europe, and the rising power of Japan in the Pacific, Evans noted that "the most phlegmatic observer cannot fail to be impressed with such a striking comparison, nor can he avoid appreciating the questionable position in which our country would be found, should any one of the many international problems of the present time suddenly force us into hostilities." Evans concluded by saying that the General Board urged "greater celerity in the completion of such vessels as are already authorized . . . while an equal or greater necessity for a further increase in our limited number of fighting ships should . . . be impressed upon Congress in the most emphatic manner."[23] Roosevelt reacted with characteristic gusto. "I am straining every nerve," he commented to a friend in the opening months of his presidency, "to keep on with the upbuilding of the Navy."[24] Roosevelt clearly envisioned needing that strength in his roles as his nation's chief diplomat and the commander in chief of its armed forces.

Roosevelt represented a quandary for European leaders. The populist nature of the American democracy led to a shifting foreign policy and inconsistent statements shaped largely for domestic consumption.[25] The more cosmopolitan Roosevelt crafted his pronouncements with domestic and foreign audiences equally in mind, however, and he was not given to exaggeration when it came to foreign policy.[26] Had the diplomats in the German and British embassies understood Roosevelt's character and reviewed his prior statements, there would have been no surprise when this staunch defender of the Monroe Doctrine interpreted a German communiqué issued in December 1901 not only as a challenge to the United States but as a personal affront as well. The message stated that while Germany and its partner Great Britain did not seek territorial gains, circumstances might require them to pursue "temporary occupation" of Venezuelan harbors and their accompanying customhouses.

Roosevelt took no comfort from these assurances.[27] After all, the kaiser's brother had recently seized territory "temporarily" in China and then negotiated (at gunpoint) ninety-nine-year leases on the holdings.[28] Rear Adm. Henry C. Taylor, chief of the Bureau of Navigation and the senior uniformed naval adviser to the president, wrote Roosevelt a memorandum in which he stated that in the likely event that Venezuela ignored the European blockade, the powers would respond by bombarding port facilities and invading. Germany's by now familiar strategy in these situations would be to demand an indemnity to cover the expense of the conflict. Secretary of State Hay had voiced his opinion of this formula a few years earlier while serving as ambassador to Great Britain: "There is to the German mind, something monstrous in the thought that a war should take place anywhere and they not profit by it."[29] In a classic European policy formulation, Taylor's memo concluded that President Castro "could offer nothing but territory," ensuring Germany's acquisition of a foothold on the South American continent.[30] With Venezuela overlooking the key approaches to the long-sought-after canal through the isthmus joining North and South America, the young American president correctly perceived the scenario of the likely establishment of a German naval base, or even an active German colony, as a clear and present threat to long-standing U.S. interests. This scenario alone would have compelled Roosevelt to act, but the historical record suggests that he also saw an opportunity to use the circumstances surrounding Venezuela's difficulties to elevate his nation and himself to the level of the other Great Powers and their leaders. To maximize this opportunity, he drew on the talents of men he understood and respected.

In June 1901 the General Board of the Navy, under the chairmanship of Admiral of the Navy George Dewey, had sent a report to President McKinley detailing the scope of influence the U.S. Navy could expect to exert in the Caribbean in the event of war with an unnamed Western European power. This unnamed power was assumed to be Germany, and in fact, the Naval War College had conducted a series of war games with negative results against the "Black" (German) Navy in 1901.[31] Now Dewey, the victor in the Battle of Manila Bay and, in Roosevelt's eyes, the nation's greatest living hero, reviewed his board's report with the new president. It stated that the "Navy can control the Caribbean and its shores in war, if we retain, in peace, vantage points on the shores of Cuba and create a strongly fortified naval base in Porto Rican waters. This control will reach Orinoco [near the present-day eastern border of Venezuela] and the Guianas."[32]

Subsequently, on 1 January 1902, a detachment of five Marine officers, one surgeon, and one hundred enlisted Marines began the permanent fortification of Culebra Island, a thickly wooded, six-mile-long islet sixteen miles east of Puerto Rico.[33] Culebra possessed no natural freshwater sources aside from that which came from the sky, but it did possess a magnificent harbor, known simply as "Great Harbor," that provided valuable protection for ships during the annual hurricane season.[34] One month earlier, in December 1901, portions of the island had been permanently ceded to the Department of the Navy. The conversion of designated areas to a fully equipped naval base now began in earnest, "in case of sudden war."[35] Named "Camp Roosevelt" in honor of the president, the camp featured barracks for officers and enlisted men, a storehouse for supplies, and a field hospital consisting of an operating room and a dispensary. The latter was deemed too small by reviewers from the Bureau of Medicine and Surgery, who recommended that it be enlarged to the standard size, providing additional sleeping quarters for attendants and a six-bed hospital ward.[36] Tiny Culebra and its harbor became the cornerstone of American naval activities in the Caribbean.

The Navy was also carefully monitoring the mounting domestic and international instability that surrounded the Castro regime. Small U.S. Navy vessels that pulled in and out of Venezuelan ports for resupply provided surprisingly detailed intelligence reports on events unfolding there. For much of the nineteenth century, naval officers such as Commo. William Bainbridge with the Barbary pirates, Commo. Mathew Perry in Japan, and Rear Adm. John Walker in Panama had functioned with proficiency and quiet expertise as the sole diplomatic representatives of their nation in many foreign ports.[37] They also served as frontline intelligence officers, acting as the eyes and ears of the United States with regard to matters critical to national interests. On 28 February 1901 the commander of the USS *Scorpion* reported that the president of Venezuela was encouraging public discontent with the United States over minor civil infractions involving American sailors. Lt. Cdr. Nathan Sargent reported that "President Castro is unpopular and his foothold is insecure; he feels therefore, that if the natural animosity to Americans can be encouraged, he can acquire popularity by his attitude and that his position will be greatly strengthened. In addition . . . he imagines he can gain the reputation of wielding a firm foreign policy without danger of being called to account for his actions by our Government." The *Scorpion*'s commanding officer suggested that the German government was using its local immigrant population to help stir up anti-American resentment: "I am also informed upon very reliable authority that the Germans are not wholly guiltless in this antagonism to everything American. They have here . . . a large colony in Venezuela, are naturally jealous of us and our trade, and have done their best to work up and accentuate this crusade against us."[38] Reports continued to arrive at the White House via the Navy Department detailing the increasing revolutionary unrest and the rising probability of European "intervention" to restore order.[39] Roosevelt knew the nature and the extent of the challenge he faced in the Caribbean, and he set about to prepare the instrument of his forthcoming diplomacy.

At the end of the nineteenth century, the U.S. Navy made a point of focusing its influence in the Caribbean. Following the Spanish-American War in 1898 the Navy commenced a series of "winter exercises," assembling various units of the fleet to carry out inspections and simulated engagements. It fell to Dewey's General Board to draft plans, assign units, and monitor the results. So it was that in May 1901 the General Board issued preliminary orders for the winter 1902–3 exercise. The conclusion of the exercise order described a simulated battle between two opposing fleets on the high seas.[40]

This proposal was refined in November 1901 by Secretary of the Navy John D. Long. According to Long's instructions, the winter exercise would begin with a series of inspections followed by combined live-firing drills (with limited expenditure of ammunition) to test the accuracy of the battleships' and cruisers' big guns and would culminate in the aforementioned simulated battle on the high seas between two large naval forces.[41] Every action ordered appears, from a professional's perspective, to be in line with standard operating procedures. As tensions between the European powers and Venezuela began to rise, however, a not too subtle "hidden hand" gradually altered the winter "exercise" to full preparation for war.

In early 1902 Ambassador von Holleben warned Kaiser Wilhelm II that Theodore Roosevelt would respond strongly to any hint of a permanent German military presence in South America. Wilhelm dismissed his ambassador's concern, saying, "We will do whatever is necessary . . . even if it displeases the Yankees."[42] The kaiser viewed the expansion of U.S. influence with alarm, fearing that it came at the expense of Germany's imperialist plans. In 1898, following George Dewey's defeat of the Spanish fleet in Manila Bay, a squadron of German ships sailed into the harbor amid rumors that it was intent on acquiring all or part of the former Spanish possession not claimed by the previously "nonimperial" United States.[43] The United States' subsequent departure from its historical imperial reluctance and acquisition of the entire archipelago, threatening to back up its stand with force if necessary, embarrassed the German commander, and by extension the kaiser.[44] Wilhelm was not one to suffer embarrassment without retaliation. At one point he even considered invading Long Island and using it as a bargaining chip to force the U.S. government to turn over certain overseas possessions.[45] Ultimately, Wilhelm backed away from that precipice and shifted his focus to other nations in the Western Hemisphere.

By the time Theodore Roosevelt assumed the presidency, Wilhelm had concluded that the Monroe Doctrine was a real threat to the expansion of German influence and territory in South America. In a government position paper he questioned the doctrine's legality. "The Monroe Doctrine has not become an international law, to which the European Nations are tied," he insisted, and he pointedly began referring to the "United States of North America" in his speeches and correspondence.[46] Contemporary observers discerned in Wilhelm's statements a strategy to "unite Europe, including England, in hostility to the Monroe doctrine."[47] Wilhelm II knew that he had to destroy the legitimacy of the United States' claims of preponderant interest in the Western Hemisphere to achieve the goals of German colonial expansion. To do that, he would have to take on Theodore Roosevelt.

Upon assuming the presidency, Roosevelt, for continuity, had asked McKinley's cabinet to remain in place. Within six months, however, the new president, who as assistant secretary had chafed under John Long's lethargy, accepted the old man's resignation, graciously describing him as as a man who was "single-minded in his devotion to the public interest."[48] Roosevelt took the traditional route of looking to the state of Massachusetts for a replacement and quickly appointed four-term congressman William H. Moody, "whose vigor, sturdiness, and temperament . . . resembled his own," as the new secretary of the Navy.[49] Moody's four years of service on the House Insular Affairs Committee had educated him on the magnitude of the challenges of carrying out a successful imperial foreign policy.[50] With Moody's help, Roosevelt quickly modified the character of the forthcoming naval exercise.

In June, Roosevelt took the highly irregular step of asking Admiral Dewey himself to assume command of the combined Atlantic Fleet for the winter exercise. Dewey, the Navy's only "four-star" admiral, seldom went to sea, and never for extended periods. He preferred to remain in Washington, where he could monitor the Navy from his office from nine until noon and then enjoy a nice afternoon nap at home before setting out for an afternoon carriage ride followed by dinner and early retirement to bed.[51] Revealing that the broader international audience was the intended target of his decision, Roosevelt wrote to Dewey: "Your standing . . . abroad, is such that the effect of your presence will be very beneficial."[52] Roosevelt demonstrated the importance he attached to Dewey's mission when, despite being bedridden with a leg injury that would ultimately result in a painful bone-scraping procedure, he invited Dewey to his sickroom to share his private thoughts on the matter. The president made it clear that his reason for assigning Dewey was twofold: He wanted Dewey commanding the fleet to "put pride in the people and [to] arrest the attention of . . . the Kaiser." The full extent of Roosevelt's instructions during this meeting are not known, but a diary entry by Dewey's wife later that evening intimates their sensitive nature: "The Prest. [sic] told G. in strict confidence—what had better not be written now."[53]

In August, Roosevelt attempted to telegraph the seriousness of his intentions to the international community. Writing to his good friend, British parliamentarian (and noted European socialite) Arthur Lee, Roosevelt stated that Dewey was training the fleet for war.[54] Lee, noted for his numerous contacts in European capitals, could be counted on to make sure that this diplomatic tidbit reached the right ears. Deeply sensitive to the significance of symbolism in diplomacy, T. R. completed his summer diplomatic foray by offering Dewey the use of the presidential yacht, the USS *Mayflower*, as his flagship.[55] Any attack on this ship, an outward symbol of the American presidency, could be seen only as a personal attack on Theodore Roosevelt himself.

Secretary of the Navy Moody had already taken steps to support Dewey in his mission to the Caribbean. Prior to the president's offer of the *Mayflower*, the swift packet vessel USS *Dolphin* had been placed at Dewey's command, along with an expert staff that included Rear Adm. Henry C. Taylor as chief of staff and the newly promoted Cdr. Nathan Sargent as Dewey's personal aide.[56] Again, from an operational perspective, Taylor's assignment as chief of staff is worthy of note.

Henry Clay Taylor was regarded as one of the most gifted men of his generation. He had served at the Naval War College in Newport, Rhode Island, acquiring a reputation as an intellectual, an administrator, and an innovator. When the position of chief of the Bureau of Navigation was vacated, Roosevelt reached far down and promoted Taylor over the heads of many of his superiors into the senior Navy position in Washington.[57] At that time there was no Chief of Naval Operations. Instead, the U.S. Navy was run by eight admirals who headed up "bureaus" (navigation, shipbuilding, ordnance, etc). While they were all equal in rank, it was accepted that the head of the

Bureau of Navigation was the "first among equals." The assignment of Taylor to be Dewey's chief of staff was thus highly unusual and could have occurred only by the direction of the commander in chief. The choice of Commander Sargent, recently the commander of the USS *Scorpion* and the source of so much intelligence concerning the political unrest in Venezuela, further underlines the importance assigned to this mission.

Moody took the additional step of ordering U.S. Navy assets in July to survey the Venezuelan coast for possible German landing zones and to submit suggestions for their defense. Later, in an internal memorandum, he informed his bureau chiefs that the president was "deeply interested" in the forthcoming maneuvers. Moody directed all involved to provide "hearty and vigorous cooperation" to ensure "that this mobilization of the fleet be successfully accomplished." He concluded by reminding the recipients "that this movement is a test of our ability to meet war demands" and assured his bureau chiefs that he would "sanction all reasonable expense within the law and regulations, in order that the vessels engaged . . . may be prepared."[58] This level of personal attention at the secretarial level leaps out at the historical and professional observer. In October the secretary issued the final instructions for the winter exercise, now just two months away. In a telling and dramatic departure from the simulated battle between two fleets on the high seas contained in previous versions of the exercise, Moody ordered a battle scenario focused on the interception of an approaching naval force intent on securing an undefended foreign harbor and mining its main ship channel.[59]

Naval power is not completely sea based, and Roosevelt's preparations did not end with Dewey and his fleet. Throughout the late summer and early fall, as the final changes were being made to the "winter exercise," the workings of the other arm of the naval service, the U.S. Marine Corps, also showed evidence of Roosevelt's hidden hand. In September 1903, on the order of the Commandant of the Corps, a battalion of Marines was constituted for possible deployment to Panama.[60] The battalion comprised 16 officers and 421 enlisted men under the command of Col. Percival C. Pope, an exceedingly experienced commander of troops whose service stretched back to the Civil War.[61] The men were embarked on board the USS *Prairie,* which remained tied up at the naval base in Norfolk, Virginia, awaiting further orders. On 23 October an additional order increased the size of the force by one company under the command of Capt. Smedley D. Butler, bringing the force to 19 officers and 522 enlisted men.[62] The size and structure of this force represented a sizable percentage of the expeditionary combative power of the Marine Corps.

On 5 November this force was ordered to participate in the winter exercise, and the *Prairie* departed Norfolk for Culebra Island.[63] The Marines reached the island on 20 November, disembarked, and began constructing three defensive artillery positions, mutually supporting in their fields of fire. They built roads strong enough to allow the transportation of heavy guns and ammunition between the emplacements and strung telephone lines between the various encampments. Rear Adm. Francis J. Higginson and Rear Adm. Joseph B. Coghlan, the respective commanders of the North Atlantic and Caribbean squadrons, inspected the positions and pronounced them satisfactory.[64] The Marines' actions constituted a major effort to establish a defensible base for fleet operations.

Kaiser Wilhelm II remained oblivious to the mounting American resistance to his plan for expansion in South America. Throughout the summer and early fall he worked to convince the British to act with Germany to coerce Venezuela into paying off its debts.[65] Two months later, in a characteristic boast, Wilhelm played up the capabilities of his navy to visiting American Army general (and known Roosevelt confidant) Leonard Wood.[66] By early November the forces of Germany and Great Britain were in position to take action against Venezuela.[67] Rear Admiral Taylor advised Roosevelt that war between the United States and the European powers was the likely outcome if the situation developing off Venezuela turned violent.[68]

On the evening of 24 November 1902 Roosevelt hosted a private dinner for a small group at the White House to honor Baron Speck von Sternburg, a German diplomat and old friend. Both men had served in Washington during the early 1890s, Roosevelt on the Civil Service Commission and von Sternburg in the German embassy. Roosevelt hoped to use the intimacy of personal diplomacy to convey his intentions directly to the kaiser's senior staff. Also at the dinner table that evening was Admiral of the Navy George Dewey.[69]

Admiral Dewey always maintained the poise and appearance of a cultured man, but inside him raged a fierce spirit with but one focus: Germany. While he publicly restrained his comments, Washington's social elite were well aware that Dewey held the Germans in particular distaste as a result of the German navy's actions preceding and following the Battle of Manila Bay.[70] Mildred Dewey, again in the privacy of her diary, stated her unvarnished opinion of the U.S.-German relationship, "The truth is, we hate each other."[71]

Roosevelt's purpose in inviting Admiral Dewey to the White House for dinner could not have escaped a professional diplomat of von Sternburg's caliber. But events in European capitals conspired to ensure that the carefully constructed guest list and dinner conversation would not have the time or opportunity to achieve Roosevelt's aim. Events were already in motion.

Germany and Great Britain had begun to consider joint action against Venezuela in the early days of 1902.[72] Great Britain wanted to seize Venezuela's gunboats as "a convenient form of coercion" and as a means of avoiding the perception of infringing on Roosevelt's Monroe Doctrine.[73] The kaiser, however, remained convinced that Roosevelt was bluffing and instructed his ambassador to Britain to communicate his intention to blockade the South American republic. Count Paul von Metternich's arguments carried the day, and on 25 November 1902 Germany and Great Britain formally announced their intention to implement a "pacific" blockade of Venezuela.[74]

Britain's participation in the Venezuelan Crisis appears inconsistent with its evolving national interests in the Western Hemisphere. After a century of acrimony and distrust between their two respective nations, the governments of Theodore Roosevelt and Arthur Balfour seemed to be successfully knitting together the destinies of the two great English-speaking nations. Given the importance it attached to its current relationship with America, Balfour's government took the precaution of forewarning Secretary of State Hay of Britain's decision to blockade Venezuela. Hay, who was either out of touch with Roosevelt's thinking or deliberately playing his role in a grand Rooseveltian diplomatic drama, responded that while he regretted "that European Powers should use force against Central and South American countries," his country "could not object to their taking steps to obtain redress for injuries suffered by their subjects, provided no acquisition of territory was contemplated."[75] Perhaps because of the tepid nature of Hay's assurance, Britain's new ambassador to the United States, Michael Herbert, felt compelled to express his own personal reservations. "I wish we were going to punish Venezuela without the aid of Germany," he wrote to his foreign minister, Lord Henry Lansdowne, "for I am not sure that joint action will be very palatable here."[76]

On 1 December Roosevelt traveled the few blocks south from the White House to the Washington Navy Yard to see Dewey off. The exact words exchanged between the two men are not known, but the substance of the conversation is clear: while Dewey did sail with the intention of overseeing the annual winter exercise, there was the very real potential for him to play an even greater role in the developing crisis off the coast of Venezuela. As her husband sailed south out of communication, Mildred Dewey recorded in her diary, "I dread there may be war over Veequela [sic] . . . how can Georg [sic] get thru three wars unscathed."[77]

39

Execution

On 7 December 1902 Germany and Great Britain instituted their "peaceful blockade" of Venezuela.[78] It did not begin well. A Venezuelan mob in Porto Cabello seized the British-flagged merchantman *Topaze* at anchor there, and German ships shelled two nearby Venezuelan military installations in response. Elsewhere, students marched in the streets displaying banners that called on the United States to uphold *la doctrina* Monroe on their behalf.[79] President Castro escalated tensions and gave his opponents a legal recipe for a declaration of war when he ordered the imprisonment of all male British and German citizens and the seizure of their property.[80] On 9 December British and German naval forces proceeded to capture the ships of the Venezuelan navy then in port.[81] The Germans, in their enthusiasm, sank one of their prizes and seriously damaged another.[82] Castro, by now convinced of the seriousness of the European threat, appealed to the American minister in Venezuela, Herbert Bowen, to intercede on Venezuela's behalf and extend an offer of arbitration.[83] Britain, increasingly aware of the concern the situation had aroused in the United States, assented, but Germany attempted to sidestep arbitration.[84]

The concept of arbitration as an element of international law emerged from The Hague Peace Conference convened by Czar Nicholas II in the spring and summer of 1899. While the conference did not achieve its ultimate, idealistic aim of achieving world peace, it did result in the establishment of a Permanent Court of Arbitration where nations could seek redress for their mutual grievances without having to resort to armed conflict. Germany, not keen to see the martial advantage arising in its shipyards and the forges of the Krupp arms factories nullified by weak nations who sought equal treatment through legal avenues, opposed the arbitration initiatives.[85] Now, as word of the Venezuelan offer arrived in Germany, the kaiser's earlier concerns seemed justified. Arbitration at this point in the blockade would not allow for the series of events necessary for Germany to gain the toehold of Venezuelan territory it needed to begin its slow expansion into South America and assert strategic prominence overlooking the approaches to the long-planned canal across the isthmus. The kaiser rejected arbitration.

According to Theodore Roosevelt's later accounts, as the *Mayflower* dropped anchor off Culebra Island on 8 December, he was in the White House welcoming a group of German businessmen escorted by Ambassador Theodor von Holleben. During this meeting, the president later recalled, he drew von Holleben aside and spoke sharply to him, issuing an ultimatum demanding that Germany either accept arbitration within ten days or face armed conflict with the United States.[86] The shocked ambassador responded that he could not forward such a demand, phrased as it was, to the kaiser. Apparently, von Holleben left the room convinced that Roosevelt was bluffing. He would not have been so certain had he been aware of the actions of Admiral Dewey during the period 9–18 December 1902.

Naval professionals will quickly discern within the stark events that occurred over the next week and a half the differences between a well-executed "winter exercise" and the actions of a veteran combatant commander preparing his forces for war. Background analysis also reveals the blunt hand of America's relatively new chief diplomatist and commander in chief. Unlike previous exercises, which focused on individual naval squadrons, the 1902–3 maneuvers gathered every available battleship, cruiser, and torpedo boat in the Atlantic.[87]

By combining the North Atlantic, South Atlantic, European, and Caribbean squadrons, Dewey was able to marshal fifty-three ships to counter the twenty-nine ships available to Britain and Germany in the Caribbean.[88] Although this number may seem excessive, it was necessary, in Roosevelt's mind, to demonstrate an ability on the part of the United States to concentrate an overwhelming force in its claimed "zone of influence." Both Great Britain and Germany possessed larger navies than the United States, but they would have had to strip units from other critical areas of their empires (leaving trade routes vulnerable to disruption) in order to exceed the combined American fleet. Assembling such a force would take weeks—weeks in which Roosevelt would be free to exercise his diplomacy.

While Dewey cruised down from Washington, D.C., aboard the *Mayflower* his task force was already exercising in the Caribbean. The individual components of the Atlantic Fleet had begun to assemble off Culebra in mid-November (Table 2). On 1 November the Caribbean Squadron under the command of Rear Adm. Joseph Coghlan had made the short transit to Culebra from its base at San Juan, Puerto Rico. Coghlan's division comprised the type of cruisers and auxiliary cruisers that had borne the brunt of action during the Spanish-American War four years earlier. The North Atlantic Squadron, largely formed of battleships and under the command of Rear Adm. Francis Higginson, arrived on 21 November 1902 from Hampton Roads, Virginia. The remaining two squadrons—the South Atlantic Squadron under the command of Rear Adm. George W. Sumner and the European Squadron under the command of Rear Adm. A. S. Crowninshield—which each comprised a

TABLE 2. U.S. ATLANTIC FLEET COMPONENTS PRIOR TO 1902
WINTER EXERCISE

North Atlantic Squadron	Caribbean Squadron	South Atlantic Squadron	European Squadron
Rear Adm. Francis J. Higginson	Rear Adm. Joseph B. Coghlan	Rear Adm. George W. Sumner	Rear Adm. Arent S. Crowninshield
USS *Kearsarge* (BB), flagship	USS *Olympia* (CL), flagship	USS *Iowa* (BB), flagship	USS *Illinois* (BB), flagship
USS *Alabama* (BB)	USS *Montgomery* (CL)	USS *Atlanta* (CL)	USS *Chicago* (CL)
USS *Massachusetts* (BB)	USS *Detroit* (CL)	USS *San Francisco* (CL)	USS *Albany* (CL)
USS *Indiana* (BB)	USS *Panther* (CX)		USS *Nashville* (GB)
USS *Cincinnati* (CL)	USS *Marietta* (GB)		
USS *Machias* (GB)			
USS *Scorpion* (GBL)			
USS *Gloucester* (GBL)			
USS *Aileen* (GBL)			
Torpedo Flotilla Lt. Cdr. Lloyd Chandler USS *Decatur* (TB), command ship USS *Bagley* (TB), USS *Barney* (TB), USS *Biddle* (TB), USS *Shubrick* (TB), USS *Thomtom* (TB), USS *Stockton* (TB)			

Abbreviations: BB, battleship; CL, unarmored cruiser; CX, auxiliary cruiser; GB, gunboat; GBL, unarmored gunboat; TB, torpedo boat.
Source: Annual Report of the Navy Department, 1903 (Washington, D.C.: Government Printing Office, 1903), 466–473.

single battleship escorted by three or four armored or protected cruisers, rendezvoused in the Gulf of Paria to form the simulated approaching opposing force in the winter exercise's main battle problem.

The objective of the exercise was for the opposing White force under the command of Rear Admiral Sumner to "secure a base" in any one of five harbors in the vicinity of Puerto Rico and Culebra by 6:00 PM on 10 December 1902. The Blue (American) force under the command of Rear Admiral Higginson had to intercept this fleet, either at sea or soon after its arrival in a port, with a superior force. The result of this exercise provides insight into the great challenges of warfare on the vast reaches of the oceans. Sumner's force transited first far to the east and then to the north of the islands before making a final swift passage down through the Mona Passage. Sumner successfully completed his task—occupying and defensively mining a harbor without resistance—on 9 December.[89]

Admiral Dewey had dropped anchor at Culebra's Great Harbor the previous day. His first step on arriving in the Caribbean was to secure fuel and ammunition for his ships as well as current intelligence on his surroundings. During his sail down from Washington Dewey had requested information on the positions of all logistical support ships in the Atlantic, and on arrival he ordered all ships to submit a list of the supplies required for them to meet "all contingencies." In the meantime, Secretary Moody had wired his naval attachés in London, Paris, and Berlin requesting the desertion rates of the respective European navies in a rough attempt to ascertain their readiness for war.[90]

Dewey continued to issue orders at odds with the planned inspection, gunnery exercise, and simulated battle. He instructed a majority of the fleet to maintain position outside Great Harbor, and all U.S. ships to "maintain sufficient steam pressure to get underway" at a moment's notice.[91] Maintaining this high readiness posture was exhausting for the men involved and used up large quantities of coal. Further, it was very difficult to perform a full material inspection of a ship with the crew manning all stations and the fires in the steam engineering plant ignited and hot. Most engine inspections were completed when the fires of the propulsion system were out and the steam plant was cold, allowing the internal workings of the boiler and gearing systems to be opened and available for visual inspection. Dewey, it seems, was not emphasizing a rigorous material review.

Perhaps the most glaring example of Dewey's novel approach to the exercise was his order on 10 December to his medical staff to establish a sixty-bed hospital ward in Puerto Rico.[92] The Marines, as previously mentioned, had built a "standard" six-bed hospital ward the year before, and the ships in Dewey's fleet maintained their own sickbays and carried doctors or pharmacist's mates to tend to the day-to-day ills and complaints of the crew. Squadrons typically carried a surgeon who would shuttle back and forth between the ships to handle the most serious cases. But Dewey took the initiative of moving his surgeons and their equipment off the major capital ships and borrowing medical staff from the growing naval base ashore to establish a land-based hospital capable of handling an inordinate number of sick or wounded. Whether that action is viewed from the vantage point of a naval professional or an archival historian, it is clear that Dewey was making every effort to ensure that all preparatory steps for combat operations had been taken.

A message from Chief of Staff Taylor to the commanding officer of the naval base adds another clue to Dewey's intent. It is customary, when a group of navy ships pulls into port, for a shore detail to be formed to assist the local command in the logistical support of the ships. This practice maintains order among the sailors allowed ashore (the dreaded "shore patrol") and also provides for the upkeep of the piers and waterfront. The local commanding officer sent a request to Dewey's flagship for just this sort of detail when the *Mayflower* arrived, but on 11 December Rear Admiral Taylor replied, "I regret to inform you it will be impracticable to give you any force of men or boats from the fleet at present. The intention of Admiral Dewey is to keep the fleet outside [the harbor] in a state of preparation to move at short notice."[93] This and Dewey's other instructions were not typical of a fleet commander preparing his ships for a set schedule of inspections, gun firings, and simulated battle. In fact, on his second day in the harbor, Dewey, a noted stickler for schedules and organization, scuttled a carefully prepared schedule and announced his intention to begin material inspections of the major combatants immediately.[94] He quickly moved through the material inspection phase, pushing on into instruction for all ships in the new system of marksmanship developed by Lt. Cdr. William S. Sims.[95]

Back in Washington—according to Edmund Morris' timeline, on the afternoon of Sunday, 14 December—Roosevelt held his second meeting with Ambassador von Holleben. After discussing the weather and exchanging other pleasantries, Roosevelt asked if von Holleben had a reply for him regarding his previous ultimatum. The ambassador replied that since he had assumed that Roosevelt was not serious, he had not sent the message to the kaiser. Roosevelt later remembered telling von Holleben that "instead of allowing the three days that remained for an answer I would order Dewey to sail [south to Venezuela] in forty-eight hours."[96] T. R. also began a series of hurried consultations with members of the House of Representatives and the Senate that were reported in the *New York Times* and *Washington Evening Star* for all to see.[97] Dewey, for his part, alluded to the focus of his attention when he wrote obliquely to his son the same day, "Things look rather equally Venezuela way, but we are not in it at present."[98]

The German ambassador understood with stark clarity his predicament. Following his 14 December meeting with Roosevelt, he hurried north to New York City to meet with Karl Bunz, the longtime German consul general there and a friend of Theodore Roosevelt. Years later, a friend of Bunz recounted that von Holleben came to ask if Roosevelt's threat should be taken seriously. Bunz replied that to the best of his knowledge, Roosevelt did not bluff.[99]

That same day, Secretary Moody wired Dewey, via a secure underwater Navy cable, to maintain a swift vessel at the ready in San Juan in order to ensure continuous communications with the fleet. He sent a similar message to the naval station at San Juan to stand by to forward instructions immediately to Dewey at sea.[100] Dewey and the combined fleet had by this time progressed into a sequence of coordinated maneuvers, beginning with divisions of four ships, then combining into squadrons, and ultimately coming together as a fleet (Table 3).The new torpedo-boat flotilla practiced stealthy night attacks against simulated opponent battleships.

Dewey confided to his journal that "some of the evolutions were rather raggedly performed, owing to new ships having joined. . . . [I] think angles and turning circles not yet having been determined."[101] The after action report noted that the "cruiser divisions were handled in connection with line of battle[ships] without confusion and without the necessity of frequent signals or signaling at great distances."

Capt. Albert Gleaves, the commanding officer of Dewey's flagship, the *Mayflower,* disagreed with that assessment. Gleaves recorded in his memoirs an attempt to steam in formation from Culebra to Saint Thomas that left an indelible image of a fleet "without form and void—so to speak." Gleaves felt that the ad hoc procurement practices of the Navy Department had resulted in such a multitude of ship designs and capabilities that the U.S. Navy was practically unable to operate in formations beyond small groups of similarly designed ships. Following the winter exercise, an attempt was made to align the fleet in accordance with the ships' capabilities.[102]

In another departure from the norms of the day, Admiral Dewey directed that the reinforced Marine battalion under the command of Colonel Pope at Culebra dispatch landing parties to the eastern and western shores of Vieques, to the bay of Ensenada Honda, and to the northern shore of Puerto Rico. Those Marines left on Culebra not tasked with logistical duties were sent into that island's jungles.[103] These reconnoitering parties, each comprising an officer and twenty-five enlisted men and supplied with a week's worth of provisions, practiced armed reconnaissance, searching out possible enemy landing sites and establishing defensive positions to repel the aggressor force. While the after action report makes no mention of Venezuela, Dewey's involvement and the magnitude and realism of the Marines' activities indicate that this, too, was no mere exercise. Dewey's final report obliquely summarized the Marines' jungle training: "These various exercises proved of conspicuous value to the officers and men engaged in them and gave us much valuable experience for later use."[104]

TABLE 3. COMBINED U.S. ATLANTIC FLEET, 10 DECEMBER 1902

Commander
Admiral of the Navy George Dewey
USS *Mayflower*, flagship

First Squadron	Second Squadron	Base Command
Rear Adm. Francis J. Higginson	Rear Adm. George W. Sumner	Rear Adm. Joseph B.
First Division	**Third Division**	Coghlan
USS *Kearsarge* (BB), flagship	USS *Chicago* (CL), flagship	USS *Vixen* (PY), flagship
USS *Iowa* (BB)	USS *Albany* (CL)	**Substitute Vessels**
USS *Massachusetts* (BB)	USS *Cincinnati* (CL)	USS *Nashville* (GB)
USS *Alabama* (BB)	USS *Newark* (CL)	USS *Machias* (GB)
USS *Scorpion* (GBL), tender	USS *Eagle,* tender	USS *Marietta* (GB)
Second Division	**Fourth Division**	USS *Bancroft* (GB)
Rear Adm. A. S. Crowninshield	Capt. Asa Walker	USS *Wasp,* tender
USS *Illinois* (BB), flagship	USS *San Francisco* (CL),	**Torpedo Flotilla**
USS *Texas* (BB)	command ship	Lt. Cdr. Lloyd Chandler
USS *Indiana* (BB)	USS *Atlanta* (CL)	USS *Decatur* (TB),
USS *Olympia* (CL)	USS *Montgomery* (CL)	command ship
USS *Hist,* tender	USS *Detroit* (CL)	USS *Bagley* (TB)
Transports	**Tugs**	USS *Barney* (TB)
USS *Prairie* (CX)	USS *Fortune*	USS *Biddle* (TB)
USS *Panther* (CX)	USS *Leyden*	USS *Thornton* (TB)
Water Supply	USS *Osceola*	USS *Wilkes* (TB)
USS *Arethusa*	USS *Potomac*	USS *Stockton* (TB)
	USS *Uncas*	USS *Nina,* tender
		Supply and Repair
		USS *Culgoa*
Colliers		
USS *Hannibal*, USS *Leonidas,*		
USS *Sterling*, USS *Lebanon,*		
USS *Brutus*, USS *Marcellus,*		
USS *Ajax*		

Abbreviations: BB, battleship; CL, unarmored cruiser; GB, armored gunboat; GBL, unarmored gunboat; CX, auxiliary cruiser; TB, torpedo boat.
Source: Journal of the Commander in Chief, Dewey Collection, Library of Congress, Washington, D.C., box 44, 15.

In reply to Moody's 14 December letter, Dewey acknowledged the order to maintain a courier boat to relay messages and, in a barely disguised request for additional information, pointedly asked, "Program of exercises called for dispersal of fleet Friday night for Christmas holidays. Shall this be carried out?"[105] Earlier that day Dewey had received an intelligence report from the commanding officer of the USS *Marietta,* operating off La Guayra, Venezuela, detailing the actions taken by the British and German war vessels *Charybis* and *Vineta* against Venezuelan military installations and port facilities.[106] Based on this information, and clearly expecting a war order, Rear Admiral Taylor sent a message to the communications center in San Juan: "Recent intelligence from Washington indicates the possibility of urgent dispatches arriving anytime . . . it is probable that such cables may be written in cipher and every precaution should be taken to expedite their delivery . . . it is advisable to avoid comment upon questions and topics in any way."[107]

Shortly after transmitting this cable, Dewey recalled all of his force's ambulatory sick from Puerto Rican hospitals in an effort to fully man his ships, and ordered all of his ships currently in or near the port to be fully loaded with stores.[108] No other indicator of the expectation of combat can be so clear as the decision to pull a sick man from his bed in order to man his battle station.

December seventeenth dawned ominously as William Moody cryptically instructed Dewey not to disperse the fleet. Such instructions along with Dewey's activities indicate that both Dewey and Moody expected the worst. Supplies of coal and ammunition had been loaded, and the force had been exercised vigorously at sea. Word from Washington indicated no change in the Europeans' position, and it was apparent that the situation was deteriorating. The U.S. Senate passed a resolution endorsing Roosevelt's public warnings to the European nations with regard to maintaining the territorial integrity of Venezuela.[109] As night fell, Dewey assembled all of his senior commanders onboard the *Mayflower* "for consultations relative to the Venezuelan question."[110]

In the United States, public reaction to events in Venezuela was decidedly anti-European, an attitude that was promptly noted in European capitals. Prime Minister Balfour learned from his ambassador in the United States, Sir Michael Herbert, "The impression prevails in Washington that Germany is using us, and our friends here regret, from the point of view of American good feeling towards us, that we are acting with her."[111] Three days earlier Herbert had cabled an encrypted message stating that the U.S. government was passing along Venezuela's renewed desire to seek a "settlement of the present difficulty by arbitration."[112] On 16 December Parliament convened to debate the situation in Venezuela and the strains it was placing on Britain's relationship with America.[113] Balfour appeared in Parliament the following day to announce, "We have no intention, and have never had any intention, of landing troops in

Venezuela or of occupying territory, even though that occupation might only be of a temporary nature."[114]

The next day the American ambassador, Henry White, presented a message from Roosevelt to Balfour's government strongly urging Britain and Germany to accept arbitration. Although Balfour was irritated by the impertinence of the suggestion, he felt it necessary to maintain the goodwill of the United States and quickly accepted it. Other officials of the government stepped forward to acknowledge and recognize the Monroe Doctrine. The prime minister also took it upon himself to contact some leading American citizens to ask them to relay to Roosevelt his desire for continued good relations with the United States. The burgeoning special relationship between the two English-speaking nations remained a high priority.[115]

In Berlin, the reaction to the United States' "suggestion" of arbitration was slightly different. Much to Lord Lansdowne's consternation, Germany's ambassador to Great Britain, Count Paul von Metternich, continued to insist that the kaiser would not stoop to arbitration.[116] The kaiser, it seems, was continuing to call what he thought was Roosevelt's bluff. Back in the United States, Ambassador von Holleben's military attachés traveled north to advise him on the strategic implications of the positioning of the American fleet.[117] Finally overcoming his "mortal terror" of the kaiser, von Holleben transmitted two telegrams to Berlin. Their contents are unknown, but their effect was immediate.[118] On the evening of 17 December Berlin signaled its acceptance of the American arbitration proposal. The kaiser had, as one observer wrote, "tested the Monroe Doctrine and discovered that it held."[119]

Soon after the crisis ended, Theodor von Holleben was recalled in disgrace by the German emperor. The Washington establishment buzzed at both the suddenness and the silence of his departure. An explanation that the ambassador's health was impaired was so at odds with his appearance and actions that speculation only increased. Some suggested that he had failed in his mission for the kaiser because he cultivated too friendly a relationship with Roosevelt rather than seek out ties with the financial community in New York so important to Germany's industrial expansion. Decades would pass before the real nature of his diplomatic demise was understood.

Following the Venezuela Crisis, the Monroe Doctrine, which the European powers had always looked on with skepticism, gained widespread tacit recognition and respect.[120] Wilhelm had blinked, ending Germany's chance to create colonies in the Western Hemisphere. On 18 December, free of worries,

Secretary Moody wired his commander at sea, "Carry out your proposed holiday itinerary. Merry Christmas."[121]

It had been Dewey's original intent to remain in the Caribbean well into January 1903, but following the Christmas port visits he apparently changed his mind. The captain of his flagship later recounted,

> One day at luncheon he [Dewey] astonished everyone by asking,
> . . . "Captain Swift, how long it would take to close up and sail for home."
>
> Captain Swift said, "By pushing everything and everybody, we should be ready in ten days."
>
> The Admiral exploded, "Ten days! Hell! Get everything ready at once. I shall sail tonight at eight."
>
> And we did.[122]

On 4 January 1903, as the *Mayflower* made its way back up the eastern coast of the United States, Admiral Dewey summarized the success of his mission in a letter to George Dewey Jr. The exercise, he wrote, "has been very interesting and I think beneficial to the Navy & Country. I have no doubt the Venezuela question would have given considerable trouble had it not been for this splendid fleet on the spot."[123] Years later, Roosevelt would sum up the role of George Dewey and his fleet succinctly during a speech given in Oyster Bay. "Dewey," the former president remembered, "was the greatest possible provocateur of peace."[124]

Edmund Morris eloquently described the vacant diplomatic record surrounding the Venezuelan Crisis as a "white shape of some vanished enormity, a reverse silhouette cut out of the gray text of history."[125] The naval record of the events associated with the crisis, both in the broader scope of Roosevelt's overarching naval policy and in the specific actions of Admiral of the Navy George Dewey in his role as the commander in chief of the combined Atlantic Fleet, support Theodore Roosevelt's later version of events as expressed in his 1915 letter to William R. Thayer.

Roosevelt's Veracity

From the outset of his administration it was Theodore Roosevelt's desire to "upbuild" the U.S. Navy, supporting the service's uniformed leadership in their desire for increased production of capital vessels. When faced with a credible threat to U.S. interests in the Caribbean and South America, he authorized the construction of a large naval base on Culebra, an island strategically located in the path of European approaches to the Caribbean. He altered the nature of a routine winter exercise—both its scenario and its composition—flooding the Caribbean basin with the near entirety of the Atlantic Fleet to ensure an overwhelming concentration of power during the critical months of the crisis. Further, Roosevelt personally made changes in personnel in key political and military positions.

He let the cautious John D. Long retire as secretary of the Navy and replaced him with the energetic expansionist William Moody, who would go on to serve as Roosevelt's attorney general and ultimately became an associate justice on the Supreme Court. Capt. Henry C. Taylor, the intellectually dynamic president of the Naval War College, was promoted to rear admiral and assigned as chief of the Bureau of Navigation, the most powerful uniformed position in the Navy. Lastly, the young president brought Admiral of the Navy George Dewey out of near retirement, clearly seeing the dual advantage of having his most famous (from the international perspective) and experienced (from the vantage of the officers and sailors at sea) combat leader in command.

At the fleet level, evidence of the combative intent of the December 1902 maneuvers is clear and conclusive. Dewey's decision to maintain the fleet at full combat readiness from the moment of its arrival in the Caribbean reflected the painful lesson he had taught the Spanish fleet at Manila in 1898 when he had caught the ships at anchor, with boilers cold, inside the confines of a bay that Dewey effectively controlled upon arrival. Taken alone, this action could be discounted as an effort to increase the "reality" of the exercise, but combined with Dewey's unique order to establish a large field hospital ashore, this order clearly demonstrates his expectation of a major fleet action.[126]

Dewey's internal personal and professional correspondence also buttresses the argument that the winter exercise portended U.S. readiness to meet the European navies in combat. Aside from Mrs. Dewey's diary entries, which imply that Dewey kept his wife fully informed of the extent of his mission in the Caribbean, we also have the evidence of Dewey's letters to his son, with their numerous circumspect references to the fleet's actions being of great "value to the Navy and Country."[127] Last, the log entries of the USS *Mayflower*'s letter book show a mounting and ever-present concern with the topic of Venezuela.

The contents of the messages being transmitted in code via the underwater telegraph cable between San Juan and the continental United States not only convey the seriousness of the situation (Moody's preoccupation with maintaining a dispatch vessel for the quick delivery of important communications to the fleet contravenes standard operating procedures during a naval exercise) but also make it possible to determine the effective beginning and ending dates of the crisis. The transmission of logistical and intelligence data commenced on 9 December, the day after Theodore Roosevelt allegedly issued his ultimatum to the German ambassador, and the message traffic and background tension rapidly decreased after Moody's 18 December message to disperse the fleet for Christmas port visits.

Finally, we have Dewey's own words from a letter written after the controversy surrounding Thayer's *Life and Letters of John Hay* came to light in 1915. Responding to a personal letter from Henry Wood, Dewey wrote, "I was at Culebra, Puerto Rico, at the time, in command of a fleet consisting of over fifty ships, including every battleship and every torpedo boat that we had, with orders from Washington to hold the fleet in hand, and be ready to move at a moment's notice. Fortunately, however, the whole matter was amicably adjusted and there was no need for action."[128]

Hence, both naval and historical records seem to provide more than enough evidence to support the proposition that the American fleet arrived in the Caribbean with the intent of coercing the European nations into accepting mediation. In order for this form of diplomacy to be successful, the naval forces involved had to be fully prepared to conduct combat operations. In the end, it was this high degree of preparation that helped to convince the Europeans of Roosevelt's seriousness and bring them to the bargaining table.

Contemporary accounts demonstrate that Roosevelt was quick to recognize Germany as a peer, competitor, and threat. Its recent actions in China coupled with its rapidly growing immigrant population in South America and solidly Mahanian naval policy suggested (correctly, as historical documents would later point out) the possibility of a larger, more permanent German presence in the Western Hemisphere. While still vice president, Roosevelt had written to Henry Cabot Lodge that Germany interpreted the United States' refusal to build up a large navy as a sign of weakness, and that "in a few years they will be in a position to take some step in the West Indies or South America which will make us either put up or shut up on the Monroe doctrine."[129] Austria, Italy, and Russia did not trouble his thoughts; Germany was his focus.[130] What Roosevelt needed, and perhaps even desired, was an opportunity to pit his will and the armament of the United States against Germany to firmly establish America's position as a leading power in the international system.

Theodore Roosevelt went to extraordinary lengths to inform European powers of his interpretation of the Monroe Doctrine, both formally through conversations with the German consul general and ambassador, and informally through back-channel personal conversations with his many contacts on the European continent. He telegraphed his intention to deploy a credible combat force by several means, not the least of which was naming Dewey the commander of the task force. Roosevelt set a time limit of ten days for the resolution of the crisis, and when his ultimatum was ignored, he heightened the sense of urgency by accelerating the timetable. Ultimately, it was his presence and force of will that convinced Ambassador von Holleben of the seriousness of the situation and led the ambassador to overcome the kaiser's personal resistance to arbitration. Roosevelt's discretion, employed throughout the process, enabled his strategy to succeed. Had the president gone public with his demands at any time, the kaiser, facing war or public humiliation, might well have chosen war. Yet the discreet nature of Roosevelt's demands allowed Wilhelm the opportunity to back down in private and preserved for the immediate present the future relations between the two nations.

The previous century of tacit cooperation with Great Britain suggested that the British would neither actively oppose Roosevelt's new interpretation of the doctrine nor stand in the way of his new activist foreign policy. Nevertheless, the events in Venezuela along with the events of the last decade of the nineteenth century suggest that conflict with the United States was not outside the realm of possibility. Documents recently declassified under the "one-hundred-year rule" at the British National Archives suggest that Roosevelt's actions with regard to Venezuela may have had another, albeit unintended, result. As the winter exercise approached and tensions increased between the United States and the European powers, the British Colonial Office drafted a secret memorandum that was forwarded to the Colonial Defense Committee, the War Office, and ultimately the Admiralty for comment. The memorandum raised questions about the defensibility of British possessions in the western Atlantic in the event of a conflict with the United States. In a response entitled "Strategic Conditions in Event of War with the United States," the Admiralty expressed doubt that "it would be possible to dispatch a sufficient naval force to maintain sea supremacy" in the western Atlantic and Caribbean "if at the time of the outbreak of war uncertain or hostile relations existed between this country and a European power." The document goes on to state that the United States would be in a position to "stop our supplies from Canada" and to secure all food imports from the United States itself, effectively cutting off two-thirds of Great Britain's food supply. The inescapable conclusion was that current realities emphasized "the necessity of preserving good relations with the United States."[131] Within two years Lansdowne and Balfour would secure an unofficial security arrangement with the United States, the beginning of what has come to be known as "the Special Relationship."[132]

Thus it was that Theodore Roosevelt established for all the world to see the two pillars on which he would construct his foreign policy: the Monroe Doctrine and the U.S. Navy. His actions during the Venezuelan Crisis established precedents for American involvement in the world throughout the twentieth century. Yet for all his "speak softly" discretion, he could be driven to "big stick" audaciousness as well, as his next excursion in statecraft would amply illustrate.

chapter three

Scalable Response in Defense of the Panamanian Revolution

I took the Isthmus, started the canal, and then left Congress . . .
not to debate the canal, but to debate me. And while the debate goes on,
so does the canal.

THEODORE ROOSEVELT, 23 MARCH 1911

17 August 1903

Theodore Roosevelt was furious. The Senate of Colombia had, to his surprise, rejected the carefully crafted Hay-Herrán Treaty, by which the United States would be granted access to a narrow strip of land across the Colombian province of Panama. Negotiated at the behest of the Colombians in January of that year with terms very favorable to the United States, the treaty had been presented to the U.S. Senate, which ratified it in March.[1] The momentum of the negotiations then passed to the Colombians, who decided to take advantage of the United States' desire for a canal cutting across the narrow isthmus. An affirmative vote by the Colombians would have authorized construction to begin on one of the greatest engineering feats in history. The creation of the canal would enhance commerce and enable the quick transfer of U.S. Navy ships from one coast to the other, doubling the effectiveness of the American fleet. The canal had long occupied the center of Theodore Roosevelt's foreign policy, and he was determined to see it built.[2]

Roosevelt and the Panama Canal are forever linked in history. His conviction that a canal must be constructed through Central America had been a common theme in his writings and speeches throughout the 1890s. His personal interest in the building of the canal compelled him to be the first chief executive of the United States to travel outside the country while in office when he boarded the USS *Louisiana* to travel to the Canal Zone. But was the canal so important that Roosevelt would "take" the Isthmus of Panama in order to see it built? More specifically, would he risk military action to achieve his goal?

Most historians agree that the Panamanian Revolution had its origins within Panama's borders and began at a moment of the revolutionaries' own choosing.[3] Regardless of the U.S. Navy's actions after the uprising began, no evidence has ever been brought forward to confirm that Theodore Roosevelt explicitly promised assistance to the rebels. Instead it is understood that the revolt was their decision to make, and that Roosevelt reserved his prerogative to respond to their actions in accordance with the interests of the United States as he saw them. Critical questions still remain, however. What did trigger Panama's movement toward independence? Was there a tipping point that initiated the fateful process of political independence from Colombia? And most important, was the revolt a popular uprising or the product of a small cabal of intelligentsia and business concerns?

A rigorous review of the operational military record reveals other events that contributed to the onset of the revolution: specifically, the actions of two young U.S. Army officers acting behind the scenes in Colombia and Panama, and the appearance of a U.S. Navy warship off the coast of the Colombian province. Additionally, close scrutiny of Navy Department correspondence reveals a plan created at the specific direction of the president of the United States. This plan, referred to as "War Portfolio No. 1," envisioned an active "defense" of the new Panamanian republic by military units of the United States. Little known and never referenced by previous Roosevelt biographers, War Portfolio No. 1 demonstrates a decisiveness and predilection for action that stands in stark contrast to the demure foreign policy statements issued by the first Roosevelt administration—policy statements that may have convinced the Colombians that they could pull the tail of the tiger during the months of negotiation that led up to their rejection of the Hay-Herrán Treaty.

Jackrabbits in Bogotá

The arrival of the ratified canal treaty in the Colombian capital relieved the pressure on President José Marroquín. Previously he had worried about the numerous interests within the United States that were actively lobbying for a canal route across Nicaragua. But with the ball now safely back in his court, it was within the Colombian leader's power to confirm the treaty outright, given the dictatorial character of his office. Instead, he chose to call the nation's legislature into session, for the first time since 1898, to consider the treaty.[4] Elections were held in May, but the Colombian congress did not convene until 20 June. The U.S. government did not anticipate problems. Despite growing populist sentiment against certain aspects of the treaty that infringed on Colombian sovereignty, an American official in Bogotá reported on 27 June that "friends of the Government have control in Congress. I believe any legislation seriously desired by the Government will pass."[5] Indications of resistance emerged soon after the congress convened.

Americans traveling to Colombia in the days before the new congress opened were surprised to be joined by Colombian expatriates returning from Europe and elsewhere. The Colombians were amazingly frank about their intentions. They hoped to gain a seat in the Colombian Senate, where they planned to sit with open pockets awaiting American bribes to buy their votes. An agent of the kaiser was supposedly also in Bogotá actively working behind the scenes to defeat the treaty in the hope that Germany might gain the canal franchise.[6]

On 26 June the American emissary in Bogotá, Arthur M. Beaupré, a lawyer from Illinois appointed minister to Colombia on the basis of his loyalty to the Republican Party, reported that while the treaty's passage in the Colombian lower house seemed assured, "unfriendly influence makes the majority in the Senate uncertain."[7] Two weeks later, Beaupré admitted to Secretary of State Hay that one of the secretary's encrypted telegrams had reached certain members of the Senate. Among other things, the telegram had stated, "If Colombia should now reject the treaty or unduly delay its ratification, the friendly understanding between the two countries would be so seriously compromised that action might be taken by the Congress next winter which every friend of Colombia would regret."[8] Beaupré had presented the substance of this telegram to the foreign minister of Colombia a few days later.[9] Two weeks after that, shortly after the Colombian congress convened, President Marroquín met with members of the nation's senate at the presidential palace and leaked the contents of the private communication between the American secretary of state and the Colombian foreign minister.[10] The disclosure, in Beaupré's words, "Created sensation."[11] Beaupré soon notified Washington that the "leak" was part of a deliberate strategy employed by President Marroquín. The motivation of the Colombian government became clear two weeks later when Beaupré communicated two "suggested" amendments that would remove any further delay in ratification. The first amendment required the French-owned Panama Canal Company to pay Colombia $10 million of the $40 million the company was scheduled to receive from the United States as compensation for the canal concession. The second amendment increased the United States' direct payment to Colombia from $10 million to $15 million.[12] Jose Marroquín and his cronies were scheming for more money.[13]

As mentioned earlier, some members of the new Colombian Senate had spent a number of years abroad in Europe. One such member who had lived in Germany asked the German chargé d'affaires if the German government would like to enter the bidding for the canal concession. Britain's diplomatic representative in Bogotá received a similar inquiry. The Colombian senators saw a potential windfall in the canal and were certain that the United States would soon see the light and agree to their terms.[14] The halls of the Colombian Senate echoed with conversation and debate about protecting the ultimate sovereignty of Colombia over the Canal Zone, populist sentiments meant to gain the support of the Colombian people, who had been swayed by the words of their leaders and now fully opposed the treaty.[15] Beaupré made it clear to his superiors in Washington that ratification could be achieved if the United States would offer more money.[16]

Secretary Hay responded in a wire sent on 29 July: "This Government has no right or competence to covenant with Colombia to impose new financial obligation upon canal company and the President would not submit to our Senate any amendment in that sense."[17] The present treaty already represented significant compromises on the part of the United States, and Roosevelt was unwilling to concede more. The original language had asked for a lease "in perpetuity," for example, and the Colombians had countered with a fixed term of one hundred years; this was accepted. The United States had asked for a canal zone ten miles wide, and the Colombians had suggested ten kilometers; this too was accepted. Roosevelt's emissary had offered a payment of $7 million, but the Colombians had demurred until the price was raised to $10 million.[18] The Americans had bargained in good faith at every stage of the original negotiations prior to the U.S. Senate's ratification vote and had already met each of Colombia's demands. When word arrived on the evening of 12 August that the Colombian Senate had rejected the treaty, Roosevelt raged that the "jackrabbits" in Bogotá must not be allowed to unilaterally "bar one of the future highways of civilization."[19] Something had to be done to remove the "bar."

Planning and Development

In the days following the Colombian vote Roosevelt mulled over his options. Officials from the State Department presented him with a proposal that

leveraged the 1846 treaty with Colombia's predecessor, New Granada, to justify the outright seizure of the proposed canal zone to ensure the uninterrupted flow of commerce across the isthmus.[20] Some commentators urged
repealing the Spooner Law, which had decreed Panama as the ultimate route,
and reconsidering an alternate route through Nicaragua.[21] Mindful of the various domestic and international interests at play, T. R. proceeded cautiously,
consulting with nearly everyone involved, and slowly composed a plan.[22]

More than fifty revolutions or uprisings had occurred on the isthmus in
the previous fifty years.[23] Ironically, Colombia had requested American assistance in squelching disturbances in Panama six times, including incidents
in 1901 and 1902.[24] In short, the United States had repeatedly acted, in the
interest of maintaining safe transit through the isthmus, to put down revolutions in Panama. Roosevelt had little reason to expect the Panamanians to
become resigned to Colombian rule, but however much he might hope for an
uprising, to publicly speak of it would be tantamount to instigation, and that
would have serious diplomatic implications with other nations of the Western
Hemisphere and Europe.[25]

On 9 October 1903 Roosevelt conducted a carefully scripted meeting with
Philippe Bunau-Varilla, an accomplished engineer and major stockholder in
the French consortium that held the current contract for building the canal
(but had so far been stymied in its construction). Bunau-Varilla, who had met
repeatedly with leaders of the Panamanian opposition as well as with members of Roosevelt's government, recounted his conversation with the president,
which began with a reference to the Dreyfus courts-martial in France.

Mr. President, Captain Dreyfus has not been the only victim of
detestable political passions. Panama is another.

"Oh yes," claimed the President, suddenly interested, "that is true,
you have devoted much time and effort to Panama, Mr. Bunau-
Varilla. Well, what do you think is going to be the outcome of the
present situation?". . . I pronounced the four words in a slow, decided
manner:

"Mr. President, a Revolution."

The features of the President manifested profound surprise. "A
revolution," he repeated mechanically. Then he turned instinctively
towards Mr. Loomis [the assistant secretary of state] . . . and he said
. . . "A Revolution! . . . But if it becomes a reality, what would become
of the plan we had thought of?"[26]

Despite this allusion to a "plan," Roosevelt remained officially noncommittal, avoiding a reply when Bunau-Varilla asked if the United States would take action either for or against the revolutionaries. The president, however, could not (or more likely would not) conceal his disgust with the Colombian leadership, stating that "Colombia, by her action has forfeited any claim upon the U.S. and I have no use for a government that would do what that government has done."[27] Bunau-Varilla left the room confident of American support for a revolution in Panama.[28] After the meeting, Roosevelt confided to a friend that he assumed the French engineer would tell the revolutionaries in Panama to expect American intervention on their side. After all, he wrote of the Frenchman, "He would have been a very dull man indeed had he been unable to forecast such interference, judging simply by what we had done the year before [in 1902]."[29]

Meanwhile, in Colombia, word of Roosevelt's dissatisfaction with the proffered amendments to the treaty and the murmurs of discontent arising in Panama were having their effect. With the possibility of a partnership with the Americans shrinking, but unable to undertake the task of building the canal alone, the Colombians began casting about among the European powers to find a suitable investor and protector. With the French already on the sidelines and the British intent on maintaining at least informal ties with the United States, Germany emerged quickly as the leading candidate. This option nominally would have created a "strictly Colombian canal" on the surface, with pure German engineering beneath the veneer.[30] This plan, and the conflict between the United States and Germany that it might have caused, never came to pass.

On 16 October two U.S. Army officers, Capt. Chauncey "Thomas" B. Humphrey and 1st Lt. Grayson M. P. Murphy, were summoned to the White House to report to the president. Earlier in March, Roosevelt had asked the secretary of war to dispatch Army officers "to map out and gather information concerning the coasts of those portions of South America which would be of especial interest in the event of any struggle in the Gulf of Mexico or the Caribbean Sea." The two intrepid young spies had done much more than that. Although they had attempted to make themselves inconspicuous by wearing civilian attire throughout their travels, it must have been difficult for these two Americans to blend in.[31] Both were experienced soldiers. Humphrey had fought in the Spanish-American War as an officer, Murphy as an enlisted man. Both had returned to the United States with orders to West Point, Humphrey as an instructor and Murphy as a plebe. In the summer of 1903 Humphrey and his former student began their odyssey, at the behest of the president of the

United States, to discover what was happening behind the scenes in Colombia and Panama.[32]

Their observations in Colombia revealed various interests, both foreign and domestic, competing for advantage in the ongoing treaty ratification process in that country's senate. Quickly moving on to Panama, the young men decided to travel as English tourists. On their arrival at the train station in Colón, they met the American railroad agent, a retired sergeant of the 6th Artillery Regiment from Fort Monroe, who informed them that there was talk of revolution, but "that no revolution had ever succeeded, and that none ever would, for there had never been a military commander who had developed sufficiently to lead or organize a successful revolt." The old noncommissioned officer handed the two men copies of the *Panama Star & Herald* to read during their trip across the isthmus. As the train chugged out of Colón, the officers were delighted to find themselves in the company of the newly appointed provincial governor.

Reading their newspapers and acting all the while as if they could not understand the conversation going on just a few seats ahead of them, Humphrey and Murphy listened as the governor and his party discussed the events unfolding in Bogotá. Their efforts at eavesdropping were quite profitable. Among other things, the Americans learned that only a narrow window of time remained for the treaty to be ratified, and that the German government was actively working to prevent its ratification. Additionally, the officers discovered that the Colombian government, not satisfied with the $10 million offered by the treaty, had decided to hold out for $20 million. Marroquín's cabinet also believed that a legal technicality would allow them to claim the $40 million being paid to the French Canal Company for its rights to the canal route. Humphrey and Murphy stifled their surprise when they heard that the Colombian government had decided not to surrender its policing power over the canal route so "that it might be possible for them to obtain, through judges, police, courts, Customs, etc., a great deal of blood money from foreigners traversing the canal." The governor's party also expressed confusion over the payment of bribes for the votes of Colombian senators. Did not the Americans understand that the support of a senator could be had for a mere $10,000?[33]

When they arrived in Panama City the two officers presented themselves to the American vice consul, Felix Ehrman, who told them that all hope of ratifying the treaty seemed to have vanished.[34] He also mentioned a great deal of local talk about a need for revolution to pave the way for Panamanian independence, a treaty with the United States, the construction of a canal, and prosperity for the isthmus. Through a series of introductions and exchanges, the two young men were drawn further and further into the depths of the local revolutionary junta, ultimately meeting with José Arango, the head of the revolutionary movement. Arango informed Humphrey that lack of past success and outside assistance had taken the heart from the movement.[35] Humphrey later remembered his response.

> Considering the political situation in its entirety I told him that if the Junta was really in earnest I might and would be glad to give them some suggestions. I would help him out of his difficulties if he and the members of the Junta would give me their word to regard it as a confidential matter. I added that if three men from the Junta who were dependable would come to my room at the Grand Central Hotel at 4:00 PM, I would suggest to them a course of action.

When the men arrived at his hotel, Humphrey asked them a series of detailed questions regarding their armament and logistical support. He also sought information about the Colombian forces on the scene in Panama and the roads and terrain of the country. Over the next thirty-six hours the information Humphrey asked for flowed into the Grand Central Hotel. Soon Humphrey and Murphy were able to piece together the information that approximately 2,500 weapons were available on the isthmus, along with a small amount of ammunition for each gun.[36]

On the day the treaty was officially rejected in Colombia, Humphrey reported that he was offered a commission as the commander in chief of the five-hundred-man revolutionary force. He declined the honor.[37] Instead he sketched out gun emplacements to cover vital approaches to critical centers of government, transportation, and commerce. He further suggested that since any new troops from Colombia "would have to land at Colón, it should be the object before any revolution was declared to endeavor to defeat this battalion. This might be done effectively by separating the soldiers from their officers after their arrival. This was considered plausible. . . . A special train could be provided for the officers and the delegation meeting them to go to Panama [City]."[38] Humphrey also established a code by which he could communicate with Arango via telegraph. After placing an order for additional arms from the United States in the name of the revolutionaries, the two officers boarded a boat and rushed home to report.[39]

Now, on 16 October, these officers stood before the president to report their activities and insights.[40] Their report must have given Roosevelt some comfort, for he had already triggered a series of events to ensure the success of the looming revolution. The officers hoped that Roosevelt would order them back to Panama to act as his agents in the revolution, but he declined that level of direct U.S. participation. Cautioning the officers to say nothing of their meeting with him, he bid them goodnight, summoned a secretary, and began dictating messages.[41] Once again he ordered the naval services into action.

A few days later, Secretary of State John Hay met with the French engineer Bunau-Varilla in private at Hay's home one block from the White House. Most of their conversation skirted the topic that was at the center of both of their minds. Themes from books and music substituted for frank talk, but eventually this dance came to an end when Bunau-Varilla had the temerity to state, "The whole thing will end in a revolution. You must take your measures, if you do not want to be taken yourself by surprise." Hay answered that far from being taken by surprise, "Orders have been given to naval forces on the Pacific to sail towards the Isthmus." Bunau-Varilla later remembered that his visit with Hay had removed the last of his personal hesitance to support the revolution.[42]

Many observers, convinced that Roosevelt hungered for the opportunity to prove himself as a wartime commander in chief, expected him to react to the impending crisis in Colombia much as he had during the Venezuelan Crisis—with an overwhelming demonstration of force. They were surprised. The Navy and the Marine Corps, Roosevelt observed, had often served as the boot on the neck of revolution in Central America. So long as Colombia had acted in harmony with U.S. interests, Roosevelt had remained willing to supply that boot. Now, faced with a situation out of tune with U.S. policies, Theodore Roosevelt made a subtle yet effective shift in his use of American power. He decided to lift the boot, opening the way for rebel activity while simultaneously denying Colombia the opportunity to land troops or transport those already present to the source of insurrection.

As darkness settled on Washington following Roosevelt's 9 October meeting with Bunau-Varilla (a week before the young spies delivered their report), encrypted deployment orders from the Office of the Secretary of the Navy made their way down the telegraph lines. The gunboat USS *Nashville*, operating near Colón (the eastern port of the Panamanian province), had been scheduled to pull into port on 11 October for coal and then transit to Saint Andrew's Island. New orders directed its captain, Cdr. John Hubbard, to carry

TABLE 4. MOVEMENT OF U.S. NAVAL VESSELS, NOVEMBER 1903

Caribbean				
Ship	Sailed From	Date	Arrived	Date
USS *Nashville*	Kingston	1 November	Colón	2 November
USS *Dixie*	Kingston	3 November	Colón	5 November
USS *Atlanta*	Kingston	4 November	Colón	7 November
USS *Maine*	Newport News, Va.	9 November	Colón	15 November
Pacific				
Ship	Sailed From	Date	Arrived	Date
USS *Boston*	San Diego	4 November	Panama City	7 November
USS *Marblehead*	Acapulco	4 November	Panama City	10 November
USS *Concord*	Acapulco	4 November	Panama City	10 November
USS *Wyoming*	Acapulco	4 November	Panama City	13 November

out his itinerary to avoid attracting attention, but then to proceed with haste to Kingston, Jamaica, for coal, thence expediting his return to Colón.[43] The letter informing the admiral of the Atlantic Fleet about these orders reported actions directing ships under his command without his oversight or knowledge. Direct civilian control of this magnitude could presumably occur only by and with the direction of the commander in chief.

The USS *Dixie,* an auxiliary cruiser laid up in reserve status, was hurriedly reactivated and assigned to the Caribbean Squadron on 15 October with orders to proceed to League Island, Pennsylvania, to take aboard a battalion of five hundred Marines. After stopping briefly in Guantánamo Bay, Cuba, and Kingston for supplies and coal, the *Dixie* was directed on 2 November to "proceed with all possible dispatch to Colón."[44] Orders were also issued to the cruiser *Atlanta,* the new battleship *Maine,* and the collier *Hannibal* to proceed to the vicinity of Colón with staggered arrivals. Other ships would follow, taking up station on both the Atlantic and Pacific approaches to the isthmus (Table 4).[45]

The commanding officers received no specific instructions on their mission, but all had in their possession several sealed packets, recently updated, with instructions covering a number of contingencies.[46] They knew enough to hold their ships and crews in high readiness in that very unstable region.

For their part, the Panamanian revolutionaries were very aware of the movements of U.S. Navy vessels in the vicinity of the isthmus. Bunau-Varilla had made a point of mentioning his exact understanding of the disposition of the U.S. military forces during a meeting with Secretary of State Hay following his meeting with Roosevelt.[47] Bunau-Varilla carefully monitored news reports of ship movements. On hearing that the gunboat *Nashville* was due to leave Kingston at the end of the month, he wired his contacts in Panama: "Pizaldo Panama all right will reach ton and a half obscure. Jones."[48] Translated, this code indicated that a U.S. Navy warship would arrive in two and a half days, and that the revolution should be timed to begin accordingly.

For two days Panamanian operatives scanned the horizon, searching for the approaching vessel. On the afternoon of 2 November 1903, the smoke from the *Nashville's* stack appeared in the distance.[49] The overjoyed revolutionary committee in Panama City declared to a crowd gathered in the plaza of the town's cathedral that independence would come at last "tomorrow."[50] One observer later remembered that in the appearance of the *Nashville* "people had seen . . . the extended hand of the powerful neighbour Republic."[51]

Guaranteeing a Revolution: Phase I

In an act of remarkable prescience, the Navy Department issued an order to the Navy commander in Acapulco on the morning of 2 November that read:

> Proceed with all possible dispatch to Panama. Telegraph in cipher your departure. Maintain free and uninterrupted transit. If interruption is threatened by armed force, occupy the line of railroad. Prevent landing of any armed force, either Government or insurgent, with hostile intent at any point 50 miles of Panama. If doubtful as to the intention of any armed force, occupy Ancon Hill strongly with artillery. . . . Government force reported approaching the Isthmus in vessels. Prevent their landing if in your judgment landing would precipitate a conflict.[52]

One U.S. ship, the *Nashville,* did not receive the "50-mile" telegram, and as a consequence, things began to go awry soon after the ship anchored at Colón.

At noon on 2 November, a telegram from the State Department arrived at the office of the American consul general in Panama inquiring if the reports of a Panamanian uprising described in the major newspapers that morning were correct. The consul general himself was absent from his post, taking his yearly leave in the United States, and his assistant tried to ascertain the answer.

The assistant, the consul general's son, took to the streets, where he happened upon an acquaintance whom he felt was close enough to members of the independence movement to be in the know. He asked quietly if a revolution had taken place, and his acquaintance informed him that independence would be declared that evening at six o'clock. This information was telegraphed back to Washington but did not arrive until 9:00 PM Washington time.[53]

In the meantime, the Colombian transport *Cartagena*, with nearly four hundred troops on board, arrived at Colón in the early evening and anchored. On the morning of 3 November the Colombians disembarked at 8:20 AM without resistance and proceeded to the train station with the intention of boarding a train bound for Panama City to put down the rebellion.[54] Local Panamanian officials, following Captain Humphrey's suggestion, conspired to delay the transportation of the troops but graciously allowed their commander, General Tovar, and his staff to board a special train and proceed ahead of the force, which he was assured would soon follow.[55] In the interim, Washington's instructions finally caught up with the *Nashville*. Hubbard was startled to learn that his orders were to "make every effort to prevent the Colombian troops at Colón from proceeding to Panama."[56] Invoking the language of the 1846 treaty, the Navy commander immediately secured the trains "in order to preserve peace and good order." Declaring his neutrality, he denied rail use to both the Colombians and the rebellious Panamanians.[57] By then, however, the events that would decide Panama's destiny were already in motion.[58] The Colombians found themselves strategically and tactically isolated.

The Colombian troops reacted angrily. Deprived of their leadership yet aware of the events transpiring around them, they threatened to "kill to the last man all Americans in Colón if General Tovar remained a prisoner."[59] Hubbard moved American women and children aboard the *Nashville* and other American-flagged vessels while the men and a force quickly assembled from the crew under the leadership of the ship's executive officer, Lt. Cdr. H. M. Witzel, took up a defensive position at an American-owned warehouse. Hubbard reported to the Navy Department, "I have landed force to protect lives and property of American citizens here against threats Colombian soldiery. I am protecting waterfront with ship."[60] A standoff ensued.

For ninety minutes the Colombian troops slowly approached the building, seeking to intimidate or provoke the American forces within.[61] Presently the commander of the Colombian forces approached the warehouse to parlay. He requested permission to send a small contingent of officers across the isthmus on the railway to seek instructions from their commander. This permission was given. Additionally, a proposal was made for both forces to withdraw—the Colombians to the edge of town, the Americans back to the *Nashville*.[62] Hubbard, perhaps feeling that this action would allow tempers to cool, returned his men to the ship for the evening, believing that there were no difficulties "of any serious nature."[63]

Morning saw the men of the *Nashville* rushing ashore again as Hubbard transmitted, "Situation here this morning again acute. Have deemed advisable to reland force."[64] The *Nashville*'s commanding officer had learned that the Colombian commander intended to reoccupy his position within the city, so he put his men back ashore, this time supported by two 1-pound guns mounted on platform railroad cars. Another day passed as the opposing commanders negotiated for an advantage. Hubbard consistently maintained that he was strictly neutral and prohibited both Colombians and Panamanians from utilizing the railroad.[65] The American-owned railroad company offered money to the Colombians if they would return to Cartagena.[66] The Colombians again demanded the return of their leaders. Both sides struggled to maintain civility. Hubbard, numerically outnumbered, knew that if he backed down, the way would be cleared for the Colombians to board the train west and quickly end the revolt. To complicate matters even more he learned from a local intelligence source that a commercial steamer carrying additional troops had left Cartagena and was en route to Panama.[67]

Just as the situation appeared untenable, the USS *Dixie*, commanded by Cdr. Francis H. Delano, appeared on the horizon with its battalion of Marines under the command of Maj. John A. Lejeune. The Colombian force, now facing an opponent in command of the port and a superior number of ground troops, boarded the steamer *Orinoco* the next morning, bound for Cartagena.[68] Two companies of Marines under Lejeune's command moved ashore to take up the positions occupied by the *Nashville*'s crew.[69]

Writing to his superiors in Washington, Hubbard praised the actions of his men, crediting their "determined attitude" and "coolness" with the Colombians' decision to leave Colón. With regard to the dramatic threat leveled by the Colombian troops at the onset of the standoff, the commander of the *Nashville* wrote with great emotion, "I feel I cannot sufficiently strongly represent to the Department the grossness of this outrage, and the insult to our dignity even apart from the savagery of the threat."[70] Theodore Roosevelt understood what the threat implied, and knew that it had not lifted with the sailing of the *Orinoco*.

Defending a Revolution: Phase II

On 6 November 1903 Washington received word from its representative in Bogotá that news of the revolution had reached the capital and that "troops are being sent to Isthmus."[71] In response, the secretary of the Navy issued an explicit order to prevent "the landing of men with hostile intent *within the limits of the State of Panama* [underlined in original]."[72] The commander of the U.S. Pacific Squadron, Rear Adm. Henry Glass, whose flagship had dropped anchor off Panama City on 10 November, amplified on this original instruction, telling his naval commanders not only to warn Colombian ships against any attempt to land troops, but also to "use any force that may be necessary to prevent such landing should it be attempted after the warning."[73] Additionally, Glass ordered the battleship *Maine* to expedite its transit to the area.[74]

President José Marroquín, realizing that the tide of events was running against him, called on the United States to render assistance: "If the Government of the United States will land troops to preserve Colombian sovereignty and the transit . . . this Government will declare martial law, and by virtue of vested constitutional authority, when public order is disturbed, will approve by fiat the ratification of the canal treaty as signed."[75] Secretary Hay answered for the president, stating that the people of Panama had chosen independence and that the United States had extended de facto recognition to the new republic.[76] Hay went further:

The President of the United States in accordance with the ties of friendship which have so long and so happily existed between the respective nations most earnestly commends to the governments of Colombia and of Panama the most peaceful and equitable settlement of all the questions at issue between them. He holds that he is bound not merely by treaty obligations but by the interests of civilization, to see that the peaceable traffic across the Isthmus of Panama shall not longer be disturbed by a constant succession of unnecessary and wasteful civil wars.[77]

Marroquín was denounced in the streets of the Colombian capital, and a crowd stoned his brother's house. Gen. Rafael Reyes, Marroquín's political ally and chief of Colombia's military, planned a hurried departure for Panama, hoping to convince the American military commanders there to assist him in recovering the province.[78] Colombia's foreign minister issued a communiqué to the American minister in Bogotá on 14 November that accused the United States of acting in direct conflict with its obligations under the 1846 Treaty of New Granada and stated that if the United States did not cease its interaction with the rebel government in Panama, diplomatic relations between the two countries would "not be possible." The minister went on to say that the Colombian "army is already marching to the Isthmus of Panama."[79] So began the second phase of U.S. involvement in Panamanian independence.

Philippe Bunau-Varilla, now the newly appointed minister of Panama in Washington, entered into immediate negotiations with Secretary of State Hay over a canal concession but received word that he was not to conclude a treaty because a delegation of senior Panamanians was en route to Washington to make their desires known.[80] Having come so close to success (and financial relief for the construction company in which he held stock), Bunau-Varilla had no desire to witness another disaster at the hands of those who would demand too much from the Americans. In great haste he drew up a treaty that provided the United States "in perpetuity" with a canal zone across Panama ten miles wide and forty miles long in exchange for $10 million cash and an annual payment of $250,000. The treaty also gave the United States the unabridged right to intervene in Panamanian affairs to maintain order.[81] Secretary of State Hay and Minister Bunau-Varilla signed the treaty on 18 November 1903, fifteen days after the start of the revolution and just hours before the Panamanian delegation arrived in Washington.

While this diplomatic soap opera unfolded in Washington, the French mail steamer *Canada* entered Colón on 19 November carrying Gen. Rafael Reyes, the envoy of the Colombian government (and now the political heir-apparent to the disgraced Colombian president). Reyes had been sent to confer with the Panamanian government "in regard to the existing situation on the Isthmus and, if practicable, arrange an amicable settlement."[82] The Panamanians, clearly uncomfortable with the thought of having the senior Colombian military commander on Panamanian soil, requested that Reyes meet with them on board an American man-of-war.[83] Rear Admiral Glass, whose flagship, the USS *Marblehead*, was on the Pacific side of the isthmus, asked Rear Adm. Joseph Coghlan to do the honors onboard the USS *Olympia* in the harbor at Colón.[84] Coghlan had arrived in the area four days earlier and had assumed responsibility for operations on Panama's Caribbean approaches.[85] General Reyes declined Coghlan's hospitality because he felt it improper to hold "peace talks" aboard a man-of-war.

The shadow Theodore Roosevelt cast over the events in Panama was clearly apparent when Reyes asked Rear Admiral Coghlan to host a tête-à-tête on "political affairs" just between the Colombians and the Americans. Coghlan demurred, citing his lack of "authority to enter into such subjects."[86] Reyes then reluctantly (and unsuccessfully) met with the Panamanians onboard the *Canada* before declaring his intention to proceed on to Washington to plead Colombia's case in person before the president of the United States. Before leaving, he asked Coghlan the extent of Roosevelt's protection of the new republic. Reyes realized his worst fears when the admiral replied that he had orders to prohibit any outside force from landing anywhere within the state of Panama.[87] Just before he sailed, Reyes informed Admiral Coghlan that his government had ordered Colombia's "forces to do nothing hostile" until he was able to ascertain the situation in the American capital.

As Reyes was en route to Washington, the Colombian army's chief of staff issued a blistering declaration in Bogotá:

> It is preferable to see the Colombian race completely extinguished than to submit ourselves to the infamous policy of President Roosevelt. It is well proved that the Chief of the American Union does not know how to interpret the boasted Monroe Doctrine; and that he does not comply, either in the spirit or the letter, with International Treaties such as the Treaty of 1846 in which the United States guaranteed that Panama should ever belong to Colombia. . . . Commanders, Officers and Soldiers of the Army let us swear to God and let us promise the Fatherland that we will defend our rights until the last drop of blood is shed."[88]

On 17 November the U.S. State Department received word from Minister Beaupré that the Colombian army was on the march toward Panama and that a special advisory council convened to assist the Colombian president during the crisis had voted ten to one to deliver Beaupré's passport to him and ask him to leave the country, a move tantamount to a declaration of war. John Hay informed his minister that he and his staff were free to leave Colombia at any moment of their choosing.[89]

The next day, Rear Admiral Glass, having previously recognized the new government in a written statement, took the next step and called on Panama's leaders in person.[90] The Navy had ensured the success of the initial revolution, but it was becoming increasingly likely that the Navy–Marine Corps team would soon be called on to defend it.

President Roosevelt had fully expected Colombia to make some attempt to regain Panama. Within a week of the revolution, Washington forwarded intelligence reports to the American commanders on the scene relating to Colombian troop movements.[91] As many as 15,000 men were estimated to be moving toward Panama.[92] Roosevelt himself received a report from a trusted observer in Colombia that an armed expedition was under way with the intention of seizing the mouth of Panama's Atrato River as a base for future operations.[93] Other sources reported plans to seize British steamers in the Colombian port of Buenaventura to transport an invasion force.[94] Another report stated that the Colombian man-of-war *Bogotá* was at Buenaventura "practicing gun firing and pressing into service all available men."[95]

U.S. Navy ships were dispatched to various locales on the Caribbean and Pacific coasts of Panama that had beaches suitable for armed landings with orders to monitor developments and to prevent Colombian forces from entering the new republic.[96] The commander of the USS *Concord* was ordered to "proceed to Parita Bay, in the vicinity of Río Dulce, and prevent the landing of any armed force approaching that place with hostile intent."[97] The USS *Boston* was dispatched to San Miguel Bay.[98] The *Atlanta* and *Nashville* had taken up station at Porto Bella and Bocas del Tora, respectively.[99] One by one, the reserve force that had been ordered to stand by just over the horizon during the unstable period of Panama's independence movement flowed into surveillance positions up and down Panama's coasts. Rear Admiral Glass ordered the prohibition against the transport of Panamanian troops via the railway to be lifted effective 11 November.[100] The new republic would be allowed to do its own part to defend itself. Commanders on the scene in early December reported to Washington that they had "a sufficient number of troops here. No chance of force advancing upon Panama until after dry season."[101]

This complacency disappeared a few days later when Rear Admiral Glass learned that an expedition of 1,100 Colombians had set out via an overland route, only to be turned back by weather, hunger, disease, and the jungle.[102] News reports from Colombia noted visceral anger directed toward Americans there.[103] It became clear that Colombia intended to reclaim its lost province and its honor despite the weather, the odds, and the obstacles. With the Panamanian government still consolidating its hold on the country, it was up to the United States to ensure the security of the new nation.

Glass dispatched gunboats to patrol the Panamanian and Colombian coasts to observe and collect intelligence.[104] The cruiser *Boston* and the battleship

Wyoming were directed to proceed to San Miguel Bay and put ashore a landing force that would go up the Tuira River "as far as Yaviza or such place as they may select for landing."[105] This force was directed to take along two Colt automatic weapons with crews to keep them in working order as well as a ship's surgeon and an ample supply of fresh drinking water.[106] Additional ships were made available to support operations along the south coast of Panama if local commanders should need them.[107] Glass recommended placing an outpost in Caledonia Harbor, owing to the support of a local indigenous chieftain there, and a battalion of Marines was dispatched to reinforce this approach.[108] The commanders of these units were directed to send word of any contact with Colombian forces immediately.[109] Such contact eventually did occur, although that fact has largely been forgotten.

The USS *Atlanta,* pursuant to its orders of 13 December, arrived at the Gulf of Darien on the morning of the fifteenth. At 7:45 AM the ship's crew observed a schooner approaching from the west. When the schooner realized that it was under observation by an American man-of-war, it altered course to avoid interception, but to no avail. The Americans were able to observe that the schooner's deck was littered with men in military uniforms. At 11:00 AM a boarding party from the *Atlanta* led by Lt. H. P. Perrill climbed the sides of the Colombian ship *Antioquia.* Once on board, Perrill's party discovered twenty-six Colombian soldiers on deck and too many to count below deck. Perrill was shocked to learn that this force intended to join up with a larger contingent already ashore under the command of Gen. Daniel Ortiz, commandant general of the Division of the Army of the Republic of Colombia.

Perrill reported to his captain that the Colombians had no information on the present situation regarding Colombia, Panama, and the United States, and that the soldiers had been restrained from firing only through the personal direction of the senior officer present. The commanding officer of the *Atlanta* strongly suspected from the Colombian schooner's sailing profile that General Ortiz's force was located somewhere near Titumati. Unable to ascertain the number of Colombian forces in the area, the *Atlanta's* captain turned for Panama to inform his superiors of the situation.[110]

The fact that the *Atlanta* chose not to confront this incursion was in keeping with Rear Admiral Glass's most recent orders, which required his commanders to avoid confrontation or even interference with the movements of Colombian forces.[111] Something had obviously changed in the month since Rear Admiral Coghlan had told General Reyes that the United States would defend all of Panama against invasion.

Earlier in December, when reports challenging the assumption that the Panamanian jungle was impassable for invading Colombian troops began to surface, Glass had wired Washington for clarification of his authority to defend the new republic.[112] The local understanding that all of Panama was to be defended by American forces needed additional scrutiny in light of the new reality suggested by the rumors from the south. On 10 December 1903, in keeping with this policy, Secretary Moody drafted a reply ordering Glass to "establish camps, seamen and marine battalions fully equipped at inland points to forcibly prevent hostile entrance by land to the State of Panama. Maintain communications between camps and vessels, cut trails, buy or hire pack animals as necessary." Below this were the handwritten words of Rear Adm. Henry C. Taylor, the chief of the Bureau of Navigation: "The above submitted by Sec Moody *to the President who directed it be not sent now but withheld till further considered* [italics added]." Taylor's signature followed.[113] This telegram represents a strategic inflexion point with regard to American involvement in Panama. Moody's communiqué, as drafted, reflected a policy consistent with the numerous telegrams sent to commanders in the arena since the onset of the Panamanian revolution. The defense of Panama, in its entirety, was the stated mission. But now a telegram extending this policy to its natural end was being held up by the president until he could consider all of the implications of his previous decisions with regard to the isthmus, the new state of Panama, and his coveted canal. Sometime during the night of 10 December 1903 Theodore Roosevelt decided to change direction in Panama.

The next day, the secretary of the Navy, acting on Roosevelt's "further consideration," ordered Glass to "establish strong posts, men and marines with artillery in the direction of the Yavisa or other better position for observation only and rapid transmission of information *but not forcible interference with Colombian forces advancing by land* [italics added]."[114]

Commandant on the Field

Moody's message signified a dramatic shift in the operational rules of engagement for the forces in the field in Panama. The next week found the secretary scrambling to translate Roosevelt's ruminations into coherent operational directives. On 17 December he wrote to Rear Admiral Glass: "My telegram of 11th December is modified so that the posts in the vicinity of Yavisa and all other established must be strong enough to resist attack positions once taken to be held by force if necessary."[115] The very next day he reversed himself, directing American military personnel in Panama to take a purely defensive role on the isthmus. Retreating from previous telegrams from Washington instructing U.S. forces to defend all territory within fifty miles of the railway, Moody cabled Glass in cipher: "Maintain posts in the vicinity of Yavisa for observation only. Do not have post beyond support from ships or launches. Withdraw your posts if liable to be attacked. It is the intention of the Government to continue active defense against hostile operations to the vicinity of the railroad line on the isthmus and for its protection. Disregard all previous instructions that may appear to conflict with these."[116]

Modern-day readers could interpret this statement as an indication that Roosevelt had been bluffing. Another possibility is that Colombia's determination to recover the renegade province had caused the American president to reconsider his long-term interests in the region. There is another possibility as well, however: Roosevelt had decided to shift his strategy toward Colombia.

The battalion of Marines that went ashore during the first half of December was composed of the same troops that had streamed off the USS *Dixie* so quickly in the first days of the revolution in November. Commanded by Maj. John A. Lejeune, they had spent the intervening month providing light security and relaying communications until they received orders on 8 December to move into base camp at point Empire, a location approximately thirty miles inland from Colón by way of the Panamanian railroad.

Lejeune, who ultimately became the Marine Corps' thirteenth commandant, had already established a reputation within the Corps for professionalism and attention to detail (and to the welfare of his Marines). Before his men moved in, he ordered an extensive reworking of the existing facilities of the former French Canal Company's buildings at Empire. Freshwater and sewage systems were installed; jungle growth was cleared, and the housing was cleaned and disinfected with healthy doses of carbolic acid.[117] Completing their redeployment on 16 December, the Marines became the backbone of the response to real and imagined Colombian incursions over the next few weeks. They stretched their observation posts and picket stations to the southeast and reconnoitered positions from which they could launch both offensive and defensive operations. Lejeune made it clear to his superiors that if the Colombians wanted a fight, he would not disappoint them.[118]

Two days after Major Lejeune's force moved into the encampment at Empire, Secretary of the Navy William Moody summoned the senior Marine in Washington, Brig. Gen. George F. Elliott, Commandant of the Corps, to receive an order from his commander in chief. The order read, "You will please proceed in person, taking passage in the USS *Dixie*, from League Island to Colón, to take command of the entire force of United States Marines and Seamen that is or may be landed for service in the State of Panama."[119] The importance of this message with regard to measuring the magnitude of Roosevelt's participation, actions, and intentions cannot be understated. The Commandant of the U.S. Marine Corps is the senior ranking active officer of that service, an officer who occupies, if not a religious, then at least a mythical position as the font of legitimate authority. No commandant had led Marines directly in the field since the legendary Colonel-Commandant Archibald Henderson campaigned against the Seminole Indians before the Civil War, and no commandant has done so again since Elliott's time.[120] Elliott's movement into the Panamanian theater of action could have come only at the explicit direction of the president, and only for a specific reason and mission.

The reason is suggested by Roosevelt's previous and subsequent reliance on the naval services when difficult diplomatic crises emerged. His prior historical and administrative immersion in all aspects of naval power gave him a pronounced lean toward the twin services of the Navy Department, despite his brief personal experience alongside the Army during the war with Spain. When he faced the possibility of conflict in the aftermath of the Panamanian Revolution, he instinctively sought the solution in sea power. This time, it was the land-borne element of the naval services that drew the responsibility for the mission he had in mind.

The mission can be viewed only as one of the most strategically audacious yet little-known initiatives of the early twentieth century. For, when George Elliott sailed south to join with the rapidly growing force of Marines on the isthmus, he carried with him plans for the invasion of Colombia and the occupation of one of its major cities.

General Elliott had assumed his position as the tenth Commandant of the Marine Corps on 3 October 1903. The only commandant to be educated at the U.S. Military Academy at West Point, Elliott made the unusual move of accepting a commission in the Marines in the fall of 1870. Subsequent duty in Cuba during the Spanish-American War and in the Philippines during the insurgency against the American occupation led to his rapid rise through the ranks.[121] It was this knowledge of tropical warfare that Roosevelt planned to draw upon. Elliott proceeded to the League Island embarkation center outside Philadelphia to begin assembling his forces.

Elliott took a personal interest in the outfitting of the troops that were to be under his command. He wanted a force that could move swiftly and easily through the dense tropical jungles. The commandant decreed that each man carry with him "one (1) blanket, two (2) suits underwear, two (2) khaki blouses, two (2) khaki trousers, one (1) pair russet shoes, one (1) blue flannel shirt, three (3) pairs socks, two (2) towels. In addition an extra blue flannel shirt is recommended and the men shall carry such toilet articles as they may desire. Tin cups will be considered a part of heavy marching order. Ponchos will be issued onboard USS Dixie after embarkation." Elliott made it clear that the men needed to set up for service in "heavy marching order." They were to be prepared in every way for rapid movement and combat operations.[122]

Another auxiliary cruiser, the USS *Prairie,* had departed Guantánamo Bay with a battalion of Marines under the command of Maj. Louis C. Lucas on 11 December.[123] Arriving at Colón on 13 December, Lucas took his 300 enlisted Marines and 11 officers into camp at Bas Obispo to extend and strengthen the security perimeter around the Panamanian railway.[124] Back at League Island, the crew of the USS *Dixie,* recently returned from disgorging Lejeune's battalion onto Panamanian soil, began loading Elliott's two Marine battalions, the first under the command of Maj. James E. Mahoney, the second following the lead of Maj. Eli K. Cole. This combined force of 635 Marines left Philadelphia on 28 December. Accompanied by an appropriately sized headquarters staff of seven officers and eleven enlisted men, General Elliott's force anchored at Colón on 3 January 1904.[125] Two days later the Marines began to leave the *Dixie* and board the train cars that would transport them to their assigned camps.[126] As the two battalions moved toward their destinations, Elliott took the formal step of establishing a provisional Marine brigade in Panama.[127] Elliott's priorities on arrival included establishing his Marines in the field, realigning his command structure to match his force size, and reporting to the senior Navy officer in country to present his orders.

The Marine Commandant ordered Major Cole's battalion into encampment at Empire alongside Lejeune's battalion. Together, these two forces became the 2nd and 1st battalions, respectively, of the 1st Marine Regiment, under the command of Col. W. P. Biddle. Major Mahoney's unit proceeded to Bas Obispo where they quartered alongside Major Lucas' Marines. These two units constituted the 2nd Marine Regiment under Col. L. W. T. Waller.[128] Both regiments, comprising together approximately 1,100 Marines, reported directly to General Elliott to form the Marines' 1st Provisional Brigade, Panama.[129] With his forces organized and established ashore, Elliott turned his attention to his fellow flag officers in the theater of conflict and the orders he carried from Washington.[130]

Shortly after coming ashore, Commandant Elliott called on Rear Admiral Coghlan, commanding the American Caribbean Squadron and the eastern approaches to Panama, at his headquarters in Colón. Shortly afterward he took the train across the isthmus to meet with Rear Admiral Glass, the commander in chief of the Pacific Squadron and, presently, the senior naval officer in Panama.[131] To each of these men he presented a letter from the secretary of the Navy: "The Department forwards herewith, in the charge of Brigadier General Elliott, U.S.M.C., a plan for the occupation of Cartagena, Colombia. As will be seen, the plan contemplates occupation against a naval enemy, but the information it contains and the strategy involved may be readily applied to the present situation."[132]

The document Elliott carried represented a bold strategy and sophistication rare in nineteenth-century U.S. planning. Recognizing the utter futility of defending Panama's numerous bays, ill-defined borders, and porous mountain passes, Roosevelt chose to forgo a defense-centric strategy in favor of an offensive action on a battlefield of his own choosing. Rather than defend Panama in the event Colombia attempted to regain its lost province, Roosevelt chose to embark his brigade of Marines on ships, sail to the port city of Cartagena (Colombia's chief source of tariff collections), and capture it, thus placing him in a position to dictate the terms of the subsequent peace settlement with the Colombians.

The plan was developed at the president's request by the Joint Army and Navy Board in November, after the revolution in Panama. Building on strategies developed at the Naval War College as part of the institution's annual war game, the plan General Elliott carried was adapted to the particulars of the current situation on the isthmus. The invasion force would be backed up by a large naval force that would stand off Colombia's Caribbean and Pacific ports, imposing an economic blockade as a complement to the Marines' physical occupation of Colombian territory.[133]

Elliott instituted a training program to maintain his Marines at a high level of combat readiness while simultaneously deploying his forces in quick expeditions that fulfilled the dual purposes of maintaining security and reconnaissance. To relieve his troops of normal housekeeping chores, Elliott paid locals to cook and clean in the Marine camps, earning their gratitude for the cash wages they received.[134]

Within ten days, weapons ranges had been constructed in the two camps where the regiments could exercise their rifles and automatic guns.

"The command is being given complete and thorough instruction in service in the field," Elliott reported, "and officers and men, many of the latter being but recruits, are profiting greatly by the experience." Elliott's Marines received training in entrenching procedures and the construction of obstructions to slow and confuse an attacking enemy force, and they experimented with the transportation of heavy guns in mountainous terrain using mules. Numerous reconnaissance parties were dispatched to map trails and paths; Capt. Smedley D. Butler, USMC, and Lt. William G. Miller, USN, headed up the two main parties.[135] Their efforts resulted in the first comprehensive survey of the isthmus.[136] Through it all, the morale and discipline of the force remained high.

The only dark spot on the horizon was a rumor that a group of Colombians planned to poison the Marines' drinking water. Elliott ordered that any individual attempting to tamper with the water supply be summarily shot on sight.[137] Rear Admiral Glass, writing from his flagship, the USS *New York,* wrote quickly to remind his aggressive colleague that "a state of war does not exist on the Isthmus of Panama" and suggested that the general simply take additional precautions to guard his water barrels.[138]

In the interim, Secretary Moody wrote to update Elliott on the situation at hand. After expressing his pleasure with the professionalism displayed by the commandant and his staff throughout their repositioning to Panama, the secretary wrote, "If Colombia actually begins hostilities against us a Brigade of the Army will proceed to the Isthmus." This force, Moody explained cryptically, would allow Elliott to withdraw his force and turn his attention to another duty that would, Moody wrote, "I believe, be important." If Colombia decided to accept the new situation on the isthmus, then Elliott's force might take part "in some operations connected with the winter maneuvers." Moody enjoined Elliott to communicate frequently with Washington.

> Let the Department know through the proper channels of your daily operations. Remember the Department is always annoyed by long silence, and please also remember that the Army, which has only a couple of officers down there, is furnishing *the President* [italics added] every day with pages of cipher cable, much of which, though dealing with small matters, is of considerable interest. Let your scouting be thorough and extending a long distance, and give us daily accounts of it.[139]

On 12 January 1904, following a cabinet meeting with the president, Secretary of War Elihu Root issued a statement denying any plan on the part of the United States to dispatch troops to the isthmus to fight Colombia.[140] This was true. There were no plans to dispatch troops; the Marines were already there. And the Marines were not intended to fight Colombia on the isthmus; they were to fight Colombia in Colombia.

Thus it was, at the end of January 1904, that Brig. Gen. George F. Elliott, Commandant of the U.S. Marine Corps, backed by ships of the Pacific and Caribbean squadrons, stood ready with his brigade of 1,400 Marines to invade the nation of Colombia to ensure the independence of Panama. Theodore Roosevelt's dedication to the creation of a canal between the Atlantic and Pacific cannot be doubted. The invasion never took place, of course. Colombia protested, probed, and negotiated, but it never invaded its former province, and hence never triggered Roosevelt's dramatic plan. Panama and the United States signed a treaty on 25 February 1904 committing the United States to protect the sovereignty of the new republic.

General Reyes, commander in chief of Colombia's army and presumptive political heir to the Colombian presidency, had continued on to the United States after his abortive negotiations in Panama during the month of November. He had been treated with every courtesy there, but when he raised the question of Panama's independence, he was given to understand, in the voice of a contemporary observer, "that what has been done could not be undone." Reyes realized that American popular opinion was solidly behind Roosevelt's policy of upholding the revolution in Panama, but he continued to press Colombia's case. He asked the United States to use its "good offices to reunite Panama with Colombia," to no avail. He also asked, again without success, that the matter be submitted to a plebiscite.[141] When he asked, for the sake of clarification, what the United States would do if Colombia attempted to recover Panama by force, Hay informed him in the diplomatic language of the day that the United States would "regard with the gravest concern any invasion of the territory of Panama by Colombian troops."[142] Reyes seemed to have better luck with his efforts to obtain for Colombia's treasury at least some of the $10 million that had been part of the original rejected treaty.[143] By the end of January 1904 rumors were circulating throughout Washington that Colombia would "receive a certain pecuniary consolation for her loss of territory."[144] When inhabitants of the Colombian province of Causa revolted in March in an attempt to join with their Panamanian brothers, the Colombian government withdrew its troops from the Panamanian border.[145]

By the middle of March the government declared its intention not to invade its former territory.[146]

In early February Rear Admiral Taylor, the chief of the Bureau of Navigation, wrote a memo to the secretary of the Navy to inquire as to the status of the Marines still in Panama: "In view of the report that, probably, the treaty with the Republic of Panama, known as the 'Canal Treaty,' will be favorably acted upon by the United States Senate on February 23rd, the Bureau asks to be informed whether it is intended that, at an early date thereafter, the marines now stationed on the Isthmus are to be replaced by a military force from the army?"[147]

Most of the Marines would not have to remain until the treaty was ratified. A large portion of the 2nd Regiment was withdrawn from Panama on 14 February and repositioned to Guantánamo Bay to take part in the annual winter maneuvers. General Elliott and his staff departed two days later, leaving Colonel Waller in command of the 800 remaining Marines. This arrangement lasted until 7 March, when Waller took a battalion home to League Island, leaving Major Lejeune behind with his original battalion of 400 men to provide security on the isthmus. Lejeune and his men remained for another nine months, until another battalion of Marines relieved them. The U.S. Marines would remain a presence on the isthmus until 1912, when Capt. John F. Hughes and his force of 389 men departed.

The Cartagena war plan, somehow overlooked by previous historians, is not a myth or a misinterpretation of historical documents. In April 1904 the commander in chief of the North Atlantic Fleet wrote the Commandant of the Marine Corps that his command's copy of the plan "has not been received yet."[148] Two weeks later the secretary of the Navy corrected this oversight, explaining that the North Atlantic Fleet commander was never intended to have a copy of the plan and that all documents referring to the plan, now referred to as "War Portfolio No. 1," should be transferred via strongbox to "the custody of the flag officer in actual command in those [Colombian-Panamanian] waters." Receipt of the instruction was to be acknowledged by the local commander.[149] Hence, there is more than ample evidence, both explicit and implicit, of a plan for U.S. Marines to invade Colombia.

Accused of Seduction, Guilty of Rape

Charges of heavy-handedness on Roosevelt's part began to crop up almost as soon as the United States recognized Panama. Neither his enemies nor his

79

friends doubted the president's role in the planning and execution of the new republic's very convenient independence movement.[150] T. R. was not immune to the criticism, which inevitably got under his skin. During a subsequent cabinet meeting he launched into a vigorous defense of his reasoning and actions throughout the incident. Arriving at the conclusion of his monologue, he turned to his secretary of war, Elihu Root, who was in civilian life one of the most highly paid lawyers in New York, and asked, "Well, have I answered the charges? Have I defended myself?" Root, known for his biting wit, answered, "You certainly have, Mr. President. You have shown that you were accused of seduction and you have conclusively proved that you were guilty of rape."[151]

Roosevelt later remarked that he "took the Canal Zone." That was Rooseveltian overstatement. He would have been more truthful had he claimed that he helped Panama and guaranteed its independence through the actions of the U.S. naval services. Compared with his use of naval power as an instrument of coercive diplomacy in the Venezuelan Crisis of 1902–3, however, Roosevelt's actions demonstrate a potent combination of sophisticated nuance and audacity.

When Capt. Chauncey Humphrey and 1st Lt. Grayson Murphy provided Roosevelt with ample warning of an impending independence movement in the Colombian province of Panama (a movement they helped to organize) that would culminate in a condition in lockstep with his conception of U.S. national interests, Roosevelt did not react by flooding the area of operations with overwhelming naval power. Instead he introduced a gunboat at Colón and an aged cruiser on the Pacific coast. This was not the extent of the sea power available in the arena, of course, for just over the horizon were troopships and heavy battleships staged to move into position if the situation warranted, as the auxiliary cruiser USS *Dixie* did when the presence of four hundred Colombian troops threatened the revolution in Colón. It is clear that Roosevelt wanted the world to see the revolution as in all aspects and appearances a Panamanian movement. It was only after the nation was recognized and a need for additional security was desired that the additional naval units appeared along the coastline, bays, and river inlets of southern Panama to guard against Colombian incursions.

When the threat of such incursions began to shift from the imaginary to the probable, Roosevelt made the audacious move of transitioning secretly from a defensive strategy to one of offensive stealth. The operational record clearly demonstrates that the change in strategic planning pivoted around the president's decision to review the rules of engagement on the evening of 10

December 1903. Before that evening the forces in the field planned a strategic defense in position. Afterward the commanding general of all Marines took to the field for the express purpose of leading an invasion force against the Colombian port city of Cartagena. The plan was never publicly revealed, and no demarche was ever given. If executed, the invasion would have altered the balance of power in South America.

The Colombians had, in his own mind, at least, betrayed Roosevelt's trust. When the Colombian Senate voted down the proposed treaty, Roosevelt could have acted in an overt military manner and not been outside the accepted Great Power norms of the day. Instead he anticipated, based on a nuanced appreciation of the historical record, a revolution in Panama and then positioned an enabling mixture of land and sea forces off the coasts of the newly created republic. The ensuing posturing between American and Colombian units provides an excellent example of coercive diplomacy, but it was Roosevelt's sophisticated strategy of positioning additional forces at increments—over the horizon but ready to make their presence known—that made the diplomacy effective. This model of scalable response still has significant implications for modern naval operations.

Similarly, when Colombia began to explore options for recovering Panama, Roosevelt had many avenues of response. He could defeat Colombia in battle if need be, and he had a plan to do just that, but he did not act precipitously; he kept his poise. He did not invade Colombia when that nation's troops came close to the Panamanian border. He created a response and the maneuvering space in which to employ it, suggesting that Roosevelt possessed a sense of the limits of military power and was not anxious to test them without cause. In the end, no action was required. Roosevelt remained true to his peaceful inclinations and guaranteed through the coercive diplomatic presence of the U.S. Navy and Marine Corps the permanent independence of Panama. The ultimate result was the creation of the Panama Canal, one of the great engineering achievements of the modern world and the cornerstone of American naval policy throughout the twentieth century.

chapter four

Morocco and the Limits of Naval Power

What does Loubet's telegram of April 30th mean? I thought
American squadron was not to touch anywhere on Continent of Europe.
Do not let the fleet alter arrangements without my sanction.
THEODORE ROOSEVELT, 2 MAY 1903

T here was an election to be won, and Theodore Roosevelt was above all else
a politician. In May 1904 he was deeply absorbed in the administrative
minutiae of the impending Republican Party National Convention, which
was scheduled to take place in Chicago in June. He corresponded with Henry
Cabot Lodge on the topic of the party's platform, and with Cornelius Bliss,
the party's chairman, about the fall campaign.[1] He took malicious delight in
watching prospective candidates for the office of vice president, which had
lain vacant since Roosevelt's own ascension to the executive office, and their
weak excuses to bring themselves to the attention of the president and his
professional acquaintances.[2] The bottom line was that Roosevelt enthusiasti-
cally looked forward to the impending contest and the opportunity to become
president "in [his] own right."[3]

His glee was interrupted late in the morning of 19 May when the telegraph keys in the State Department chattered with a cable from Samuel René
Gummeré, the American consul general in Tangier, Morocco. Gummeré, a successful lawyer from Trenton, New Jersey, had served the United States in various diplomatic capacities since 1881. Posted to Tangier in 1898, largely owing to
the influence of Ion Perdicaris, another American citizen of some importance
in the city, Gummeré had experience dealing with local issues.[4] On the previous evening, the cable reported, a Moroccan brigand known as Raisuli had
broken into Perdicaris' country home just outside Tangier and had kidnapped
Perdicaris and his son-in-law and carried them off into the mountainous wilder-
ness. Although no demand for a ransom had yet been presented, the practice of
kidnapping prominent individuals for financial or political profit was common
in Morocco. Five years earlier, Gummeré had faced a crisis with the sultanate

that the arrival of an American warship had quickly solved.[5] Now, once again, the native of Trenton, who irritated local expatriate Americans with his British manners and dress, wired home that it would be of "immense importance to have a war vessel here to show what gravity my Government consider the situation and support me."[6] Given his well-evidenced predilection for employing naval power, the president happily obliged.

The kidnapping incident, best known historically for Secretary of State John Hay's famous cable, "This government wants Perdicaris alive or Raisuli dead," which was announced to thunderous applause at the Republican Convention, provides yet another opportunity to assess the subtlety of Theodore Roosevelt's use of the naval services as instruments of his particular brand of coercive diplomacy.[7] The incident also establishes the absolute control T. R. maintained over the movement of the fleet and the flexibility of his responses to international incidents.[8]

Theodore Roosevelt's form of naval diplomacy had continued to evolve since the crisis with Colombia over Panama's independence. During the summer and fall of 1904, he intended to combine the ships of the Battleship Squadron under Rear Adm. Albert S. Barker with those of the European Squadron under Rear Adm. Theodore F. Jewell for a "show the flag" tour of the Mediterranean. While these ships visited Portuguese, French, and Austrian ports, the South Atlantic Squadron under Rear Adm. French E. Chadwick was to cruise the North African coast before passing through the Suez Canal and steaming down the eastern coast of Africa (Table 5).[9]

The cruise was intended to demonstrate the capability of the American Navy to operate as a credible combat force far from home bases. Roosevelt felt that a strong U.S. Navy was essential to maintaining good relations with the Great Powers of Europe. "If we quit building our fleet," he noted with regard to the greatest of the naval powers, "England's friendship would immediately cool."[10] The fleet's cruise would also further American interests in certain corners of the Mediterranean, namely Turkey, where schools run by American evangelical societies had come under increasing threats.[11] Secretary of State Hay, alluding to this aspect of the summer cruise, informed the American representative in Constantinople on 24 May that "an imposing naval force will move in the direction of Turkey. You ought to be able to make some judicious use of this fleet in your negotiations without committing the Government to any action."[12] This was the plan in place before the kidnapping of Ion Perdicaris sidetracked the itinerary and redirected the fleet toward Morocco as the first stop of its odyssey.

TABLE 5. PARTICIPANTS IN THE SUMMER 1904 MEDITERRANEAN CRUISE

Battleship Squadron	European Squadron (Protected Cruisers)	South Atlantic Squadron
Rear Adm. Albert S. Barker	Rear Adm. Theodore F. Jewell	Rear Adm. French E. Chadwick
USS *Kearsarge* (flagship)	USS *Olympia* (flagship)	USS *Brooklyn,* armored cruiser (flagship)
USS *Iowa*	USS *Baltimore*	USS *Atlanta,* protected cruiser
USS *Alabama*	USS *Cleveland*	USS *Castine,* gunboat
USS *Maine*		USS *Marietta,* gunboat

During the last decade of the nineteenth century, Ion Perdicaris published a series of articles that appeared in the *Imperial and Asiatic Quarterly* in which he predicted the demise of the Sultanate of Morocco as an independent power and argued for British intervention.[13] By 1904, Morocco had, by all means of measurement, disintegrated from within. Banditry and chaos in the countryside further undermined the central government ruled by young Sultan Abdelaziz, who had ascended the throne in 1894 at the age of ten. Romantic characters such as the bandit Moulay Ahmad el Raisuli, scion of one of Morocco's most distinguished families, captured the hearts of the people. A descendant of Moulay Idriss, Raisuli was entitled to style himself a sharif and claimed lineage back to the Prophet Muhammad as well as the founder of the Kingdom of Morocco.[14] In his youth he had been a cattle rustler. His lineage, manner, and looks contributed to his celebrity among Morocco's numerous poor. As time went by, his challenge to authority became too great, and betrayal by a friend led to his incarceration for nearly five years—years that scarred his soul as well as his flesh.[15]

The death of the Moroccan regent, Bou Ahmad, in 1900 led to Raisuli's release, and he left prison determined to take his revenge on those who had betrayed him and to become a protector of the common people. "Against Europe on one side," he later recounted, "and the Sultan on the other I protected the rights of the people, for they were my people."[16] His chosen method of "protecting" the people was to kidnap notable Europeans and hold them for ransom, knowing that their home countries would bring pressure to bear against the sultan.[17] In 1903 he captured Walter Harris, a reporter for *The Times* of London, and demanded the release of certain of his associates from prison as well as a "remittance" for damage done to his property.[18] The speed of the sultan's response encouraged Raisuli to look for another prominent westerner to capture and bargain for, hence his encounter with Perdicaris.

Ion Perdicaris owned two homes in Morocco, one in Tangier and the other, a former royal residence named Aidonia (the Place of the Nightingales), outside the city among expansive grounds surrounded by a cork forest.[19] Perdicaris, his British wife, and his stepson, Cromwell Varley, were dining there on the evening of 18 May 1904 when they heard loud screams coming from the servants' area.[20] Perdicaris and Varley hastened to the scene, believing they were responding to a quarrel among the domestic help, only to find that a group of bandits had overcome and bound the servants. Perdicaris attempted to drive off the bandits but was beaten, cut by a knife, and himself bound.[21] The elderly man and his stepson were trundled to the stable where they met their captor, Moulay Ahmad el Raisuli. Within hours, Perdicaris and Varley had been hidden away in the maze of mountains east of Tangier.[22]

Initial Movements

Samuel Gummeré's initial communication to the U.S. State Department was terse and to the point: "Mr. Perdicaris, most prominent American Citizen here, and his stepson, Mr. Varley, British Subject, were carried off last night from their country house . . . by a numerous band of natives headed by Raisuly [sic]. . . . Earnestly request that a man-of-war be sent at once . . . situation most serious."[23] Assistant Secretary of State Francis Loomis, standing in for Secretary John Hay, who was representing the president at the Saint Louis Exposition, was certain that Theodore Roosevelt would accede to Gummeré's request but thought it wise to check with the commander in chief anyway.[24] A year earlier, T. R. had noticed that Hay had modified the mission of a Navy squadron without first checking with him and had briskly cautioned the older man against ever doing so again. By now, every individual who worked for Roosevelt knew that the naval services fell within his private purview. His initial reaction confirmed, Loomis consulted with the Bureau of Navigation's chief, Rear Adm. Henry Taylor, who transmitted orders to the coaling station at Tenerife in the Canary Islands.[25] Loomis telegraphed Gummeré that ships currently steaming in the Atlantic would be diverted to Tangier and could be expected to arrive in "three or four days."[26] The desk-bound Washington diplomat grossly underestimated the time of travel.

The Navy squadrons had departed San Juan, Puerto Rico, on 14 May for what was to be a leisurely Atlantic crossing, averaging only 9.2 knots in smooth to moderate seas. This pace brought them to the coaling station at Tenerife on 27 May. On arriving there, Rear Admiral Chadwick, commander of the South Atlantic Squadron, had expected to take on coal and stores and then cruise across the northern coast of Africa, through the Suez Canal, and southward to make a port call at Djibouti, at the southern entrance to the Red Sea, before proceeding back to the Atlantic via the southern tip of Africa.[27] Chadwick's original orders from the Navy Department had contained a series of prints of Turkish flags and signals that were not included in the orders of the other two squadrons, suggesting that Chadwick's squadron had a specific target for its diplomacy: the Ottoman government in Turkey.[28] In all probability, his squadron's presence in the western Mediterranean had been intended to serve as a signal to Turkey, but all that was forgotten when Rear Admiral Chadwick's squadron arrived in Tenerife and received its new orders.[29]

Theodore Roosevelt's views on America's place in the world continued to expand as he became more comfortable with the office and trappings of the presidency. In May 1904 he wrote to his son Theodore Jr., "I do not think that any two people ever got more enjoyment out of the White House than Mother and I . . . we like Washington. . . . I work until between four and five, usually having some official people to lunch—now a couple Senators, now a couple of Ambassadors."[30] Whereas in his first years in office he had been content to confine himself to the Western Hemisphere and his pet project, the Panama Canal, he had begun looking beyond this horizon to a broader field of play. Three squadrons of the U.S. Navy were set to show the flag of the United States in the Mediterranean during the forthcoming summer months. With news of the Perdicaris kidnapping not more than a day old, the president wrote to Elihu Root, his secretary of war, that if nations acted within the norms of international conduct they would have no need to fear the United States. If they strayed from those norms, however, the United States would consider intervening to restore order both internally and internationally.[31]

On being informed of the president's wishes with regard to Perdicaris' kidnapping, the Navy Department had sent orders to Tenerife: "Vessel which can reach Tangier quickest proceed there immediately, remaining vessels follow soonest practicable."[32] Chadwick's ships began coaling immediately, and each departed as soon as it had taken on enough fuel for the trip. The squadron comprised the armored cruiser USS *Brooklyn* (flagship), the protected cruiser USS *Atlanta,* and the gunboats USS *Machias* and USS *Marietta.*[33] Proceeding at their best speed, all arrived in the Moroccan port within hours of each other on 30 May. On entering the harbor, each ship fired its guns in ceremonial salute to the fort overlooking the bay and received a retort from Moroccan cannon.[34]

By now the American people were well informed of the plight of their fellow countryman in faraway Africa. The *New York Times* had carried its first story on 20 May.[35] Washington was abuzz with conversation regarding the possible landing of Marines to search out Raisuli's lair. *Harper's Weekly* came closest to the actual strategy that the Americans would follow when it printed, "We can quickly place a fleet strong enough to bombard or occupy not only Tangier, but every seaport in Morocco."[36] While this did not happen, the mere presence of the American ships was enough to remind the Moroccan government that the potential existed.

Theodore Roosevelt enjoyed working with Rear Admiral Chadwick, who possessed an enviable martial reputation and a lucid pen. After entering the naval service during the Civil War, Chadwick quickly carved a niche for himself as one of the Navy's foremost intellects. Tours as an instructor of mathematics at the Naval Academy, naval attaché in London (seven years), chief of the Office of Naval Intelligence, and president of the Naval War College refined and demonstrated the admiral's ability to handle complex issues. Numerous articles in the U.S. Naval Institute's *Proceedings,* as well as three published books, honed his composition skill to a fine edge.[37] Appropriately, his most important work was a two-volume history that covered the diplomacy and military operations of the Spanish-American War.[38] Had his career not coincided with Alfred T. Mahan's, French Chadwick probably would have emerged as the premier American naval writer of his age. As it was, he established a reputation as a warrior that Mahan never had, and was repeatedly advanced in seniority in recognition of his performance under fire. The Spanish-American War found Chadwick serving as chief of staff to Rear Adm. William T. Sampson.[39] The fact that Sampson's ships had such success off Cuba even though numerous current historians believe that Sampson was suffering from the onset of Alzheimer's disease suggests that Chadwick had more to do with the American victory in the Caribbean than was believed at the time.[40] Regardless, he arrived in Tangier well prepared to be the conduit of Theodore Roosevelt's diplomacy.

The Limits of Coercive Diplomacy

Within twenty-four hours of his arrival, Chadwick sent off an impressively concise two-and-a-half-page report to the secretary of the Navy. He covered the particulars of the kidnapping, Perdicaris' background and that of his family, the general location where the prisoners were being held, and the extent of Raisuli's demands. Additionally, he gave his assessment that whatever action the Americans took must be "wholly against the Sultan, or more immediately against the Sultan's representative in this region." Chadwick continued, "There is but one outcome which can be insisted upon, which is a yielding by the Sultan to Raisuli's demands . . . the former knows he is powerless to accomplish anything against Raisuli's people in the mountain region . . . such an attempt would be a signal for the immediate death of the two captive men."

The admiral continued with a description of the local terrain and its tactical implications, then outlined his plan to coordinate with Consul General Gummeré and with the other foreign plenipotentiaries in Tangier.[41] Subtle corrections on the typewritten pages in Chadwick's own hand suggest that he produced it himself, in one sitting, at the desk in his flag cabin on board the USS *Brooklyn*.

Raisuli's demands had from the beginning been carefully targeted to undermine the authority of the sultan and his representative, Si Abd al-Salam, the pasha of Tangier. Raisuli had a long-standing feud with al-Salam, who had lived in the home of Raisuli's father as a child and had been a lifelong friend until his betrayal led to Raisuli's arrest in 1896.[42] Nearly five years in prison left Raisuli with a powerful thirst for vengeance. When he discovered on his release that his betrayer had confiscated his property and had been appointed pasha (governor) of Tangier, his anger knew no bounds. Raisuli, seeking legal redress, had applied for the recovery of his property but was laughed out of the sultan's court.[43] Now, finally, with an American prisoner in his hands and American warships staring down the sultan's representatives, he issued his demands.

In his first communication with the sultan, released simultaneously to the representatives of the foreign governments, he demanded a payment of $70,000 for himself and his followers to cover their recent losses to the pasha's troops. He explicitly stated that the money be raised from the sale of property belonging to the pasha of Tangier and his cousin, the pasha of Fez. Next Raisuli demanded the outright removal of the pasha of Tangier and the withdrawal of the troops that had been deployed against him in the city and surrounding territories. These territories were to be ceded to Raisuli for his control. Additionally, the brigand demanded the release of his followers previously captured and imprisoned by the government and a pardon from the sultan for all of his previous actions.

The sultan responded with an offer of $20,000, to come from unspecified sources. Additionally, the pasha of Tangier would be dismissed, the government's troops withdrawn, and Raisuli's people released from prison. No mention of a pardon accompanied this initial reply.[44] Raisuli responded by increasing his demands and threatening, for the first time, to kill the hostages if his demands were not promptly met.[45]

Raisuli had killed captives before. After his capture by Raisuli in 1903, *London Times* correspondent Walter Harris had been taken to the bandit's hideout and treated to the sight of a dead man whose ransom had not been paid.

> It was a ghastly sight. The summer heat had already caused the corpse to discolour and swell. An apple had been stuck in the man's mouth, and both his eyes had been gouged out. The naked body was shockingly mutilated, and the finger-tips had been cut off, to be worn, the tribesmen told me, as charms for their women. The hands were pegged to the ground by sticks driven through the palms, about a yard in length, bearing little flags . . . the village dogs had already gnawed away a portion of the flesh of one of the legs. I was jokingly informed that that was probably what I should look like during the course of the next couple of days.[46]

Everyone in the expatriate community was familiar with Harris' account and took Raisuli's threat very seriously.[47] The ripples of concern had reached as far as Washington. At the time of Harris' kidnapping Secretary of State John Hay had inquired if there were any American citizens who wished transportation out of Tangier, and if the missionaries at Larache, Morocco, felt secure.[48]

Consul General Gummeré became increasingly despondent about the rapidly destabilizing situation. By 25 May, twice the time allotted by Loomis in his reply to Gummeré's request for naval assistance, no ship had yet arrived. The diplomat again telegraphed the State Department, giving full vent to his anxiety and concern.[49] His cables were ultimately read by Roosevelt himself, and the commander in chief sent for his secretary of state on 28 May "in a hurry."[50] Their quick conversation, no more than an interruption in Roosevelt's thoughts about the impending political convention, led to the dispatch of the European Squadron to join Chadwick's force in Tangier.[51]

At the coaling station at the Portuguese Azores Islands in the mid-Atlantic, Rear Admiral Jewell, commander of the European Squadron, received orders via wireless telegraph to separate his ships—the cruisers *Olympia* (flagship), *Baltimore,* and *Cleveland*—from Rear Admiral Barker's Battleship Squadron and proceed to Tangier at best speed.[52] Jewell's squadron dropped anchor at Tangier on 1 June. One of Raisuli's observers in Tangier journeyed into the hills east of the city to report the ships' arrival to his master. Rather than being intimidated by the American vessels, Raisuli was pleased, hoping that their presence would force the sultan to accede to his demands.[53]

Chadwick himself took the same view in a report to the secretary of the Navy, noting that the seizure of Perdicaris had been intended "to bring pressure on the Sultan of Morocco to secure the demands of [Raisuli's] tribe. Our sense of the gravity of the case is shown by the presence of the American Squadron and will undoubtedly cause the earlier yielding of the Sultan of Morocco to the demands of the Chief. Which is the only safe means of releasing captive. An attack will cause their immediate murder."[54]

The admiral's ominous cable attracted the president's attention. At noon on 1 June Roosevelt again summoned John Hay as well as the secretary of the Navy, William H. Moody, to the White House "for a few words about Perdicaris."[55] The Perdicaris incident had been discussed during a cabinet meeting the previous day, so all three men were familiar with the background of the ongoing standoff.[56] Chadwick's report had provided no sense of impending success from an American standpoint. It was becoming clear that the American military presence was unlikely to have any influence on the brigand in the hills east of Tangier. The nation's youngest president had lately begun feeling the tendrils of age creeping up on him, and he was noticeably anxious for action.[57]

At Roosevelt's direction, Hay composed a brusque missive addressed to the sultan via the American consul general but did not send it. A communiqué from the American ambassador in London convinced the secretary of state that ongoing European initiatives would not be helped by a disrespectful tone, so Hay altered his message to state that the "President wishes everything possible done to secure the release of Perdicaris. He wishes it clearly understood that if Perdicaris is murdered, this government will demand the life of the murderer . . . you are to avoid in all your official action anything which may be regarded as an encouragement to brigandage or blackmail."[58] Having viewed and signed off on Hay's message, Roosevelt knew he was both increasing the pressure on the sultan and putting the situation very much in the hands of Raisuli himself. The sultan and his foreign minister reacted with despair.[59]

Back in Washington, John Hay found himself in an uncomfortable predicament. On 1 June, coincidental with his last meeting with the president, the State Department had received a disturbing letter from Mr. A. H. Slocomb of Fayetteville, North Carolina. Mr. Slocomb alleged that he had met Perdicaris during a visit to Athens, Greece, in 1862. In the course of their conversation Perdicaris had informed Slocomb that he had foresworn his American citizenship to become a Greek—as was his right as the son of a Greek citizen—in order to avoid either serving in the Confederate Army or surrendering part of his million-dollar inheritance from his father, which included property in South Carolina. Hay knew that this information portended international embarrassment and domestic political disaster. He cabled the American diplomatic representative in Athens to ascertain the truthfulness of the allegation.[60]

In Tangier harbor, Rear Admiral Jewell placed himself and the Mediterranean Squadron under the command of Rear Admiral Chadwick, the senior admiral present.[61] Chadwick continued to assess the situation and began to realize that the problem in Morocco went beyond Raisuli's immediate personal agenda to an issue that lay festering at the nation's heart. The growth of Christian influence in the sultan's court combined with the incursion of Western powers into Moroccan territory and culture had undermined the legitimacy of the sultanate and encouraged lawlessness. The unrest grew every day, and the presence of the armed American ships was fast becoming a two-edged sword. While the ships were a force that subdued the enthusiasms of the mob during the daytime, they served as a focus of national embarrassment and unrest for Moroccans at night. In a brief telegram to the secretary of the Navy on 3 June, Chadwick described a "fanatical feast" that left the natives restless and endangered Morocco's foreign community. "The presence of ships is the only protection of the Christian population," he warned. The next day, in his second lengthy report to Roosevelt via the Navy Department, Chadwick again issued this warning: "The danger to the Christians here is an unknown quantity. There is some danger and there may be very considerable [danger]. Truth in such a region is difficult to reach."[62]

The admiral also informed his superiors that he had placed armed Marines outside the Perdicaris residence and the American consulate.[63] Burly sailors accompanied the consul general as bodyguards.[64] Navy signalmen were posted to the American consulate "in order to be able to communicate with the vessels in case of attack and need of assistance."[65] Unpreparedness was to be avoided at all costs. Expecting continued unrest, Chadwick requested that the senior Marine present in the squadron ready all of the Marines embarked on ships in the harbor as well as a company of sailors for an armed landing, "if it should be necessary." Chadwick took the additional step of inviting a number of the local leaders of the various tribes aboard the American warships, hoping that the display of technology and firepower might erase any thoughts of resistance.[66] In the meantime, the consul general asked Chadwick to land some additional Marines ashore, with embarrassing results.

The wife of the absent Belgian minister in Tangier was an American citizen and the daughter of Gen. John Patton Story, a senior U.S. Army artillery officer posted to Washington.[67] She felt threatened by the local Moorish population, which had begun to exude aggression and intimidation toward its European neighbors, so two Marines were ordered ashore to stand guard at her residence.[68] When news of the posting leaked out, the *New York Tribune* led its front page with "American Marines Have Landed in Africa," and the *World* drew overblown allusions to Capt. Stephen Decatur's actions against the Barbary pirates.[69]

French Chadwick, perceptive as always, had received word that a new British battleship, HMS *Prince of Wales,* had arrived at Gibraltar. Anxious to bring the maximum amount of diplomatic and military pressure to bear on the situation, the admiral requested permission to contact the British to ask that the battleship be moved to Tangier. "I think it policy that England should be required under the circumstances to make public exhibit of interest," he explained.[70] After all, Perdicaris' son-in-law, Cromwell Varley, was a British citizen.

By now, other Great Powers were becoming concerned about the size and duration of the American presence in Tangier. Spain, so recently the victim of American martial prowess, feared that its recent enemy was intent on finding a reason to seize the port of Tangier as a permanent coaling station.[71] Such a move would be yet another blow to Spanish pride because Morocco had historically been within Spain's sphere of influence. The Spanish government decided to move Spain's sole remaining battleship, the *Pelayo,* south to the port of Cádiz to improve its potential to respond.[72] Other European nations quietly began to consider their own responses to the developing diplomatic situation.

The French were also unsettled. They had been working quietly for years to increase their influence in Morocco. Military moves in the eastern oasis had met with success, and diplomatic subterfuge was currently undermining the British influence at Fez.[73] Perdicaris himself had recognized the slow progression of French influence, writing in early 1904, "any day, any hour now may give the Sultan's tottering authority the last fatal [blow] which will send him at last, all unwilling though he may be, reeling into the arms of France."[74] Almost overnight, however, the upstart North American republic and its navalist president threatened to negate the careful machinations of the French.[75] At first, the French thought they would be able to capitalize on the situation by pushing through a plan to create a pan-national security force to reestablish order in Morocco. Indeed, Roosevelt, possessing no motives beyond the recovery of Perdicaris, had reached out to the French and asked for their support and ideas. As time passed and U.S. military pressure came to bear, the French began to consider whether the American initiatives would undermine their own influence by stirring up local resentment against Western nations. The French minister at Fez, St. Rene Taillandier, began to encourage the sultan to draw out the ordeal, endangering the lives of the kidnap victims.[76]

The Germans, on the other hand, were not the least bit concerned about stirring up local resentment. Their fear was that they were once again about to lose out to the Americans in the crucial contest of colonial conquest. All were mistaken. Roosevelt wanted Perdicaris back. He may have seen the issue as a way to stir the imagination of the American electorate at this particular time, but he did not want a colony in Africa.

Chadwick called on the British minister in Fez, Sir Arthur Nicholson, on 5 June to discuss bringing HMS *Prince of Wales* to Tangier. He was pleased to learn that Nicholson had already arranged it; the battleship would arrive on 8 June.[77] Nicholson, the son of a British admiral, had entered the British Foreign Service in 1870 and had served with distinction in Berlin, Peking, Constantinople, Athens, and Teheran before being appointed Britain's minister to Morocco in 1895.[78] He was a mature diplomat who quickly realized where his nation's interests lay. From this perspective, he extended to Chadwick the privilege of reading all of his correspondence with London concerning the Perdicaris matter, informing the American admiral that he felt it urgent that the force currently in place in the Bay of Tangier "should not be reduced."[79] Rear Admiral Chadwick found himself acting as a second conduit for diplomatic negotiations.

As the second week of June began, the situation had not improved. The American consul general reported that all efforts that could be made were being made, but to no avail. He had not attempted direct negotiations with Raisuli and advised that he thought it best to maintain the pressure on the sultanate to obtain Perdicaris' release. The Moroccan government's only option at this stage, however, was total acquiescence to the bandit's demands. Gummeré was informed that "the government has no authority, for the present at least, over these mountaineers."[80]

Later, Gummeré felt compelled to report information suggesting that the elderly American captive was seriously ill. He and the British chargé d'affaires in Fez both hastened to acquaint the Moroccan government with the consequences should Perdicaris meet an untimely demise. The British representative, writing to his superior at Tangier, recounted,

> I pointed out the grave risks to the lives and health of these gentlemen, especially Mr. Perdicaris, whose age and state of health could ill bear such strains by any prolongation of their captivity, and I stated that one could not be sure of what a man like Raissuli [sic] might do in a moment of impatience and under undue pressure from others and that he might proceed suddenly to extreme measures. It was therefore absolutely necessary that the captives' liberation be procured at once.[81]

Realizing that Perdicaris' death could very well trigger American armed intervention, the Moroccan minister of foreign affairs suddenly reported that the sultan's government was ready to meet all of Raisuli's demands. Chadwick reported to the Navy Department that "the prisoners, money and everything are in readiness for the exchange of captives."[82]

The stillness of the morning of 7 June was shattered in the harbor of Tangier by a twenty-one-gun salute fired at the harbor's entrance. Such was the speed of the sultan's capitulation that the new governor had already arrived to take the place of Si Abd al-Salam as the pasha of Tangier.[83] Raisuli, staring success in the face, decided to increase his demands once again. Fearing that the sultan would double-cross him as soon as he released the captives, the brigand demanded that the British and American governments stake their national honor to guarantee the sultan's compliance.[84] They refused. In the meantime, reports circulated that Pedicaris had recovered from his ailment.[85]

The ever-observant Rear Admiral Chadwick continued to study the situation and report to the president via the Navy Department. On 12 June he commented on the weakness of the current Moroccan government's institutions and military power. He warned of "the powerlessness of the government to do anything more than concede; it cannot punish; there is practically no army. . . . We should thus look in vain to the government should events unfortunately require a punitive expedition. I cannot make this fact too strong."[86] Apparently the admiral never lost sight of the possibility that it might become necessary to introduce an armed American force into Morocco, either to attempt to rescue Perdicaris or to exact retribution for his death.

On 15 June Consul General Gummeré received yet another communiqué from the Moroccan minister of foreign affairs informing him that Raisuli was, again, increasing his demands. The kidnapper by now knew that the sultan's government was trapped between his elusiveness and a Great Power that was holding it responsible for the ultimate health of his kidnapped victim. This time he demanded the release of additional prisoners, the immediate arrest of his archenemy—the by now former pasha of Tangier—and the cession of four additional districts surrounding Tangier to his control. The sultan's minister meekly reported that these new demands would also be met.[87] Raisuli, still sniffing betrayal, again asked the United States and Great Britain to guarantee that his demands would be faithfully met. When he heard the particulars of the latest demand, the American secretary of state opined that Raisuli had developed "a bad case of megalomania."[88]

Chadwick, for his part, requested that HMS *Prince of Wales,* which had appeared in Tangier's harbor only briefly before suddenly setting course for the docks at Gibraltar for repairs, make another appearance in Tangier. The American admiral wanted it to be abundantly evident to the Moroccan government that the two great English-speaking nations were working closely together on all aspects of the negotiations.[89] The British representative assured him that the capital warship would soon make another appearance.[90]

In the meantime, the French, increasingly disturbed about the mounting American-Anglo presence in Tangier, began bringing pressure on the sultan's government at Fez. The French minister belittled the American naval presence in Tangier and the British battleship's brief visit to the bay. Behind the scenes, he urged the sultan to ask the Americans to send some of their ships away. Later, he suggested that the young leader send a punitive expeditionary force from Casablanca to end the situation, hoping that the presence of the Moroccan force would mitigate any need to land a foreign force either to provide protection for the local European population or to search for Raisuli.[91] On hearing of the planned Moroccan troop movement, Chadwick immediately realized both that any Moroccan force would greatly outnumber and outgun his own meager troops and that this fact would be readily evident to the local population.[92] He feared the move would backfire and encourage simmering local resentment against the West to flare into violence.

The introduction of a Moroccan force would also violate the sultan's earlier agreement to withdraw the Moroccan forces present in Tangier. Under the current circumstances, Gummeré had every right to fear that the brigand, so far successful in his bargaining with the government at Fez, might seek any excuse to prolong the negotiations to gain additional advantage for himself. He asked the State Department's permission to formally warn the kidnapper that any further delay in the release of the kidnap victims would trigger a response by the United States and Great Britain. Gummeré emphasized that this warning, once made, would have to be carried to its conclusion: "In order not to jeopardize the lives of all Christians in Morocco it would be necessary that such a threat of punishment should be fulfilled to the letter."[93]

Gummeré was trying to signal Washington that the United States was dealing with an Arab culture, and that Arab rules had to be followed. It was important to get President Roosevelt to focus on the problem in the context in which it was being played out. Roosevelt's distraction with domestic politics was quite evident by this time, and Gummeré saw a critical need to bring the president's significant intellectual focus to bear on the situation in Morocco. This was not a test of will and wits against another European power. Nor was it a contest against an upstart Latin American "democracy." U.S. interests were being threatened by a rogue acting outside the boundaries instituted and recognized in the West. The local state's representatives, diplomatic and military, were attempting to achieve a solution within the confines of a government characterized by weakness at every point. Gummeré wanted Roosevelt to be prepared to pursue a military option if the situation deteriorated further.

Back in Washington, John Hay and Theodore Roosevelt exchanged notes with regard to the new information. Hay was struck by Raisuli's escalating attempts to destabilize the sultan's government. "You see," he wrote Roosevelt, "there is no end to the insolence of this blackguard."[94] Both T. R. and Hay agreed that the United States could grant no guarantees to the kidnapper. In reply to Hay's note, the president wrote, "Of course, it would be out of the question to surrender to the demands of the Morocco brigands. We have gone just as far as we possibly can go for Perdicaris. Our position must now be to demand the death of those that harm him if he is harmed."[95] How to punish Raisuli in the event that Perdicaris was not returned was becoming a chief concern among the decision makers.

Roosevelt, for his part, was already cautiously approaching this decision. On 15 June, concurrent with receipt of his consul general's report, the president wrote a second note to John Hay stating that the time had come "to enter into negotiations with England and France, looking to the possibility of an expedition to punish the brigand if Gummeré's statement[s] with regard to the impotence of the Sultan are true." The stalled nature of the negotiations and his previous commitment of U.S. prestige in the form of Chadwick's naval battle group were leading Roosevelt toward a solution using force. Historian Barbara Tuchman summed up the situation concisely: "America's fleet, flag, and honor were committed."[96]

French Chadwick took the initiative and began active preparations for armed confrontation. He gathered the commanding officers from the *Cleveland, Marietta,* and *Castine*—Cdr. H. H. Southerland, Cdr. Henry Morrell, and Cdr. F. J. Dorn—and directed them to "collect information and prepare without delay a plan of military operations of a foreign force in Morocco, based upon possible necessity of a punitive expedition directed against the bandit Raisuli and those allied with him." The admiral put his force's intelligence capabilities at their service and warned those involved that the plans must be kept secret.[97] Chadwick also offered the services and experience of the senior Marine officer embarked in his task force, Capt. John Twiggs Myers.[98]

At the age of thirty-four "Handsome Jack" Myers was already an international hero. A graduate of the U.S. Naval Academy (class of 1892), Myers had served in the Navy for three years before transferring to the Marine Corps in the spring of 1895. In May 1900, while attached to the USS *Newark,* Myers led a force comprising forty-eight Marines and three sailors to relieve the American legation in Peking during the "Boxer" rebellion. The ensuing fighting was bloody, sweaty, and hand-to-hand. Myers was seriously wounded when a spear lodged in his thigh. Two U.S. Marines were killed in the action, but Myers' force saved the legations of several European nations. He was brevetted to the rank of major and advanced four numbers on the Marine Corps' seniority list. President McKinley mentioned him by name in his annual State of the Union message to the Congress, and when the British erected a monument to commemorate the relief of the legations, Myers' image was carved in bas-relief leading the charge. He was a Marine of unique standing within both his own service and the international community.[99] He was just the type of officer that might be needed in Tangier.

The plan that emerged from Chadwick's three ship commanders called for an armed assault on Tangier's critical positions to include the fort, dockyards, and customhouse by a combined force of 1,200 sailors and Marines backed by five 3-inch guns and assorted automatic weapons. The 1,200 men were subdivided into two brigades drawn from the European and South Atlantic squadrons, respectively. The South Atlantic Squadron brigade, including its Marines under the leadership of Captain Myers, would conduct the initial assault and take the wharf area and customhouse. The warships in the harbor were to be prepared to shell the batteries at the custom pier and the northeast battery if the landing were opposed.[100]

After the sixteenth, negotiations appeared to break in the Americans' direction. The sultan's government offered terms, and a negotiator returned from Raisuli's lair on the seventeenth announcing that Perdicaris and Varley would be released upon receipt of $50,000 in Spanish promissory notes and $20,000 in Spanish gold. Raisuli's message did not mention a requirement for American or British guarantees of his safety.[101] Although the U.S. government remained skeptical, success appeared to be at hand.[102] The day of release would be 21 June 1904, more than one month after the men had been abducted.[103] Roosevelt's ships and the threat posed by their Marine contingents appeared to have done the trick again. Then, on 19 June, rumors began to circulate that "complications had come up in the Perdicaris case."[104]

Raisuli's representative approached the government's representative on 20 June with the intent of tying up the last loose ends of the negotiations, only to be informed that some of the territory that was to have been transferred to Raisuli's oversight would remain under the sultanate's control after all. Fear that he might exact retribution against some of the local population who had opposed him in the past blocked the transfer. Gummeré, in a fit of frustration, informed the sultan's minister of foreign affairs that "the manner of the negotiations was not satisfactory; that it could not be conceded that the Government had no authority over a petty chief, and that for every hour's further delay he would be held responsible."[105]

Gummeré reported home that his position as consul general for the United States vis-à-vis the negotiations with the Moroccan government had become personally "humiliating." He requested permission to issue an ultimatum to the Moroccans to claim an indemnity for each additional day's delay in delivering Ion Perdicaris safely to the American authorities. Furthermore, he wanted permission to threaten the Moroccans with the possibility of landing Chadwick's two naval brigades and seizing Tangier's customhouse.[106] He ended this cable by stating that he had spoken to Rear Admiral Chadwick, and that the admiral agreed "to the same effect."[107]

Before Washington could reply to that cable Gummeré wrote again, this time reporting that the process for returning the kidnap victims had begun and all seemed to be in order, although he was not "entirely confident" in the outcome of the day's proceedings. Eager to obliterate his self-perceived humiliation at the hands of both the Moroccan government and the brigand Raisuli,

Gummeré asked the president's authorization to use the force assembled by Chadwick to pursue and punish "all who were implicated in the abduction." He went on to say that asking the sultan's government at Fez to pursue this aim would be useless. "As the government is without sufficient power, some means should be considered to enforce such a demand."[108]

Rear Admiral Chadwick was also not willing to let down his guard. Since formulating his plan for the occupation of critical sectors of Tangier, he had been working with Gummeré and the British representatives to bring about a peaceful outcome. However, the constant delays and the shifting demands of the parties involved had tried his patience to the limit. Cdr. Edward Dorn, commanding officer of the *Castine,* recorded in his diary, "Admiral signaled for us and read us the telegram he was having sent in cipher to the Navy Department stating that negotiations being thwarted by the authorities, he considered it advisable to seize the Customs House as indemnity for each day's delay in delivery of the Captives."[109] Dorn learned that he was to lead the battalion of sailors and Marines who would be executing the plan. He and Captain Jack Myers "went at once on shore to lay out the principle points to be seized and the route to be followed on landing—very hard afternoon but tramped over miles, but have a clear enough idea now of the surroundings."[110]

The *Castine's* commander was very excited about the prospect of combat. In the turn-of-the-century Navy, success in such operations could lead to fame and advancement in seniority over one's peers. Unfortunately, he and Myers were unable to agree on the tactics to be employed.[111] Dorn felt compelled to consult with the admiral, but on returning to his gunboat at the end of his day of reconnaissance he was confused to learn that he had received orders to take his ship and proceed the following morning to Gibraltar to take on stores. Signaled to come aboard the *Brooklyn,* Dorn hurried over to see Chadwick, who explained that "he had not sent the [first] dispatch but another one he read me which was the result of sleeping on the order and [was] much milder." The warrior-scholar had decided to take a less confrontational tone than the diplomat. Even a bystander like Commander Dorn felt uncomfortable about this conflict of approaches.[112]

In a coded message to the Navy Department Rear Admiral Chadwick concurred with Gummeré's representation of the situation. It appeared to him as well that negotiations had broken down owing to the scheming and maneuvering of local officials seeking to expand their influence or find a way of profiting from the ongoing crisis. Additionally, Chadwick endorsed Gummeré's idea of demanding an indemnity for every day that passed without the safe return of the captives. The admiral did, however, hedge on the use of military force: "After further consultation active pressure at present is regarded as dangerous to captives."[113]

Hay, alarmed at the gloomy reports coming out of Tangier, approached the president with more disquieting news. The State Department's minister in Athens, John B. Jackson, had wired that records there appeared to confirm that a Mr. Ioannis Perdicaris had, in fact, been naturalized as a Greek citizen in March 1862. Hay faced the uncomfortable prospect of informing Theodore Roosevelt, in the midst of an election campaign, that he had committed the prestige of the nation to the recovery of a man who had apparently surrendered his citizenship to avoid military service. As was the prerogative of the old man, he sent his assistant, Gailand Hunt, over to the White House to brief the president on the current situation and ask his permission to respond to Gummeré's request for an ultimatum. A draft response was included in the briefing folder. Hunt later reported that the president found the information regarding Perdicaris' citizenship "quite unwelcome" but would allow the situation to play itself out. No word of Perdicaris' citizenship was to leak out.[114] Hunt returned to Hay's office with the president's assent to send the message Hay had drafted.[115] Thus, with the approval of Theodore Roosevelt, Hay issued his famous directive that the United States "wants Perdicaris alive or Raisuli dead." Although that is the part of the message remembered today, the rest of Hay's communiqué reveals the president's real intent: "Further than this, least possible complications with Morocco or other powers is desired. Mr. Gummeré is instructed not to arrange for landing marines or seizing customhouse without Department's specific directions."[116]

The president, so seemingly bent on the employment of martial force, so bellicose in his choice of words throughout the negotiations, had pulled back from the brink, perhaps so as not to offend the other Great Powers, or perhaps because he had learned that Perdicaris was possibly not even a U.S. citizen. Gummeré, unaware of the secret knowledge swirling in the background of the diplomatic correspondence, replied the next day that he would take no action that would alter the balance of power in Morocco without first receiving explicit instructions from the Department of State. In the meantime, he reported that negotiators carrying the ransom money had departed for a remote village where the exchange of money and prisoners was to occur.[117]

Recognizing the Limits of Force

Perdicaris and his son-in-law were led out of the mountains by their captor and met by the ransom party, which was carrying the payment in boxes on the backs of thirty pack-mules. Following the exchange, Perdicaris and Varley continued on toward Tangier. Although he arrived in town after darkness had fallen, Perdicaris was quick to make out the signal lights of the American Navy ships riding at anchor in the harbor and to discern the reason for their presence. Overcome by patriotism, Tuchman noted, he welcomed "such proof of his country's solicitude for its citizens, and for the honor of its flag!"[118] He quickly wired the U.S. State Department to thank John Hay for the nation's efforts on his behalf.[119] Perdicaris did not remain in Morocco. His wife insisted that they move away from the horrid place that now held so many bad memories for her, and the couple moved to England. They lived out their remaining days there, with occasional trips to the United States.[120]

With regard to Ion Perdicaris' citizenship, it was later decided that his action in 1862 did not void his American citizenship, but merely recognized his right, as the son of a Greek national, to have dual citizenship.[121] This ruling, however, was rendered years later. Roosevelt had decided to go forward with his pressure on the Moorish government at Fez knowing that Perdicaris might not be a U.S. citizen. Perhaps he did not want to deal with the embarrassment of having committed a substantial portion of the Atlantic Fleet to a fool's errand. Perhaps he felt umbrage at the fact that Raisuli had captured someone who at least had the reputation of being an American citizen. More than likely, he was just exhibiting his predilection to never let rules stand in the way of his chosen outcome. As his attorney general once replied to a legal inquiry about a past event, "Ah, Mr. President, why have such a beautiful action marred by any taint of legality."[122]

On 25 June Rear Admiral Chadwick informed the secretary of the Navy that the captives had been released and that HMS *Prince of Wales* had left once again for Gibraltar.[123] Chadwick's South Atlantic Squadron would follow two days later to recoal and resupply at the British naval base.[124] Chadwick received congratulatory telegrams from the Navy Department and the State Department, which assured him that it had not had the "least doubt of your judgment and discretion."[125] He also received an accolade from his commander in chief.[126] French Chadwick did not make his Mediterranean cruise and then circumnavigate Africa after the Perdicaris "interruption." He was instead ordered to proceed down the western coast of the continent after refueling.[127]

He turned over command of the South Atlantic Squadron in November 1904 and returned home. Placed on the retired list in 1906, he continued to be a prolific writer.[128] He died on 27 January 1919 in New York City, twenty-one days after the death of the president he had served in the summer of 1904.

Consul General Samuel Gummeré received a telegram of congratulations from Secretary of State John Hay on 25 June as well.[129] He would render great service to his president a year later during the crisis surrounding the Algeciras Conference, when the Great Powers of Europe came to the precipice of war over the internationalization of Morocco.[130] Roosevelt's behind-the-scenes mediation, with Gummeré's local assistance, did much to mute the tocsins of war.[131] As a reward, and in recognition of Morocco's increased strategic importance in the world, the president elevated Gummeré's status in Morocco from consul general to minister, a rank just shy of ambassador.[132]

On 10 July, less than a month after letting Perdicaris go and riding into the mountains with his seventy thousand Spanish dollars, Raisuli attempted to abduct the British journalist Walter Harris again but did not succeed.[133] His achievement in forcing the sultan's government at Fez to bow to his every demand both heightened his sense of power and further undermined public support for the young sultan. The Algeciras Conference in January 1906, in which eleven European nations and the United States dictated that the Moroccan economy be opened to European involvement, removed whatever public reverence remained for the sultan's hereditary position.[134] His elder brother soon replaced him in a coup.[135]

Theodore Roosevelt emerges from the Perdicaris affair in a new light. While Hay's famous cable to Gummeré did ring out with the energetic bellicosity that had characterized much of Roosevelt's earlier years of power, T. R.'s actions behind the scenes demonstrate a more thoughtful and restrained diplomatic approach to the problem at hand. Most of those involved had expected the arrival of the U.S. warships to bring about the quick return of Perdicaris and his son-in-law. When this did not occur, Roosevelt, distracted by the upcoming domestic political campaign, instinctively called for more ships. When they arrived and there was still no progress, he briefly shifted his attention away from the political stage in Chicago to focus his intellect on the problem in Tangier.

After due consideration and consultation he directed his chief diplomat to send a message to the Moroccan government that he held them responsible for the life of Ion Perdicaris. The threat of naval force, so far directed at the brigand Raisuli, swung to point instead at the sultan's throne at Fez. T. R. also set about engaging other Great Powers in the situation so that they might bring their influence to bear at the sultan's court. This appreciation of local political influence and the Moroccan government's inability to bring about any solution short of total capitulation demonstrates a diplomatic sophistication matched only by a select few of Roosevelt's predecessors.

Roosevelt's use of the advice of the two senior American officials in Tangier reveals much about his thought processes at the time. Samuel Gummeré, a diplomat with extensive knowledge of local customs and personalities, had recommended an active, overt, and immediate military response. French Chadwick, who was the epitome of the type of military officer Roosevelt appreciated but possessed limited experience in local matters, advanced the idea of an indemnity, demurring on the option of force. Roosevelt ultimately listened to the latter.

Having committed the fleet and American prestige, he could not, and did not, remove it. But the forgotten second half of Hay's famous message, the part that forbade the introduction of force without express sanction from the State Department—which is to say the president himself—demonstrates that Roosevelt possessed a clear view of the limits of military power.[136] Diplomacy, always a component in Theodore Roosevelt's foreign policy, was on the ascendancy.

chapter five

The Unlikely Location
Making Peace at the Portsmouth Navy Yard

There was difficulty in getting them to agree on a common meeting place;
but each finally abandoned its original contentions in the matter,
and the representatives of the two nations finally met at
Portsmouth, in New Hampshire.

THEODORE ROOSEVELT

The impetus for peace began at sea. The victory had not been unexpected, but the magnitude of Adm. Heihachiro Togo's defeat of the Russian naval force on 27–28 May 1905 exceeded even Theodore Roosevelt's active imagination. "No wonder you are happy!" he wrote Baron Kentaro Kaneko, a fellow Harvard alumnus who served as an informal liaison between Roosevelt and the Japanese government. "Neither Trafalgar nor the defeat of the Spanish Armada was as complete." Roosevelt's understanding of the full implications of Japan's success is evident in the message he issued to his secretary of war later that same day: "I hope that . . . you will direct the attention of the Senators and Representatives . . . to the need of fortifying Subig [*sic*] Bay [Philippines]. It seems to me this country must decide definitely whether it does or does not intend to hold its possessions in the Orient—to keep the Philippines and Hawaii. If we are not prepared to build and maintain a good sized navy . . . and . . . establish a strong and suitable base . . . in the Philippines, then we had better give up the Philippines entirely."[1]

Roosevelt wanted a peace treaty between the two combatants, and the sooner the better. Japan's mounting victories threatened the fragile balance of power in Asia, and Roosevelt was determined to establish a new equilibrium before the United States' long-term interests in the region were damaged. Throughout the war Roosevelt had urged Great Britain, Germany, and France to use their influence to convince the two belligerents to recognize the strict neutrality of China. He did not want the conflict between Japan and Russia to serve as an excuse to further carve up the already decaying Chinese empire.[2]

Within four months of Togo's victory, Roosevelt would mediate a peace conference at Portsmouth, New Hampshire, that resulted in his desired treaty and also garnered him a Nobel Peace Prize.

Many historians have questioned the propriety of this award. Some have pointed out the irony between the recognition of Roosevelt's peace-making efforts and his very public persona as an advocate of the martial spirit in national life.[3] Others, perhaps more substantially, have charged that Roosevelt's absence from the actual negotiations rendered him, at best, an interested bystander and thus unworthy of the distinguished international honor.[4] Both viewpoints stem from a flawed understanding of Roosevelt's methodology and effectiveness.

In many ways the decision to hold the negotiations that formally ended the war between Russia and Japan at the Portsmouth Navy Yard in New Hampshire represents the pinnacle of Theodore Roosevelt's effective intertwining of foreign and naval policies. Considered in that light, it should be no surprise that he chose a naval setting when he was approached to mediate between the two warring parties. Yet the question of how the negotiations came to Portsmouth has generally been either largely unexamined, unexplained, or conveniently accepted, missing the decision's broader implications and what it says about the overall success of Theodore Roosevelt's foreign policy.[5]

Preliminary Negotiations

Theodore Roosevelt had hoped to head off the war between Russia and Japan before it began. He had approached first the Japanese and then the Russians to propose his by now familiar diplomatic preference for mediation as a means of settling their differences. The Japanese responded that they would regard any "attempt at mediation as unfriendly," perceiving diplomacy as a means to give Russia additional time to prepare. The government of Czar Nicholas II, for its part, stated that mediation was beneath it and that any diplomatic overture must come from Japan.[6]

Roosevelt was an interested observer throughout the conflict that ensued. Repulsed by Russia's earlier arrogance, T. R. privately cheered Japan's early military success.[7] As Japanese land victories inexorably mounted, however, and Roosevelt recognized the potential of Japan's growing power, his attitude shifted. In June 1904 he confided to his British friend Cecil Spring Rice that "the Japs interest me and I like them. I am perfectly well aware that if they win out it may possibly mean a struggle between them and us in the future."[8]

By December, Roosevelt had decided to send the experienced American diplomat George von Lengerke Meyer to Saint Petersburg as his new ambassador. While he remained contemptuous of Russia and generally supportive of Japan, Roosevelt cautioned Meyer, "Japan is an oriental nation, and the individual standard of truthfulness in Japan is low. No one can foretell her future attitude." Recognizing that the American Navy was only halfway through its modernization process, Roosevelt wished to avoid conflict in the Pacific for the present and follow the path of diplomacy. The United States, he told Meyer, needed to be ready, if necessary, to "play our hand alone."[9]

In early February 1905 Roosevelt again suggested mediation to both warring parties as a means of extricating them from an increasingly difficult situation.[10] The war was proving to be a military disaster for Russia and was putting an extreme strain on the Japanese economy. He also feared that the fragile balance of power in Asia was tipping decidedly in Japan's favor. Japan's victories over an established Western power appeared to embolden Japanese nationalistic pride, and Roosevelt's correspondence began to focus on the need to "put our naval and military preparations in such shape that we can hold the Philippines against any foe."[11] Admiral Togo's crushing victory in the Battle of Tsushima Strait moved the issue of a peace settlement to the highest priority. Japan's momentum, in Roosevelt's view, had to be stopped before it further threatened recently acquired U.S. territorial holdings in the Pacific. The time for the participants to arrive independently at a mutual agreement had passed.

Following their victory at Tsushima Strait, the Japanese felt that they had satisfied their strategic goals in the war at hand. They had undisputed control of Korea and the Liao-tung Peninsula, including the naval base at Port Arthur, and Russia's presence in Manchuria had been neutralized. Japan felt that the Russians' position in the Far East had been compromised enough that the czar could be compelled to accept a demand for an indemnity, and the nation's faltering economy needed that infusion of money. Japan's minister to the United States approached Roosevelt within days of the battle to ask that he offer to act as a mediator. For the sake of Japan's honor, however, the minister stressed that the initiative should appear to be the president's own.[12] Roosevelt sent a message to his representative in Saint Petersburg to ascertain whether the czar would consider an offer of mediation. He also sent messages to the governments of Great Britain and Germany, which had significant influence in the courts of Japan and Russia, respectively.[13]

Russia's initial response to Roosevelt through its ambassador in Washington was blunt. The czar's government "desired neither peace nor an offer of mediation."[14] Soon after this reply was received, however, Roosevelt's back-channel efforts began to pay off. Kaiser Wilhelm weighed in so heavily with his cousin Nicholas that the czar accepted "a meeting of Russian and Japanese plenipotentiaries, without intermediary, in order to see if it is not possible for them to agree to terms of peace," even though he preferred to continue the war rather than settle on dishonorable terms. Meyer confided to the secretary of state that the czar had been made aware, presumably by the kaiser, that while Japanese forces had not yet stepped on Russian soil, the situation was unstable and it was "therefore important to get Japan's consent [to a conference] at once."[15] Japan agreed to the meeting, and the two nations set about deciding how and where to settle their differences.

The following day a confidential cable from the U.S. State Department moved across the globe requesting that the warring parties meet at The Hague.[16] Russia, presumably to save face, countered with a proposal to confer in Paris. Not to be outdone, and eager to promote its new strong position in Asia, Japan suggested the Chinese city of Chefoo.[17] In the end, the only mutually agreeable location was Washington, D.C.

This agreement set the stage for the first major international peace treaty to be mediated on the North American continent.[18] Realizing that the dates in early August suggested for negotiations overlapped the American capital's hottest and most humid period of the year, a representative of the Japanese government forwarded his hope that "Newport [Rhode Island] or some other place in the United States may be selected."[19] Roosevelt set out to find an alternate site, preferably one near his own summer home in Oyster Bay, New York.[20]

Preparations for Peacemaking

As early as 15 June, Roosevelt had established some parameters for the ultimate location of the negotiations. In particular, he sought a place "where the conditions will be agreeable, and there will be as much freedom from interruption as possible."[21] The task of finding the location fell to Third Assistant Secretary of State Herbert H. D. Peirce, who was standing in for the ailing head of the State Department, John Hay. Peirce, the son of famed Harvard astronomer and mathematician Benjamin Peirce, owed his position in the State Department to the patronage of Senator Henry Cabot Lodge of Massachusetts.[22] He was selected to coordinate the peace conference largely on the basis of his previous service as the secretary in the embassy in Saint Petersburg.[23]

Peirce began the search for a host site immediately. Mild weather and a small surrounding population were important criteria, and the site needed ample access to communications and suitable accommodations for the negotiators. State Department officials reviewed the advantages and disadvantages of locations throughout the Northeast as mayors and governors along the New England coast publicly lobbied for the honor of hosting the event. The towns of Bar Harbor and Portland, Maine, weighed in, as did the larger resort towns of Atlantic City, New Jersey, and Newport.[24] New Hampshire's governor, John McLane, suggested the Mount Washington Hotel in the town of Bretton Woods, high in the White Mountains, a generous offer conveyed to the U.S. State Department in person by New Hampshire's own secretary of state, Edward N. Pearson. Pearson's actions following his meeting with Peirce suggest that Roosevelt had already decided on another venue. Pearson reported to Peirce on 3 July, "Immediately upon my return from Washington I visited Portsmouth and conferred with the owners and managers of the Hotel Wentworth and the Rockingham, and also with some of the leading citizens of the place. I have the honor to report that every possible courtesy and convenience will be afforded the peace plenipotentiaries."[25]

President Roosevelt formally recommended the Portsmouth Navy Yard to the representatives of Japan and Russia on 25 June, but it was not until 7 July that the *Portsmouth Herald* reported that the city's leaders had been responding to inquiries from Washington about local accommodations.[26] The town was small compared with the others under consideration, having a population just under 11,000, but it also had an active Navy yard, and that made all the difference. On 10 July the official announcement was made.[27] The site for the negotiations was set, but Roosevelt still had to get the delegations to show up.

Two aspects of Roosevelt's particular form of diplomacy emerge as the critical elements of the ultimately successful negotiations: his personal level of involvement throughout the process and his use of "back-channel" communications. After both parties had acknowledged interest in a negotiated peace, Roosevelt instantly and consistently applied both of these techniques throughout the process that followed. The first opportunity for his participation required Roosevelt to employ these tools to save the peace process from an early demise. From the very beginning, the two sides disagreed about the composition of the delegations. The issue came down to two separate but intertwined topics: the prestige of the individuals assigned, and their level of authority to negotiate on their nation's behalf.

Japan, a nation that had modernized itself after centuries of isolation, was still relatively unsure of international protocol. The Japanese were anxious to avoid the national embarrassment of sending individuals close to the imperial court if Russia did not do likewise. Japan announced its intention to send two plenipotentiaries of the first rank and floated the name of Ito Hirobumi, the nation's leading statesman and a senior political adviser to the emperor.[28] Ito, a member of the informal ruling council known as the Genro, had opposed the war on the Asian continent.[29] Russia made the mistake of inquiring whether Ito would be appointed, feeling that he was "peacefully disposed and would . . . be a good selection."[30] This attitude ultimately seems to have precluded Ito's participation. The British minister in Tokyo told his superiors in London that the "Minister for Foreign Affairs said that Russians were evidently very anxious that Marquis of Ito should be a plenipotentiary and pretty plainly inferred that from an unofficial point of view he might be too pro-Russian."[31]

Meanwhile the Russian foreign minister, Vladimir Lamsdorff, initially proposed Alexander I. Nelidoff, Russia's ambassador to France, as the czar's representative. Nelidoff, however, begged off, citing his advanced age and unfamiliarity with the English language. Lamsdorff then turned to Michael Mouravioff, the czar's emissary in Rome.[32] Mouravioff acquiesced and returned to Saint Petersburg for consultation, only to suddenly back out of the mission, claiming ill health, when he realized that the peace negotiator would likely become a scapegoat for Russia's defeat.[33]

Behind the scenes, Roosevelt conversed daily with representatives of the two imperial courts in an attempt to assuage concerns of diplomatic one-upmanship. He spoke repeatedly with Russia's outgoing ambassador at the White House and sent numerous telegrams to the American ambassador in Russia imploring Czar Nicholas to send a top-notch emissary to meet with the Japanese. In Japan's case, he carried on a continuous verbal and written dialogue with Baron Kentaro Kaneko, who made it clear that Japan would no longer accept the previous European practice of sending third-class officials to meet with Asian leaders. The Japanese believed they were winning the war, and they would not submit to any indignity while negotiating the peace.[34]

Ultimately Russia turned, reluctantly, to Serge Witte, one of the empire's most competent public officials. Witte had established the nation's modern railway system and reformed its finances, but by 1905 he had earned impe-rial disfavor by opposing the government's expansionist policies in the Far East.[35] Witte would be assisted by Russia's newly appointed ambassador in Washington, Baron Roman Rosen, who had previously served as secretary to the embassy in Washington and had most recently served as his nation's minister to Mexico.³⁶ Japan in turn named its wartime foreign minister, Baron Jutaro Komura, another Harvard graduate, as its representative.³⁷ He was seconded by Japan's ambassador to the United States, Kogoro Takahira.

While negotiations over the delegations' rosters proceeded, a simultaneous dialogue regarding the extent of the powers of the plenipotentiaries to negotiate in the name of their government developed. Roosevelt's original message to both governments had used the deliberately vague invitation "to see if it is not possible for these representatives of the two powers *to agree to terms* [italics added] of peace," broad language that would allow the powers to participate at any level in any form of negotiation. Japan's response indicated that its delegates would meet with Russia's representatives "for the purpose of negotiating and *concluding terms* [italics added] of peace."³⁸ Russia's response, however, followed Roosevelt's original language, stating that its delegates would meet with their Japanese counterparts "to see if it is not possible for these representatives of the two powers *to agree to terms* [italics added] of peace," leaving open the question of the Russian delegation's authority to act in the name of its home government.³⁹ Japan found Russia's statement "evasive and unpromising" because it left open the option for the Russians to simply receive Japan's demands and draw out the negotiations while Russia's forces regrouped on the battlefield.⁴⁰ China had employed the same tactic against the Japanese during the negotiation of the Treaty of Shimonoseki in 1895.⁴¹

Roosevelt's personal approach to diplomacy again came to the fore. In a strident conversation, he reminded Minister Takahira that the term "plenipotentiary" itself, properly translated, meant "someone who is authorized to negotiate and conclude peace subject to ratification."⁴² He added that the issue of "the powers of the plenipotentiaries is not in the least a vital question." The critical object of the proceedings was for the two warring parties to meet. If "there is a real chance for peace," Roosevelt told Takahira, "it makes comparatively little difference what the formal instructions to the plenipotentiaries may be." T. R. closed out the conversation by stating that if the Russians did not arrive with full powers to negotiate, that would not, in his opinion, give Japan a legitimate reason to break off the negotiations.⁴³ Roosevelt cabled his ambassador in Russia to ask for clarification on the authority of its representatives, and Russia responded on 13 July by announcing that Witte would sail from Cherbourg on 25 July with "full powers" to conclude a peace with Japan. Witte would arrive in New York on 1 August 1905.⁴⁴ While these back-channel negotiations unfolded, Roosevelt also focused his unique powers of

FIGURE 1. Assistant Secretary of the Navy Theodore Roosevelt, a young man in a hurry. *(Courtesy of Theodore Roosevelt Collection, Harvard College Library)*

Figure 2. Capt. Alfred Thayer Mahan, Theodore Roosevelt's intellectual partner in the development of a new national strategy. *(U.S. Naval Institute Photo Archive)*

FIGURE 3. Secretary of the Navy John D. Long. Roosevelt had to ease him out in order to bring about the changes he desired. *(U.S. Naval Institute Photo Archive)*

FIGURE 4. Theodore Roosevelt at the Naval War College in Newport, Rhode Island, after addressing the student body on the topic of "Washington's Forgotten Maxim." *(U.S. Naval Institute Photo Archive)*

FIGURE 5. Admiral of the Navy George Dewey. Roosevelt was eager to use the hero of Manila Bay's international reputation for fierceness to get his point across to Europe's Great Powers. *(U.S. Naval Institute Photo Archive)*

Figure 6. Rear Adm. Henry C. Taylor, the highly professional and gifted intellectual leader of the Bureau of Navigation during the early years of T. R.'s presidency. *(U.S. Naval Institute Photo Archive)*

FIGURE 7. Roosevelt and Secretary of the Navy William H. Moody seated with Admiral Dewey (standing center behind them). *(U.S. Naval Institute Photo Archive)*

FIGURE 8. Cdr. John Hubbard, USN, commander of the USS *Nashville* during the critical days immediately following Panama's declaration of independence. Hubbard's quick thinking and steady nerves were critical to the movement's success. *(Navy Historical Center)*

FIGURE 9. Capt. Chauncey B. Humphrey, one of two intrepid spies sent to Colombia and Panama to uncover information about a future uprising in the province. *(Courtesy of Ms. Mary Waldron)*

FIGURE 10. Secretary of State John Hay, author of the "Perdicaris alive or Raisuli dead" statement. He ordered the movement of Navy ships on his own once, and suffered the president's wrath. *(U.S. Naval Institute Photo Archive)*

FIGURE 11. Rear Adm. French E. Chadwick, the commander of the American naval force in Tangiers, Morocco, who turned out to be more diplomatic than the diplomats. *(U.S. Naval Institute Photo Archive)*

FIGURE 12. The Russo-Japanese War peace treaty negotiators on board the presidential yacht *Mayflower*. Left to right: Russian diplomats Serge Witte and Roman Rosen, Roosevelt, Japanese diplomats Jutaro Komura and Kogoro Takahira. *(Courtesy of Theodore Roosevelt Collection, Harvard College Library)*

FIGURE 13. Building 86, site of the negotiations at the Portsmouth Navy Yard. *(Courtesy of the Charles Doleac collection)*

FIGURE 14. The Wentworth Hotel, a luxurious resort hotel in Portsmouth, New Hampshire, that hosted the delegates to the peace conference. *(Courtesy of the Charles Doleac collection)*

FIGURE 15. Protected cruiser *Chicago*, one of the United States' first modern steel hull warships. Built from a European design, she represents the beginning of the United States' naval renaissance. *(U.S. Naval Institute Photo Archive)*

FIGURE 16. Cdr. William Sims, naval gunfire expert, Roosevelt's naval aide, and a lead agent for the technological transformation of the American Navy. *(U.S. Naval Institute Photo Archive)*

FIGURE 17. The battleship *Connecticut*, flagship of the Great White Fleet, and the backbone class of the American Navy prior to the advent of dreadnoughts. *(Navy Historical Center)*

FIGURE 18. The USS *Wyoming*, the all-big-gun, centerline battleship that was the realization of Roosevelt's and Sims' efforts. *(U.S. Naval Institute Photo Archive)*

FIGURE 19. Theodore Roosevelt and Rear Adm. Robley "Fighting Bob" Evans, meeting on the day the Great White Fleet began its round-the-world voyage. *(U.S. Naval Institute Photo Archive)*

FIGURE 20. T. R. in all his glory, welcoming his fleet home just prior to leaving the presidency. *(U.S. Naval Institute Photo Archive)*

concentration on the process of hosting the plenipotentiaries. To aide him in this endeavor he turned to two individuals, Rear Adm. William W. Mead and Assistant Secretary of State Herbert H. D. Peirce.

Mead was a naval officer more experienced ashore in Navy yards than he was at sea. He had been flying the two-star flag of a rear admiral in front of his headquarters for only ten days when a letter from Assistant Secretary of the Navy Charles Darling instructed him to provide the Honorable Herbert H. D. Peirce with "such aid and . . . such courtesies as you are able."[45] While Peirce had led the effort to select the site for the negotiations, it had not been originally expected that he would serve as the U.S. representative in Portsmouth during the actual discussions. A series of events led to Peirce's appointment as the critical man-on-the-spot in Portsmouth.

The first of these was the illness throughout the first months of 1905 that preceded the death of Secretary of State John Hay, a holdover from the McKinley administration. Hay had been a personal secretary to Abraham Lincoln and a friend of Theodore Roosevelt's father, and Roosevelt had maintained a close personal relationship with the elder statesman, despite their numerous differences with regard to American foreign policy. Hay's health had forced him to return to his estate on the eastern shore of Lake Sunapee, New Hampshire. His absence left Roosevelt alone to initiate the series of communications that ultimately led to the peace conference. Hay's sudden and unexpected passing on 1 July 1905 did nothing to alter the president's participation in the process.[46] Roosevelt quickly appointed former secretary of war Elihu Root to the State portfolio, but Root's first days on the job were focused on an ongoing dispute between the United States and Great Britain over the fishing grounds off Newfoundland and a reorganization of the State Department.[47]

A second official who would be all but absent during the critical coming months was Secretary of the Navy Charles J. Bonaparte, who was dealing with the repercussions of a tragic engineering plant explosion on board the USS *Bennington* that had killed several officers and enlisted men. The subsequent investigation led to the inspection and refit of the engineering plants of many of the older ships of the fleet during the following months, including the presidential yacht *Mayflower*. Bonaparte was also deeply involved in another event that held the attention of the president: the return of the remains of the Revolutionary War naval hero John Paul Jones from France. Jones' body was to be brought with great honor and reinterred, after a magnificent ceremony, in a crypt beneath the newly built chapel at the Naval Academy in

Annapolis, Maryland. Bonaparte's absence was particularly felt because his lineage as a great-nephew of Napoleon Bonaparte gave him unique insight into European diplomatic practices.⁴⁸ The combination of Hay's illness and demise, Bonaparte's other duties, Root's attention elsewhere, and Roosevelt's decision to foster the effort from a distance gave Assistant Secretary Peirce the chance of a lifetime.

Rear Admiral Mead and his staff had already answered numerous inquiries from Washington regarding the general condition of the yard and the availability of a suitable structure to host the delegates. Mead's correspondence during the twenty-three days that followed the announcement that Portsmouth would host the negotiations sheds a great deal of light on the logic behind the selection of Portsmouth as well as on several themes underlying Roosevelt's diplomacy. These themes can be roughly summarized under the banners of security, communications, and protocol.

"Some Retired Place": Securing the Negotiations

Rear Admiral Mead's most immediate concern was the physical security of the shipyard in general and Building 86 in particular. He had been directed by the Navy Department to turn his "new storehouse building" over to Assistant Secretary of State Peirce for use by the peace delegates.⁴⁹ The building's outer façade of brick gave it an appropriate air of sturdiness. Although plain by modern standards, it would still inspire one member of the Russian delegation to remark, "One cannot help but admire the contrast of the American surroundings and ours especially as compared to the poor premises of the Russian Foreign Office."⁵⁰ Secretary Peirce had ascertained from plans of the building that the structure would "offer every facility requisite for the sitting of the conferees." It lacked furniture, but Peirce was certain that "arrangements could be made for the hire of such furniture as may be needed without very great expense to this government."⁵¹ The rented furniture, hastily erected interior walls, and strategically hung curtains created a "Potemkin" illusion of grandeur that the Russians surely must have appreciated.

To protect his yard, the storehouse building, and the peace delegates, Rear Admiral Mead called in the Marines. In a letter to Brig. Gen. George F. Elliott, the Marine Corps' commandant, Mead requested a detail of two sergeants, six corporals, and forty-two privates to supplement the yard's existing Marine security detachment. The admiral explained the importance of his request. "It is needless to say that it will be necessary to afford the Commission absolute protection against interruption by outside people, and as the building is quite a large one, a number of sentries will be required to properly guard it."[52] The commandant granted the admiral's request for the six noncommissioned officers but drew the line at twenty-five privates, stating that the detailing of the other seventeen Marines was "impracticable."[53]

Mead took the additional step of closing the yard to visitors during the conference. Department heads were ordered to provide civilian employees with passes bearing their names for admittance to the facility.[54] Applicants for employment were advised to apply by mail. Veterans applying for jobs were granted the favor of being allowed to appear during a four-hour window on Monday and Tuesday at the yard's front gate, where they would be met and escorted to the application window and then returned to the front gate under guard. Even individuals applying for enlistment received similar, exclusionary, treatment.[55]

Lastly, Mead limited the presence of the press in the shipyard. In the days following the official announcement of the conference, reporters and photographers swelled the population of the small New England town by several hundred. The admiral established a formal application process for press access to the delegates. A limited number of passes were issued, "as nearly as possible," Mead later wrote, "in the order in which their applications were taken," much to the chagrin of the larger press population and the major American media outlets, who felt they should have special privileges.[56] Many of those denied passes filed protests with the Navy Department.[57] Mead calmly justified his actions.

> The necessity for closing the Yard to visitors arises from the fact that, if it were not done, the Yard would be over-run by curious people, possibly many of them "cranks," and it is only by having passes that the matter can be kept under control at all. There are hundreds of correspondents in Portsmouth and vicinity now, and I am informed that over at the Hotel Wentworth, where the Peace Commissioners have their quarters, it is hardly possible for one of the ambassadors to leave his room without being surrounded by reporters seeking interviews. It would appear to be extremely important that any such interference while on Government reservations should be absolutely prevented, and it can only be done by absolutely excluding all correspondents from the Yard.[58]

The draconian nature of Mead's orders with regard to public and press access and his use of Marines to provide security for the yard fulfilled President Roosevelt's wish to provide "some retired place" for the peace negotiations, but security was only one aspect of Roosevelt's use of the military in this diplomatic effort. He also planned to use the unique communications capabilities resident in the Navy yard to carefully monitor the ongoing negotiations.

Listening from a Distance: Portsmouth Communications

When H. D. Peirce of the State Department first surveyed Portsmouth as a site for the peace conference, one of his initial questions was whether the local Western Union could expand the number of wires into the town.[59] Communications, secure and unsecure, were critical to the success of the conference, and Portsmouth was superbly equipped. Rye Beach, just down the coast, was home to the country's first transatlantic telegraph cable. Western Union was present in ample force, and the town had telephone service as well. And what the town had in communications, the Navy yard far exceeded. The yard was also equipped with a wireless telegraphy station that could relay messages up and down the coast and to ships at sea.[60]

Roosevelt was well aware of this capability; as assistant secretary of the Navy he had been keenly interested in all types of new technology. It was a resource that would allow the Navy, and by extension Roosevelt, to exercise a great deal of control over the flow of communications into and out of Portsmouth and to channel information in such a way as to keep the president fully informed in Oyster Bay. In short, he would possess knowledge of every communication going into and out of the Navy yard. There is no evidence that he actually read the emissaries' messages; nor is there evidence to the contrary. What the historical record does support is that the Office of Naval Intelligence (ONI) had no greater supporter or customer than Theodore Roosevelt. He depended on ONI to provide him with reports to justify his naval building plans.[61] With regard to the negotiations at Portsmouth, Theodore Roosevelt was, at the very least, aware of who sent telegrams, when they were sent, how long they were, and how many were sent; all of this would be registered in the yard's logbooks. This information alone could tell an informed observer a great deal about the tempo and direction of the negotiations.

Within days of the announcement of Portsmouth's selection as the conference site, Mead began fielding requests from local telegraph companies to string more wires into the yard. At first, Mead simply delayed the decision by passing it on to the Navy Department in Washington.[62] It took nearly half of the time remaining before the conference for the secretary of the Navy to reply, granting permission. Even then Mead carefully controlled access by directing the new lines to an ad hoc communications center, allowing each telegraph provider only one line and one operator inside Building 86.[63] These lines were to be used primarily by the members of the peace delegations and Assistant Secretary of State Peirce. By controlling the size of the communications stream out of the shipyard, Roosevelt hoped to be able to "take the pulse" of the activities within the secured confines of the shipyard's walls.

A Sense of Style: Protocol in a Republic

In the imperial courts of Europe, diplomacy came with its own sense of style. Members of the diplomatic community possessed court rank and at state functions wore uniforms denoting their relative position within the court. Great conferences were held in fine palaces, surrounded by the treasures and booty of antiquity, denoting the sum total of a nation's past and present greatness. Admiral Mead, on behalf of his president, faced the prospect of hosting representatives of rank-conscious courts while still upholding the anti-aristocratic traditions of the American republic. Fortunately, the elements and traditions of the naval services were more than up to the task.

It was understood that the presidential yacht *Mayflower* and the dispatch vessel *Dolphin* would provide transportation for the delegates after the president welcomed them at his home in Oyster Bay. Often used by Roosevelt, the secretary of the Navy, and the various commanders of the fleet, these were small, swift vessels with comfortable accommodations and robust communications capabilities. Mead's responsibilities began when the delegations disembarked in Portsmouth. To transport the distinguished visitors from the ships and to transport them daily during the conference from the Wentworth Hotel to the yard, Mead ordered into service two navy cutters, boats approximately twenty-five feet long and manned by enlisted crews of five sailors.[64] A few days later the admiral ordered a third boat and then a fourth, as well as two additional crews, into service in the event one of the boats broke down or in case shuttle runs between the hotel and the yard extended far enough into the day that additional shifts of men might be required.[65]

While the boats were being refitted for the distinguished passengers, Mead inquired as to the official diplomatic status of his guests. He had been given to understand by Secretary Peirce that the leaders of the two delegations would carry the title of ambassador. This in and of itself presented certain requirements on his part. He wrote the chief of the Bureau of Equipment in Washington,

My dear [Rear Adm. Henry] Manney:

Article 158, U.S. Navy Regulations, provides that when a diplomatic official of the United States or and above the rank of chargé d'affaires pays an official visit afloat in a boat of the Navy, the Union Jack of a suitable size shall be carried on a staff in the bow.

The foreign peace commissioners who are to meet at this yard next month will have, I understand, the rank of ambassador, and I can find no provision of the regulations which direct as to the flag which shall be carried in the bows of boats in which they may be, but I am under the impression that in foreign navies they use their own jacks on such occasions, and I am in doubt as to whether our own Union Jack should be used, or that of the nation to which the ambassador belongs. Can you give me or get for me any enlightenment on this question, and if foreign jacks are to be used, that is, the Russian and Japanese for their respective commissioners, will you order a set sent here.[66]

The Bureau of Navigation, two days later, replied that the envoys should receive the full honors due to the office of ambassador while in the United States.[67] Two flags, one Russian and one Japanese, arrived in due course, and each was mounted prominently on the jack-staff at the bow of one of the two cutters. Mead was ready to receive the two delegations. It was up to Herbert Peirce to see that they arrived.

Confrontation and Compromise: The Negotiations

Once the president established 5 August as the date for his meeting with the two delegations in Oyster Bay, Assistant Secretary Herbert H. D. Peirce began making arrangements for their reception. The plenipotentiaries would travel from Oyster Bay to New Hampshire aboard the naval vessels *Mayflower* and *Dolphin*.[68] Transportation in this manner would not only avoid reporters and the noisy and hot alternative of going by rail from New York to Portsmouth (with a perfunctory stop in Boston), it would also "add to the honors with which the plenipotentiaries would be received."[69] Both of these lines of reasoning reflected the now firmly established synergy between Roosevelt's diplomatic and naval policies. Having established these vessels as the mode of transportation, Peirce turned his attention to the delegates' meeting and dinner with the president.

Given both delegations' well-known sensitivity to any hint of an insult, the meeting at Oyster Bay presented numerous challenges. The question of whom the president would receive first was decided by Roosevelt, based on who arrived first in the United States (the Japanese delegation), but other issues such as who would sit on the president's right (the place of honor) at dinner remained unsettled.[70] Roosevelt's back-channel discussions with the two governments, and with the members of the two delegations after their arrival, only served to exacerbate his concern that the negotiations would not go smoothly. He had met privately with Komura and Takahira at Sagamore Hill on 27 July, and with Witte and Rosen on 4 August.[71] From those conversations Roosevelt gathered that Japan would not be talked down to in its moment of victory, nor would Russia admit that it had been conquered.[72] Roosevelt hit on an ingenious solution to the dinner question: there would be no dinner, no seats, no place of honor. He would greet the two delegations standing; they would partake of a buffet, again standing; and the entire meeting would take place aboard the recently inspected and refurbished presidential yacht, *Mayflower*.

At noon on 5 August 1905 Roosevelt was transported from Sagamore Hill to the *Mayflower*, which was riding at anchor in Oyster Bay.[73] When his flag broke out on the ship's mast—he was the first president ever to fly a presidential flag—the ships supporting the ceremony began the carefully timed dance of diplomacy. Half an hour later, with competing ship's bands playing in the background, the Japanese delegation's boat came alongside and Baron Komura and Minister Takahira along with ten others scrambled up the steps to meet the president as their national flag rose up a halyard. After an hour-long meeting during which Roosevelt discussed his recent conversation with Witte (the two men had not hit it off; Roosevelt thought Witte stubborn, and Witte thought Roosevelt somewhat crass), the Japanese were escorted into the ship's library to wait while the Russian flag climbed to its own position above the *Mayflower*.[74] On greeting the Russians, Roosevelt proposed introducing Witte and his party to the Japanese delegation, who appeared from behind a door opened by Assistant Secretary of State Peirce.

A member of the Russian delegation later recorded that the Japanese entered the room "very triumphantly and very importantly."[75] Witte would forever remember the moment as a jolt of physical and spiritual pain.[76] Roosevelt, attempting to exert his larger-than-life personality to break the ice, invited everyone to enjoy the buffet. As the two groups filled their plates with cold meats and other dishes, T. R. took a seat in the corner of the room and invited the lead diplomats from each delegation to join him. No serious discussions were attempted; it was too early for that, and the delegations had made it clear that they wished to solve their difficulties among themselves, without outside assistance. After a few minutes that must have seemed like an eternity, champagne was poured and Roosevelt rose to say, "Gentlemen, I propose a toast to which there will be no answer and which I ask you to drink in silence, standing. I drink to the welfare and prosperity of the Sovereigns and the Nations whose Representatives have met one another on this ship. It is my most earnest hope and prayer, in the interest not only of these two great Powers, but of all civilized mankind, that a just and lasting peace may speedily be concluded between them." Perhaps it was paranoia, but Witte's secretary would later remember that the president looked directly at Serge Witte as he spoke.[77] Despite this perception, Ambassador Rosen felt that the popularly elected leader of the American republic had handled a very sensitive ceremony with "admirable tact."[78]

After a quick photograph was taken of Roosevelt and the leaders of the two delegations on the deck of the *Mayflower*, the president slipped over the side to return to Sagamore Hill with the sound of a twenty-one-gun salute echoing in the background. Minutes later the Japanese delegation followed, transferring by boat to the slightly smaller dispatch vessel *Dolphin* with their own prerequisite number of salutatory salvos, leaving the *Mayflower* to the Russians for the journey up to Portsmouth.[79] Only bad weather could mar their journey now, and it did. Fog slowed their advance to a crawl, and the two ships were forced to anchor at night for fear of collision at sea. Witte used the delays as an excuse to abandon his team at Newport. He made the rest of the journey by rail and surreptitiously reboarded the *Mayflower* on the morning of 8 August in time to participate in the ceremonies associated with its delayed arrival in Portsmouth.[80]

Rolling Out the Red Carpet

Mead's preparations for the arrival of the delegations ashore clearly indicate that his initial letter to the Commandant of the Marine Corps had two purposes. To be sure, he desired the unique security capabilities the Marines could supply, but he also hoped to provide the type of ceremonial presence that U.S. Marines embody on formal occasions. Marines on duty at the commandant's headquarters in Washington were frequently detailed to high-level White House events and were trained in just the type of presentation Mead desired, but they were under the personal command of the commandant. Consequently, Mead contacted General Elliott rather than base commanders in nearby Boston, Newport, or New York, each of whom had a healthy supply of Marines on security detail. These Marines could have arrived in Portsmouth more rapidly and with less difficulty, but the admiral was after the spit-and-polish appearance and ceremonial ability that only the Washington Marines could supply. Once he had them, he put them to work.

On 4 August 1905, with the arrival of the delegations just three days away, Rear Admiral Mead published a special order governing the arrival of the peacemakers. He ordered his staff into dress uniform, and the Marines into full dress. Directing that the plenipotentiaries be received "with all honors," Mead went so far as to specify that ceremonial gun salutes be executed "just as the ambassador reaches the upper platform of the [pier] landing."[81] To round out the arrival ceremonies, the admiral arranged for an official reception of the two delegations in Building 86, which had been gaily decorated with flags to mark the occasion.[82] Outside the Navy yard, Governor John McLane ensured that the ceremonial welcome continued. Members of the New Hampshire National Guard lined the streets between the Navy yard and the Wentworth Hotel, the fashionable five-star resort where the two delegations were ensconced.[83]

Begin the Beguine: Roosevelt in the Background

The meeting of the leaders of the two delegations on 9 August was understood to be merely a preliminary exercise. The four men were to exchange their credentials and set a schedule for subsequent meetings. When the moment came to exchange the documents, the embarrassed Japanese had to explain that their papers had been left behind at the Wentworth but would be brought the next day. Oddly enough, after all the consternation over the negotiating powers of the two delegations, the Russians arrived with the stronger hand, having been deputized by the czar to conclude a treaty, whereas the Japanese delegates' negotiations were subject to ratification at home.[84] Witte and Komura decided that henceforth they would hold two negotiating sessions per day, morning and afternoon. With these decisions out of the way, they lunched with local officials before returning to the hotel. As they departed, Assistant Secretary of State Peirce climbed the steps to the small telegraph office of Building 86 to send out the first of many telegrams to the eagerly waiting president in Oyster Bay. Peirce concluded, "So far all the relations are as cordial as could possibly be expected."[85] The cordiality would not last.

After formally exchanging credentials at the beginning of the first substantive meeting, on 10 August, the Japanese got down to business. The question of the terms of peace had kept the back-channel diplomatic circuits buzzing since early June. Japan itself had begun considering terms of peace soon after its crushing victory at Mukden in March 1905. On 21 April the consensus-driven imperial cabinet received the emperor's sanction for a list of terms that fell into two categories: absolutely necessary and relatively necessary. The former included Russia's recognition of Japan's preeminent interests in Korea, Russia's withdrawal from Manchuria, and Japan's assumption of Russia's lease and interests in the Liao-tung Peninsula. Among the latter demands were reparations for Japan's war expenses, transfer of ownership of Russian warships interned in neutral ports, cession of Sakhalin Island, and granting of fishing rights off Russia's Pacific coast.[86] Two additional lesser demands were added in June: a proposal to limit the number of Russian naval vessels in the Far East and the demilitarization of the port at Vladivostok. These were Japan's demands, but there were other agendas at play.

Japan's demand for an indemnity payment from Russia to cover the costs of the war followed the precedent set by France and Germany after the 1870 conflict. Lord Rothschild in London had made it known that he could raise a $500 million loan for Russia to pay the indemnity. Half of the money would remain in his bank in London, one-fourth would be paid in cash, and the remainder would be remitted in Russian bonds.[87] Japan asked both Roosevelt and the British government if they thought the indemnity a realistic demand.[88] Roosevelt hedged from the beginning, pointing out that unlike the Germans in 1870, Japanese military units were not encamped around the capital of their enemy.[89] Japan continued to discuss the indemnity nevertheless, compelling Roosevelt to reach out to Japan's closest friend, Great Britain, for help.

On 12 June he called the British ambassador, Sir Henry Mortimer Durand, to the White House for consultation. He asked Durand to convey to London his wish that the British government establish a dialogue with Japan and convince the Asian power to moderate its demands. Durand demurred, feeling that Britain would not want to become involved. After all, Russia was a perennial rival in the game of Great Power politics, and it suited Great Britain's purposes to see Russia on the ropes. Throughout the process that followed, Roosevelt would continue to urge Britain to exert a restraining influence on Japan and the British would continue to ignore him.[90] It would become a point of some irritation. Roosevelt was able to convince the Japanese at least to leave the amount of the indemnity open to negotiation.[91]

The indemnity was only one of numerous demands that the Japanese laid on the long table inside Building 86 of the Portsmouth Navy Yard. Komura began the deliberations by stating that "he desired to discuss all questions in full sincerity," adding that the government of Japan was "ready to do all in order to arrive at a peaceful agreement." With these words he pushed a memorandum across the table with the list of Japanese terms.[92]

1. Russia must acknowledge Japan's paramount position in Korea.

2. Russia must evacuate all of its military forces from Manchuria within a specified period.

3. Russia must transfer its lease of the Liao-tung Peninsula, received from China, to Japan.

4. Russia must cede to Japan the island of Sakhalin and all of its associated islands.

5. Russia must pay Japan's war expenses in the form of an indemnity.

6. The Russian naval base at Vladivostok must be dismantled and the port converted for purely civilian use.

7. Russia's naval strength in the "Extreme East" must be limited so as not to be a threat to Japan.

8. Russia must surrender to Japan as prizes of war all Russian vessels of war that had sought refuge in neutral ports after suffering damage. One battleship, two cruisers, and no less than four destroyers had been interned in Chinese, Vietnamese, and Philippine ports during the war.[93]

9. Russia must grant to Japan and its subjects full fishing rights along the coasts and in the bays of Japan, Okhotsk, and the Bering Sea.[94]

Komura asked Witte to read the memorandum carefully and to answer each clause with a written reply. The Russians received the conditions quietly, announcing that the delegation would review them and reply the next day. Witte felt that any delay at this early juncture in the deliberations would be detrimental to Russia's standing in the international arena.[95] After the Japanese left the building to return to the Wentworth, Witte and his staff removed their coats, rolled up their sleeves, and set to work under air currents generated by electric fans. The Russian delegation found most of the conditions expected and acceptable. The demands had been translated quickly and were being telegraphed to the czar even as the delegates sat down to plan their responses. Witte asked for an additional day to consider his reply and, not coincidentally, to await word from Saint Petersburg. It can also be surmised that a member of the Russian delegation took the opportunity to leak Japan's list of terms to the press, for the demands were published the next morning, to Japan's great consternation.[96]

Since Witte's departure, Czar Nicholas II had increasingly come under the influence of hard-liners within his government who favored continuing the war with Japan. Many of their arguments involved intangibles such as Russian pride and dignity, which had been grievously insulted by the upstart military power Japan and the upstart diplomacy of the United States. In a show of strength and resolve, the czar sent a short telegram back to Witte directing him to refuse five of Japan's demands outright, including the demand for an indemnity and the surrender of Sakhalin.[97]

Witte did not entirely agree with the czar's decision. He thought the Russians should evacuate Manchuria as far as the railroad line that they were empowered by international treaty to protect. In addition, he felt Japan could have the fishing rights without harming Russia, which had only a small commercial presence on its Pacific coast anyway. Witte agreed, however, that Russian congeniality must stop short of the demands for Sakhalin, the surrender of its combatant vessels, and, most of all, the indemnity.

Russia had controlled Sakhalin for thirty years and was eager to come out of the negotiations without surrendering any Russian territory. Witte would offer to recognize Japan's "economic rights" on the island, but that was as far as he was prepared to go, initially. With regard to the warships sheltering in neutral ports, Witte believed that Japan's demand for their surrender had no support in international law and would begin his response accordingly. Finally, there would be no indemnity. In summing up his staff's deliberations, Witte confided his view that acceptance of Japan's terms in their present state would engender such resentment as to guarantee future conflict.[98] That opinion considered along with the czar's strong note did not bode well for the peace process. Witte asked his assistant to inquire quietly as to the steamship schedule to Europe in the event the negotiations fell apart immediately.[99]

Witte gave his reply to Komura on 12 August in the form of a memorandum with clauses. Because the Russian document was in French, the Japanese requested time to translate it. As the day went on and the Japanese progressed in their efforts, the mood at the Navy yard and at the Wentworth Hotel noticeably soured. It was clear to everyone that the Japanese were not pleased with Russia's response. It was at this point that the full effect of Roosevelt's form of diplomacy came to the fore.

The president received information from Portsmouth through several channels. Witte and Komura, as well as a number of their personal assistants, dined with Assistant Secretary of State Peirce throughout the process, and Peirce conveyed their views and concerns via telegraph and courier.[100] Although the delegates did not know it, Roosevelt was also receiving information via a more unconventional source. John Callan "Cal" O'Laughlin, a reporter accredited to the *Chicago Tribune,* had developed a strong personal relationship with Theodore Roosevelt. On 13 August 1905 he wrote the first of several long, wide-ranging letters to the president giving his impressions of the events unfolding in Portsmouth. Because many of his observations drew on his day-to-day experiences at the Wentworth Hotel, where the delegates relaxed and socialized, his letters offered a unique insight into the positions and moods of the two delegations. In his first, nine-page report O'Laughlin warned Roosevelt that the mood was "gloomy" but also noted that Witte's actions at this point were a mixture of bluff and a play for the sympathy of the American public.[101]

Twenty-four hours later, after the Japanese had deciphered and read the Russians' response to their demands, "gloom" was not a powerful enough word to convey the mood in the Wentworth. In a four-page missive dated 14 August the reporter noted that most of the Japanese demands had been accepted, although details had yet to be worked out. "Korea, Manchuria and Lao ting [*sic*], including Port Arthur . . . have been disposed of," he wrote. However, Russia's refusal to budge even an inch on Japan's claim on Russian territory or Russian money had surprised him: "Sakhalin and indemnity continue to be the grave articles and the Russians insist with a vigor I had not expected that never will they cede the island or give money to Japan."[102] The Russians' stoic adherence to this stand caused Japan's Komura to state, "You talk as if you represented the victor." Witte answered, "There are no victors here, and, therefore no defeated."[103] Roosevelt, who understood the degree to which the Japanese government had publicly committed itself to bringing home an indemnity payment, saw trouble looming on the horizon.[104]

Rear Admiral Mead and Assistant Secretary of State Peirce did their best to cast oil upon the troubled waters of the negotiations by holding a gala social event on the evening of 16 August. In Europe, gatherings of diplomats were accompanied by great balls characterized by court dress, the latest Paris fashions, and military uniforms festooned with flashing medals and jangling swords. Portsmouth's gathering was more subdued but no less glamorous. Military officers wore evening dress, the ladies wore the latest available fashions, and the Navy band from the *Mayflower* provided musical accompaniment.[105] While no diplomatic breakthrough coincided with this event, it did demonstrate that the conference's local hosts were dedicated to doing everything within their power to bring about a successful conclusion. As it was, the conference's national host, monitoring events from his home in Oyster Bay, was about to end his period of silence and jump feet first into the negotiations.

Back Channel to Front Stage

Businessman Oscar S. Straus, who would later serve in Roosevelt's cabinet as secretary of commerce and labor, urged Roosevelt to insert himself into the negotiations after Straus met with Serge Witte in Portsmouth on 15 August. He learned at that meeting that Witte had received explicit instructions from the czar that there was to be no compromise on the questions of the indemnity and the cession of Sakhalin.[106] By now the government and the Russian people were energized to reenter the field of armed conflict, but Russia needed money to continue. The purpose of Witte's meeting with Straus had been to inquire about the availability of a large loan. Straus came away from the meeting convinced that the Russians had come to the United States with the intention of utilizing a failed peace negotiation as a cover for seeking loans to cover future war operations. Now Straus believed that the proceedings would succeed only if public knowledge of the negotiations—and at the same time public embarrassment in the event of failure—were increased.[107] With the *Portsmouth Herald* announcing in its Friday, 18 August 1905, headline, "Peace Negotiations May End at Any Moment," Roosevelt swung into action and asked Japan's behind-the-scenes emissary, Baron Kentaro Kaneko, to come to Oyster Bay.

Roosevelt urged Kaneko to advise the Tokyo government to abandon its demands to limit the Russian navy's presence in Asian waters and to transfer the interned warships to Japan, and to moderate its demands for an indemnity and the acquisition of Sakhalin. In return, Roosevelt would make a direct personal appeal to the czar, and ancillary appeals through the leaders of Germany and France, to increase the pressure on the Russian autocrat to moderate his own position.[108] Following this interview, Roosevelt telegraphed Assistant Secretary of State Peirce to ask that either Witte or Baron Rosen take an early-morning train to New York to meet with him at Sagamore Hill.[109] Rosen received his summons at two o'clock in the morning on 19 August and surreptitiously boarded a train bound for New York.

A very irritated Rosen arrived at Sagamore Hill in the afternoon to find Theodore Roosevelt playing tennis. Roosevelt took a break from his play to advise the ambassador that Russia needed to come to grips with the fact that Japan currently occupied Sakhalin and had a historical claim to the island. If Russia would agree to cede Sakhalin, the American president assured Rosen that he could get Japan to drop the two demands that affected the Russian navy. As for the indemnity, Roosevelt suggested that Russia and Japan seek conciliation by having two powers, one selected by each side, negotiate a financial settlement. Roosevelt requested that Rosen relay these thoughts to the czar, not as a formal communiqué but as an informal, personal suggestion.[110]

Rosen brusquely responded that he did not feel free to speak frankly with Roosevelt because the president's close relationship with Kaneko made his discretion unreliable. He added that Russia would not budge on the indemnity and Sakhalin questions.[111] Witte later reiterated Rosen's comments to Roosevelt, saying that he, too, was confident that the czar would reject the proposals.[112]

A chagrined Roosevelt took the negotiations out of the hands of the individuals in Portsmouth two days later and formally communicated a proposal directly to the czar through Ambassador Meyer.[113] In the meantime, Kaneko had returned to Sagamore Hill with a brilliant compromise solution. Japan had decided to drop its demand for the interned Russian ships. Additionally, Japan would offer to sell back to Russia the northern half of Sakhalin, removing the czar's argument that a war indemnity was insulting and beneath Russia's dignity. Word soon leaked out that Witte himself felt this to be a reasonable offer.[114] Roosevelt transmitted the essence of these proposals to Kaiser Wilhelm in Berlin in the hope that he might bring his influence to bear on his cousin, Nicholas II.

The U.S. ambassador to Russia was taken aback when he met with the czar on 23 August. Nicholas sprinkled his statements with emotional, spiritual protestations, convincing Meyer that he was dealing with a weak mind at best. The czar insisted that "peace was impossible if Japan insisted upon any war indemnity." When Meyer countered that the offer to sell the northern half of Sakhalin eliminated any demand for an indemnity, Nicholas responded that the sale "would be interpreted as a war indemnity differently expressed." Nicholas relied on his conscience, he told Roosevelt's emissary, which told him that he was right and that he had the support of the Russian people. Nicholas closed out the interview by telling an astonished Meyer that if need be, he would join his army at the front and continue the war against Japan.[115]

Back in Portsmouth the atmosphere continued to deteriorate. The Japanese delegates felt that they had made all of the concessions they could make. Japan had arrived in Portsmouth as the undisputed victor and had graciously given up its demand that Russia limit its naval presence in Asian waters, had relinquished its claim to the interned Russian vessels, and had even moderated its demand for unlimited fishing rights. Yet the Russians refused to budge an inch on the subject of Sakhalin or the indemnity. In truth, it was not the fault of the Russian delegation. On the evening of 23 August, after Meyer had met with the czar in Russia, Cal O'Laughlin had cabled Roosevelt some unsettling news. Witte had confided that he no longer held plenipotentiary powers, and that henceforth all issues related to the peace conference were to be settled in Saint Petersburg.[116] O'Laughlin added that the discussions would continue out of respect for Roosevelt, who had directly committed the prestige of his office, in his home country, and could be expected to suffer great embarrassment in the event of a catastrophic failure.

Roosevelt, however, was not willing to allow the negotiations to move toward inevitable failure. He directed Meyer to approach the czar again. One day after their first meeting, the ambassador again came into the presence of the Romanov monarch. The American was more successful on this visit. While Nicholas remained adamant on the subject of an indemnity, the ambassador was able to convince him to move away from his refusal to surrender a foot of Russian territory by pointing out that "Saghalin [sic] had been, like Port Arthur, merely temporary Russian territory." Faced with this fact, the czar agreed to the partition of the island and showed an openness to discuss paying for the return of the northern half when Meyer suggested, apparently on his own initiative, that the payment could be structured along the lines of the American purchase of Alaska from Russia some fifty years before.[117]

Roosevelt continued to bring pressure to bear on the Japanese as well. Witte, pondering the proposition that Russia pay for the northern half of Sakhalin as a means of covering Japan's war debt, had asked openly if Japan would forget the indemnity entirely if Russia ceded the whole of Sakhalin.[118] At that, Roosevelt suggested that the Japanese were edging toward the very untenable diplomatic position of continuing the war for the sake of money if they refused to accept Russia's offer.[119] He communicated this observation to the Japanese government and again wrote letters asking Japan's British allies to exert their influence for the sake of peace.[120] On 27 August Baron Kaneko wrote Roosevelt that he feared "that the last day has come. If you should suggest any advice to our Government, I am at your command."[121]

O'Laughlin wrote Roosevelt that same day that the next meeting of the delegations had been postponed, but the Russians had received authoritative direction from the czar never to pay any form of indemnity.[122] The czar's advisers had convinced him that the Russian army in Manchuria was once again ready to face the Japanese in battle and would emerge victorious.[123]

Both nations were operating under certain misconceptions, and both had come to the bargaining table counting on the weakness of their opponent to ensure their own success. Japan had entered the negotiations convinced that the constant threat of internal revolution within Russia would force the czar to pay an indemnity in exchange for a quick peace. The Russians, for their part, believed that Japan's strained economy made it impossible for Japan to continue the war.[124] In that they were not far wrong. Japan was indeed facing economic ruin and hoped that Roosevelt or Kaiser Wilhelm would be able and willing to sway the czar. The problem was not making an unreasonable man see reason, however. The czar was determined to stay the course because he simply lacked the imagination to conceive the disaster that loomed ahead.[125] Roosevelt increased the pressure on the Japanese by stating that he had to prepare the American press for the breakdown of the negotiations. He craftily assured the Japanese that he would explain to the newsmen "that it is Russia's fault" and that he hoped to see Baron Komura before he returned to Japan.[126]

Roosevelt had, by personal intervention, gotten the negotiations to their present state. He had convinced the czar to recognize Japanese ownership of Sakhalin. The next move was up to Japan. The only substantive demand remaining on the table was the indemnity. Did Japan want to return to the battlefield solely for money? Just as he had deftly inserted himself into the process when the negotiations had bogged down, now Roosevelt removed himself from the scene. Herbert Peirce wired in cipher that there were some indications that Japan would present a new compromise proposal when the plenipotentiaries reconvened,[127] but Cal O'Laughlin asserted that all was lost. Peirce kept the special telegraph lines between Oyster Bay and Building 86 at the Navy Yard open deep into the night of 28 August, but they remained silent.[128] The next meeting was set for the morning of 29 August. The breakup of the negotiations seemed all but inevitable.

Half a world away, the words of Theodore Roosevelt were resounding off the walls of another imperial palace. The war cabinet of Emperor Meiji had assembled in his divine presence along with the emperor's three senior advisers (collectively known as the Genro) to consider the disaster looming in front of them. Their intelligence indicated that the Russians had been reinforcing their positions in northeast Asia during the lull afforded by the peace conference. Soon the Russians would have in excess of twenty divisions available to renew the conflict. While Japan remained confident that it could defeat these forces, matching Russia's troop commitments would cost some 1.3–1.8 billion yen. Even then, the cabinet advised the emperor, "we cannot guarantee that we shall not be deeply bogged down in financial difficulties."[129] On the table before them were two letters sent by Theodore Roosevelt urging Japan to forgo the indemnity.

Japan had consciously adopted the German model when it had emerged from self-imposed isolation in the mid-nineteenth century. Having successfully prosecuted a war, it had expected to reap the same type of financial rewards that Germany had gained from its war with France. Now the leader of the American republic had forced them to confront the fact that they risked appearing to be money-hungry imperialists rather than an aggrieved nation that had honorably sought justice on the battlefield. Faced with the prospect of widespread international condemnation, the Japanese emperor "decided to withdraw his demand of money payment for the cost of the war entirely," for "the sake of Humanity and Civilization."[130] The Japanese delegation in Portsmouth received word that a special delivery communication was coming through the telegraph lines via the Japanese ministry in Washington and asked for a delay in the start of the scheduled conference.[131] Komura received the message, decoded it, and then walked into the meeting room.

First the Japanese plenipotentiary asked for Russia's formal reply to Japan's demand for an indemnity. Witte replied that there would be no payment. Komura then moved on to the issue of Sakhalin, stating that Japan would withdraw its demand for an indemnity if Russia would agree to recognize

Japan's ownership of the entire island. Witte declined, even though Nicholas II had authorized this concession, because he believed that the Japanese were ready to make the peace regardless. After a lengthy pause when the only sounds in the room were the spinning electric fans, Komura, Japan's wartime foreign minister, made his final offer. Would Russia recognize a division of the island, he asked? Witte replied in the affirmative. In that case, Komura replied, Japan withdrew its demand for an indemnity.

Roosevelt's man-on-the-spot in Portsmouth, Assistant Secretary of State Peirce, sent off a telegram in cipher from the small communications room on the second floor of Building 86 to Oyster Bay: "All the main points have been definitely settled," he wrote. "The plenipotentiaries will now proceed with discussion of details."[132] Peirce would send another telegram later that afternoon in which he firmly placed the laurels for the success of the negotiations on Roosevelt's head, offering his "heartfelt congratulations upon the successful issue which has crowned your efforts on behalf of humanity and the world's welfare."[133] Baron Kentaro Kaneko echoed this opinion: "Our Emperor has decided on the line of policy you suggested in your letters. . . . Your advice was very powerful and convincing, by which this peace of Asia was secured. Both Russia and Japan owe to you this happy conclusion; and your name shall be remembered with the peace and prosperity of Asia."[134]

Diplomatic Afterglow

History records the successful conclusion of the negotiations in Portsmouth. A treaty was signed on 5 September 1905 to the accompaniment of ceremonial naval cannon and church bells.[135] A year later, Roosevelt learned that he was the 1906 recipient of the relatively new Nobel Peace Prize. The prize committee cited Roosevelt's ability to "infuse the ideal of peace into practical politics" as one of the prime reasons for his recognition.[136] As he was still in office, T. R. directed Herbert H. D. Peirce, now the U.S. minister in Norway, to accept the prize on his behalf.[137]

Aside from exemplifying his overriding commitment to arbitration and mediation as a means for settling international conflicts, what do the negotiations at Portsmouth and Roosevelt's role in them tell us about his style of diplomacy? First, we can establish that it truly was *his* style of diplomacy. Secretary of State John Hay was desperately ill throughout most of the first half of the year and died on 1 July, right in the middle of the Portsmouth preparations.[138]

Roosevelt's second secretary of state, Elihu Root, did not assume the reins of office until after the negotiations were well under way.[139]

Style mattered to Roosevelt, and he knew it mattered within the context of traditional diplomacy as well. As the head of a republic that shunned court dress and aristocratic titles, and had been in existence for less than a century and a half, Roosevelt faced many hurdles when it came to impressing his guests with the greatness and dignity of their host nation. His familiarity with the Navy and Marine Corps presented him with a solution. When it came to ceremony and honors, the U.S. naval services excelled, and Rear Admiral Mead used the forces under his command to the best possible effect. Establishing the degree of success is a matter of pure conjecture, but it is a fact that the one area of the peace conference that Serge Witte did not complain about in his memoir was protocol and ceremonies.

Second, Roosevelt set more than the style of his diplomacy. Portsmouth demonstrates that he was, in fact, deeply involved in its execution. We know that Roosevelt paid intense attention to the communications out of Portsmouth. His normally voluminous written correspondence came almost to a complete halt during the ten days that followed the opening of the negotiations as he focused his attention squarely on the Navy yard.[140] So well aware was he of the activities within the yard that he summoned representatives of each government at key moments to meet with him in Oyster Bay. His comments to them during these meetings were informed enough to restart negotiations as well as to influence their individual governments back home.[141]

Roosevelt's overwhelming reliance on "back-channel"—now more popularly labeled "multitrack"—diplomacy is also evident. He reached out to the participants in Portsmouth through various means, official and unofficial. Simultaneously he sought to influence the imperial courts of Japan and Russia through requests to their close allies in England and Germany, respectively. Lastly, he was not above using individuals such as Baron Kentaro Kaneko and Kaiser Wilhelm II to directly appeal to the leaders of the home governments to listen to reason and moderate their demands. Roosevelt, as the elected leader of a democratic republic, had only a limited amount of personal capital to spend in this process, and, despite the fact that he carried a higher risk of failure than his contemporaries in Europe and Asia, he committed that capital fully.

Yet it is in the choice of a Navy yard for the peace conference that we can discern something more than Roosevelt's style, level of participation, or commitment; his fingerprints are all over this favorite talisman. By 1905 the pattern, the formula, of his diplomacy was set: he faced a crisis and he reached for the naval services. That would have been perfectly normal in conflicts involving the United States, but the fact that it remained true even when he was presented with a purely diplomatic situation (at least from the American perspective) tells us a great deal about the depth of Roosevelt's attachment to the naval services. They had become as much a part of his "speak softly" as they were of his "big stick."

chapter six

T. R., Technology, and Transformation

My dear Commander Sims . . . Evans insists that we ought to have on
our battleships merely big twelve-inch guns and fourteen-pounders,
with nothing between. What do you think of this?
THEODORE ROOSEVELT, 1904

A colloquial expression often applied to problem solving says that "when all you have is a hammer, everything looks like a nail." When Theodore Roosevelt first began to practice foreign policy, the application of naval power was often ill defined or expressed in terms of brute force. As his ideas regarding naval power as an adjunct to diplomacy evolved, he became increasingly aware of gaps—some large and some small—in the spectrum of military engagement. Some of these gaps limited the United States' ability to operate in certain environments, such as close in to land. Some represented an inability to operate at great distances from U.S.-controlled shore bases; others represented a tactical shortfall that restricted the United States from going toe-to-toe with certain foreign navies. As his understanding of these gaps came into focus, Roosevelt realized the extent to which they undermined or limited his foreign policy. Not willing to accept these handicaps, he took an active role in filling the gaps with new technology.

It is impossible to appreciate Theodore Roosevelt's impact on the direction of the Navy at the dawn of the twentieth century without considering his influence as a forceful advocate of rapid technological improvements that transformed the service. The only modern president who has come close to Theodore Roosevelt in this respect is Ronald Reagan, whose eager embrace of the war-altering potential of space-based missile defense systems changed the focus of U.S. defense strategies; and even Reagan falls short in that he played no role in the original conception of the idea.

In his public and private advocacy of transformational technology, Roosevelt exceeded every other navalist of his age, including Alfred T. Mahan, who lagged far beyond Roosevelt in his grasp and appreciation of the

132

capabilities of post-*Dreadnought* battleships. Theodore Roosevelt was a self-educated technical expert who sought to change the very design and capabilities of the ships under his command. Perhaps more than any other political leader of his day, he recognized the need to pursue new avenues of technology to back up his use of naval power as a means to advance U.S. interests.[1]

Protected by the seemingly insurmountable barriers of two oceans, and focused on the step-by-step conquest of a vast continent, the U.S. military trailed other nations in technology during most of the nineteenth century. Even in those brief moments when American innovation pointed the way for a technological leap ahead, such as the invention of the steam-powered warship, Americans passed up the opportunity and allowed others to reap the initial benefits. When invention was necessary, however, the United States proved itself quite capable. The simultaneous development of ironclads by both the North and the South during the Civil War is a good example. Following the Civil War, U.S. technological advancement slowed once again. The United States continued to produce ironclads for the next thirty years, even as Great Britain and France introduced the first iterations of the modern battleship.[2] The historical record suggests that this condition might have continued indefinitely had Theodore Roosevelt not stepped to the fore. The United States had plentiful resources to supply its own needs, and although there was a growing desire to develop overseas markets for domestic products, a situation often historically accompanied by the development of a strong navy, it remained all too easy to "freeload" on British naval supremacy. The rise of American naval power at the crossover point between the nineteenth and twentieth centuries was not an automatic outcome of history's flow; it represented the concerted efforts of a small group of individuals, most notably Alfred T. Mahan, Henry Cabot Lodge, and Theodore Roosevelt.[3]

Roosevelt's upbringing established him as a technological neophyte in early adulthood, but just as he rebuilt his body to deal with childhood infirmities, he undertook an intellectual exercise regimen that enabled him to master the arcane nuances of modern shipbuilding. The knowledge he gained allowed him to make substantive contributions to the decision-making process that resulted in the creation of modern *Dreadnought*-style battleships in the United States and the growth of the U.S. Navy from a fifth-rate power to a force with international standing second only to the Royal Navy. Roosevelt's private correspondence, professional articles, and public statements establish a link between technology, military power, and diplomacy and demonstrate his commitment to transform the American military as a whole and the Navy in particular. These efforts culminated in the final years of his administration, when, as commander in chief, he was at last able to overcome the combined resistance of naval officers, shipbuilders, and legislators and have keels laid and ships launched that were equal to or better than any contemporary design in the world. The marriage of Roosevelt's ideas on the employment of naval power with his support of seaborne assets in their most destructive and efficient form set the course for American naval and foreign policies for decades to come.

Emergence from Stagnation

Most post–Civil War naval vessels in the United States represented an unbalanced amalgam of technologies. Possessing both sail and steam capabilities, American ships were commanded by men more comfortable with the old ways who viewed the employment of sail power as a team-building exercise that built esprit de corps even as it saved money on coal.[4] Through an unconscious effort that bordered on deliberate neglect, the U.S. Navy in 1881 would have struggled to come up with a major warship eligible materially for wartime service. In fact, it had no more than a handful of ships able to carry out normal peacetime high-seas patrols. The 1879–84 conflict between Chile and Peru and Bolivia forced American lawmakers to realize that the navies of these three South American nations were more effective than their own.

In 1881 and 1882 the secretary of the Navy empanelled a board of naval officers to develop a strategy to modernize the U.S. Navy. Their report, released in 1883, recommended the construction of four ships of the most modern designs and specified that they be built of steel. The cruisers *Atlanta, Boston,* and *Chicago,* and the dispatch vessel *Dolphin* (collectively known as the ABCD ships), built from designs purchased from British shipbuilders, were the result. The four ships sailed together as a squadron, developing modern tactics and maneuvering techniques.[5] Fourteen additional steel-hulled cruisers followed. Vested interests within the Navy demanded designs that included both sail and steam-propulsion capabilities. These American hybrids were no match for their European counterparts.[6] The first two American battleships were funded in 1886, although they would not be commissioned until 1895.[7] The *Texas* and the *Maine* were in reality armored coastal cruisers, displacing only 6,500 tons each and possessing small coal bunkers. They carried two 12-inch and four 10-inch guns, respectively, but they were a step in the right direction.[8]

Two factions were at odds over U.S. naval strategy at the turn of the century. Secretary of the Navy Benjamin Tracy favored a force with international capabilities. In path-breaking annual reports, Tracy declared in 1889 and 1890 that the United States needed twenty battleships—twelve of them stationed in the Atlantic and eight in the Pacific—to meet the nation's interests.[9] His opponents argued against a seagoing navy, suggesting that a new fleet of Civil War–type monitors able to defend America's coasts and harbors would suffice. Blue-water navy advocates returned fire, pointing out that a successful blockade of either coast of the United States would have a tremendous economic impact on America's vital overseas trade. In the end, Tracy was able to cajole Congress into purchasing four battleships.[10]

The first three—the *Indiana, Oregon,* and *Massachusetts*—displaced 10,255 tons each, cruised at 15.5 knots, and carried four 13-inch guns, all mounted on the ship's centerline. Each also had a secondary battery of eight 8-inch guns and a tertiary battery of four 6-inch guns.[11] These vessels, bristling with multicaliber firepower, were clearly designed to meet the enemy at sea. As a concession to those concerned that the United States might be viewed as an imperial power, however, they were outfitted with limited coal bunkers, decreasing their effective cruising range.[12] Only with the commissioning of the *Iowa* in 1892 did the nation get its first true blue-water battleship.[13]

In 1895 the U.S. Congress directed that two additional battleships be built. Commissioned in 1900, the *Kearsarge* and *Kentucky* were 375 feet in length, displaced 11,500 tons, and boasted a top speed of 16 knots.[14] Each carried four 13-inch guns mounted in two "cheesebox" turrets reminiscent of John Ericson's *Monitor* turret from the Civil War. Oddly, the designers chose to mount the ship's secondary armament, four 8-inch guns, in a protected enclosure on top of the 13-inch gun turrets, restricting their aiming capability to the direction in which the larger guns were pointed. It was an abysmal design. The smaller guns' location deep within the assembly required large gun port openings to enable the barrels to be trained up and down freely. These larger openings left the guns and their crews unusually vulnerable to incoming shellfire. In addition, there were no safety measures or armored bulkheads between the gun turrets and the ammunition room three decks below. Lt. Cdr. (later Admiral) William Sims wrote in a 19 May 1901 criticism of the design that "a baseball tossed into one of the ports of the *Kentucky* class would fall directly into the 13-inch handling room opening . . . below which are some of the 8-inch magazines."[15]

The ships were the product of a disconnected design process in which the various bureaus of the Navy Department designed various ship components without close coordination. The Bureau of Construction designed the turrets, the Bureau of Ordnance designed the guns, and then the Bureau of Construction stepped in again to design the hoists to bring the ammunition up to the guns.[16] Writing to the Navy Department in 1897, young Commander Sims stated, "The *Kentucky* is not a battleship at all. She is the worst crime in naval construction ever perpetrated."[17] Sims' reports were ignored at first, but the arrival of Theodore Roosevelt as assistant secretary of the Navy in 1897 brought into the Navy Department an eager reader of Sims' observations and a strong proponent for transformation.

The Maturation of Roosevelt

Sworn in as the number two man in the Navy Department on 19 April 1897, Theodore Roosevelt lost no time in digging into the minutiae surrounding the capabilities and limitations of the battleships available for national tasking.[18] One week later he sent a report to President William McKinley covering the current disposition and capabilities of the major capital vessels of the U.S. Navy. His report included recommendations as to where the ships could be most effectively assigned based on their relative strengths and weaknesses, not only compared with each other, but also based on their most probable opponent platforms in each theater of operations. It was a professionally insightful letter, especially given the shallow depth of the author's experience.[19]

One of Roosevelt's most immediate undertakings was to counter the McKinley administration's fiscal conservatism, which tended to decrease funding for the Navy in general and for shipbuilding in particular.[20] John D. Long was Roosevelt's immediate superior in the Navy Department. The onetime head of Massachusetts' Peace Committee, Long seemed an odd fit for his job, although his views were in accord with McKinley's on the appropriate size of the U.S. Navy. In a letter recommending that new ship construction be cut back to just one battleship, Long wrote it would be a mistake "not to recognize that our naval power has more than doubled within the last few years; that the case of an emergency beyond our present resources is the very rare case; that until it comes ships will be gradually taken out of commission and put into reserve in order to reduce running expenses; and that due regard is necessary to the relation of national expenditures to national resources."[21] These words reveal the fragility of the "new" U.S. Navy at this point in history. Support for naval power had waxed and waned throughout the eighteenth and nineteenth centuries as the political leadership of the United States altered its calculations of the nation's domestic and foreign commitments. Theodore Roosevelt would be the first to establish a durable dedication to naval power. The explosion of the *Maine* in Havana Harbor in 1898, however, guaranteed that shipbuilding would go on, at least for the time being.

T. R. evinced a particular interest in the nuances of shipbuilding, especially in the areas of armor, guns, and ordnance. The subject of the day during his time as assistant secretary was the design of the *Illinois*-class battleships; more specifically, the question was whether the Navy should continue to superimpose 8-inch mounts on top of the 13-inch main batteries as had been done on the *Kearsarge* class. Roosevelt, new to the job and vigorously nationalistic, thought the design granted certain advantages to American ships that rendered them superior to their British counterparts. To his regret, the shipbuilders designing the *Illinois* class did not agree, and the ships were built with separate primary and secondary batteries.[22] In nearly every respect aside from the placement of the guns, the three ships of the *Illinois* class mirrored the *Kentucky's* design.

Roosevelt's personal views of the efficiency of the *Kentucky*-type turret began to change after he traveled to the Newport News, Virginia, shipyards in mid-May to meet with naval engineers. While Roosevelt arrived, by all accounts, a supporter of the superimposed turret design, he left a changed man. Writing to Richard Dana on 21 May, Roosevelt confided, "Ever since I have been here I have been going over them [the turret designs] and I hope that I may yet get them taken off." He went on to say that his efforts along this path were being blocked by leaders in the Bureau of Construction, including the well-respected Capt. William Sampson.[23]

The trip to Newport News was indicative of Roosevelt's "I'll see for myself" approach to business. In the fall of 1897 he went to sea during the fleet's annual gunnery exercises. Most civilian political appointees would not have gone out of sight of land for the three days that Roosevelt volunteered for, and those who did probably would have been happy to watch the firing of the large guns from the vantage of an observation deck and then go below for a nice dinner with the ship's officers in the wardroom. Roosevelt did these things, but he also apparently soiled good suits going from ship to ship, climbing in and out of turrets, investigating the machinery and mechanisms that made them work. He wrote to his friend Henry Cabot Lodge, "I saw for myself the working of the different gear for turning turrets—electric, hydraulic, steam, and pneumatic. I was aboard the Iowa and the Puritan throughout their practice under service conditions at the targets, and was able to satisfy myself definitely of the great superiority of the battleship as a gun platform."[24] One can only assume that Roosevelt was comparing the battleships to the old monitors, but it is clear that he instinctively grasped the tactical implications of the increased capabilities inherent in the battleship design. Roosevelt even took a turn at firing a naval gun during his time under way, remarking to his friend William Bigelow that he was most successful at hitting his target "by shooting when the ship's side was rising, getting the gun in position, and then, just as the front sight touched the target on the way up, pulling [the] trigger."[25] Theodore Roosevelt's subsequent quick transitions from assistant secretary of the Navy to Rough Rider, and thence to governor of New York, vice president, and president did not diminish his interest or his knowledge of naval technology. Instead, he arrived in the White House a remarkably well-informed chief executive.

Agent of Change

When Congress authorized the construction of three new battleships in March 1901, the Navy's Board of Construction was tapped to choose their design. The board, which comprised the leaders of the major Navy bureaus, was unable to reach a consensus on the types and placement of guns onboard the new class of battleships. Two documents, a majority report and a minority report, were referred to Secretary of the Navy John D. Long for his decision.[26] Ultimately, as discussed above, Long decided to go with superimposed turrets, with 8-inch guns mounted atop the 12-inch main battery.[27] That decision did not go unnoticed.

Lt. Cdr. William Sims had been studying U.S. armaments for years and comparing them with those of the European powers. He particularly admired the theories of Capt. Percy Scott of the Royal Navy, who had invented what he called "the continuous aim technique." Sims became enamored of this technique and many of Scott's other innovations while serving in the USS *New York*.[28] The more Sims learned, the more dissatisfied he became with the standard operating procedures of his own fleet. He wrote a number of critical reports to the Navy Department that suggested solutions in construction and gunnery procedures. These reports were shelved and forgotten. When he heard about the Construction Board's divided report to the secretary of the Navy, he took the liberty of sending in an unsolicited recommendation to John D. Long. He also took the dangerous step of writing directly to the commander in chief.

Roosevelt received Sims' letter with bemusement and sought the advice of his brother-in-law, Capt. William Cowles, USN. "Will you write back what you think I ought to do? Sims is a good man, but a preposterous alarmist. . . . Nevertheless, I am inclined to think we are deficient in target practice."[29] Roosevelt requested that the Navy Department send him all of Sims' reports; 11,000 pages were delivered.[30] Roosevelt pored over the information with zeal, corresponding with Sims periodically as he went along.[31] The president immediately began to pressure the Navy's senior leaders to "perfect, or rather immensely improve, the standard of our marksmanship."[32] These senior officers were none too happy that Sims had gone over their heads with his "recommendations." In April 1902 the president directed the Navy Department to condense Sims' reports and circulate them for comment.[33] This overt presidential sponsorship of Sims' "radical" new ideas initiated the transformation in American naval power.

Sims' observations convinced T. R. that improvements in big gun accuracy were possible. Scott's continuous aim technique allowed British gun teams to keep targets in the gun sights continuously rather than having to time gunfire with the roll of the ship. At first, U.S. Navy admirals refused to believe Sims' reports and manufactured reports of their own refuting his observations. British gun crews were hitting 85 percent of their targets, however, while American ships "fired for five minutes at a hulk only 2800 yards distant, and [made] only two hits." It was clear to Roosevelt that Sims was on to something.[34] Hoping to encourage gun crews, in August 1902 the president asked the secretary of the Navy to establish a method to recognize and reward superior performance.[35] The Battle Efficiency, or Battle "E," program that is still practiced on U.S. Navy ships was the result. In the spring of 1903 Roosevelt instituted a program whereby superior performance as a gun pointer resulted in advancement and increases in pay. Competitions between ships became fierce, and trophies and promotions came to officers whose gun crew performed on an advanced level.[36]

The president eagerly sought other ways to bring U.S. Navy ships up to par with the Royal Navy. Writing to the commanding officer of the presidential yacht *Mayflower,* Roosevelt inquired what could be done to "use the *Mayflower* as, in a certain sense, an experimental vessel for marksmanship. As you know, I am greatly interested in bringing the marksmanship of our navy up to the highest standard. It seems to me something could be done in the way of making the *Mayflower* not only an example to all the ships of the navy as regards marksmanship, but a vessel upon which we could experiment with a view to finding out what system secures the best results."[37] Roosevelt's interest in the progress of American gunners in their utilization of the continuous aim method continued unabated in the months that followed.[38] He remained particularly interested in how the U.S. Navy stood relative to the navies of Great Britain and Germany.[39]

In October 1903 Roosevelt intervened in Navy Department affairs to break a three-year bureaucratic logjam surrounding the selection of a new gun sight for the fleet's large-caliber weapons. When the uniformed leaders of the fleet claimed that installing the new sights would take four years, Roosevelt stepped in again and the Navy was fully equipped in twelve months.[40] The president took every opportunity to "impress upon the Navy the interest I take in the target practice," increasing his presence at fleet gunnery exercises and personally reviewing the results.[41]

When on 13 April 1904 a "flareback" in one of the turrets on the USS *Missouri* caused an explosion that killed thirty-three men, senior admirals quickly cited Sims' techniques as the root cause of the explosion, pinning the origin of the combustion on Sims' requirement for rapid fire. Roosevelt would have none of it. "The test is not the number of ill-aimed shots," he explained in a letter to Secretary of the Navy William Moody, "nor the percentage of hits among shots fired slowly, but the number of shots that hit in a given time."[42] Despite his interest and energetic support, however, T. R. still did not understand the full strategic implications of Sims' improvements. Clarity would soon emerge.

American armament designs such as the superimposed turrets on the *Kentucky* class and later the *Virginia* class accorded with the accepted doctrine that smaller-caliber guns were more effective at shorter ranges. Following that logic, ships were equipped with guns of three or even four different calibers. There was simply not enough room on some of the earlier designs for each set of guns separately, and thus the superimposed turret was created. Sims' research, however, suggested that the enemy could be successfully and accurately engaged at long range, rendering the requirement for smaller calibers moot. In December 1902 a ship blueprint drawn by Lt. Homer C. Poundstone, a friend of Sims, made its way to the president.[43] The blueprint depicted a ship equipped with three turrets containing 12-inch guns mounted on the ship's centerline, with no accompanying subcaliber armament. Poundstone whimsically called his ship the USS *Skeerd-o-Nothin*. Roosevelt wrote the lieutenant that he found the design "excellent; though I am not sure that I can get Congress to take the view I should like it to take on the subject."[44]

Lieutenant Poundstone continued to make significant contributions to the ongoing debate about the physical size of battleships and the type of armor and armament they should carry. One year later Poundstone's report appeared in the pages of the U.S. Naval Institute's *Proceedings* in two articles. In them, Poundstone elucidated the relationship between a ship's size and its speed and presented an engineer's analysis of the relative throw weights of various configurations of armament. His nearly irrefutable finding was that big ships, with more exposed surface area and more internal room for fuel and propulsion, could go farther and faster.[45] Poundstone further showed that increasing the overall battery size, within the limits imposed by reloading cycle time, would bring an 18 percent increase in the ship's potential firing energy in battle.[46]

Poundstone's articles invigorated battleship design. The recent crisis over Venezuela in the Caribbean had spurred Congress to appropriate funds to build five new battleships: three of 16,000 tons (the *Kansas, Minnesota,* and *Vermont*), a continuation of the *Connecticut*-class ships authorized the year before; and two at 13,000 tons (the *Idaho* and *Mississippi*), throwbacks to the earlier *Illinois* class and obsolete even before they were launched. The *Connecticut*-class ships, capable of 18 knots and sporting four 12-inch guns as well as the now normal complement of lesser calibers, were fast becoming the backbone of the American fleet. They compared very favorably with their European counterparts, including the Royal Navy.[47] While the United States did not seek a navy as large as Great Britain's, Secretary of the Navy Moody had no compunction about informing the German ambassador that the kaiser's fleet had become "the measure for us." Theodore Roosevelt was going after a prominent position among the leading naval powers in the world.

In October 1903 Admiral of the Navy George Dewey, on behalf of the General Board, presented a building plan that would provide the United States with forty-eight battleships and escorts by 1920.[48] The number of these behemoths to be constructed was restricted only by the availability of space in construction docks.[49] The strategic focus was on the number of ships, however, not their capabilities; no one knew how the ships would perform in wartime conditions. Virtually every interest group associated with naval shipbuilding weighed in with an opinion on what the ships' capabilities should be. William Sims and his rapidly growing group of followers favored an all-big-gun approach to construction, placing their faith in advances in gun targeting. Alfred T. Mahan and his acolytes remained committed to the multicaliber approach, believing that ships needed to be prepared to fight in close as well as at long distance.⁵⁰ The outcome of two decisive battles during the Russo-Japanese War seemed to settle the dispute.

The negotiations that ended the Russo-Japanese War are discussed at length in chapter 5, but that account largely ignores the battles that defined the conflict. Three significant sea battles were fought. The first involved a concentrated, surprise torpedo boat attack on the Russian Pacific fleet at anchor in Port Arthur. What remained of the Russian force attempted to break out on 10 August 1904 and proceed to Vladivostok, and six Russian battleships met four Japanese battleships and four armored cruisers in pitched battle. The Japanese opened fire at 20,000 yards and began to observe effective hits at 14,000 yards. A foreign observer on one of the Japanese ships later said, "For all the respect they instill, 8-inch or 6-inch guns might as well be pea shooters."⁵¹ It was an all-big-gun battle, and the Japanese, having mastered the continuous aim techniques developed by the British, overwhelmed the Russians. The third battle, which took place nine months later in Tsushima Strait, is discussed later.

On 5 October 1904, two months after the defeat of Russia's Pacific fleet, Roosevelt wrote Sims a short letter in which he stated that Rear Adm. Robley D. Evans, one of the Navy's preeminent ship captains, had come down solidly behind the idea of an all-big-gun battleship. Sims added his own forceful argument on behalf of the new design, claiming that a ship armed with twelve 11-inch guns could "pierce the armor of any battleship in the world at long ranges."⁵² Roosevelt read and considered the views advanced by Evans and Sims carefully, and wrote a letter to Secretary of the Navy Paul Morton on the afternoon of 6 October: "I am sorry that the *New Hampshire* is to have 12-inch, 8-inch, and 7-inch guns. It seems to me that her armament should be composed simply of 12- or 11-inch guns, and of a secondary battery of 3-inch guns. In other words, I am inclined to believe that it is unwise to have 3- and 1-pounder guns, and 7- and 8-inch guns. I should like a full report on this from the proper authorities."⁵³ On 8 October the president himself weighed in on the technological argument, asking the Navy's Board of Construction to consider substituting a main battery of single-caliber guns for the *New Hampshire*. But the board and its parent organization, the Bureau of Construction, wanted nothing to do with the ideas of Roosevelt and his acolytes.⁵⁴

At first, the Bureau of Construction simply attempted to ignore Roosevelt. A request for the bureau to draft a design for a twelve 12-inch-gun battleship languished for eleven months. Faced with the bureau's resistance Lieutenant

Poundstone drafted his own plans for three variations of an all-big-gun ship, naming them the *Feasible,* the *Probable,* and the *Possible.*[55] Ultimately, in a play of bureaucratic brilliance, the board lit upon Congress' legislative restriction that the new ship be limited to 16,000 tons of displacement. A ship of that size, the board argued, would not have the internal infrastructure to support an all-big-gun battery. Additionally, the head of the Bureau of Ordnance, Rear Adm. Charles O'Neil, had recently returned from a tour of Europe and pronounced the current American standard design, the *Connecticut* class, to be equal or superior to any ship he had seen. "After prolonged and mature consideration," the Board of Construction wrote in reply to its commander in chief on 17 October, "nothing has transpired during the past year which would justify extensive changes in the main battery of vessels building or recently designed." It was the board's decision to build the *New Hampshire* as another *Connecticut*-class battleship.[56]

Roosevelt was not pleased. Rear Adm. Royal Bradford, chief of the Bureau of Equipment, a position he had occupied increasingly as a sinecure since 1897, was ordered back to sea to live with the equipment he had procured. Rear Admiral O'Neil, late of the fact-finding trip to Europe, was relieved of his responsibilities in the Bureau of Ordnance without follow-on orders. He retired from active service in late 1904.[57] Roosevelt emphasized in his end-of-the-year message to Congress on 6 December 1904 that "the main reliance, the main standby, in any navy worthy of the name must be the great battleships, heavily armored and heavily gunned."[58]

Those words reveal a man who had come to grips with the diplomatic implications of the war-altering technology inherent in the battleship design. Battleships had transcended their component parts to become tangible symbols on the chessboard of the international system. Great Britain's empire, the envy of the world, depended on the power contained within the Royal Navy's floating arrangements of complex and expensive hulls, engines, armor, and guns not only to exert influence, but also to deter others from challenging for supremacy. Roosevelt understood that battleships were now the decisive components of international competition, and he meant to build them in their most effective form.

Early the following year, on 3 March 1905, Congress authorized the construction of two new battleships. Once again there was dissension over their design. Admiral Dewey and the other members of the General Board wanted ships displacing 18,000 tons—large enough to carry a main battery of ten 12-inch guns, with no secondary battery. The Board of Construction insisted on keeping the 16,000-ton-displacement hull already well proven in the *Connecticut* class, but agreed to mount only 12-inch guns, lowering the allotment to eight to offset the ship's less-than-adequate displacement.⁵⁹ These ships later slid down the ways as the *Michigan* and *South Carolina*.⁶⁰

In Theodore Roosevelt's mind, the construction of these two all-big-gun ships represented a turning point and lured him toward a strategic blunder with regard to securing congressional authorization for additional battleship construction. He had worked hard to modernize the Navy; surely, he thought, inertia would continue to propel it along the path he had chosen while he focused his attention elsewhere. On 9 March, less than a week after the authorization of the two new battleships, he wrote his old friend and former commanding officer from his Rough Rider days in Cuba.

> When I became President three years ago I made up my mind that I should try for a fleet with a minimum strength of forty armor-clads; and though the difficulty of getting what I wished has increased from year to year I have now reached my mark and we have built or provided for twenty-eight battleships and twelve armored cruisers. This navy puts us a good second to France and about on a par with Germany; and ahead of any other power in point of material, except, of course, England. For some years now we can afford to rest and merely replace the ships that are worn out or become obsolete, while we bring up personnel.⁶¹

Two events later in the year would cause Roosevelt to reassess the strategic position of the U.S. Navy in relation to its competitors.

The czar, having lost his Pacific fleet, decided to dispatch his Baltic fleet to make the long trip through the Suez Canal, around India, through the Strait of Malacca, and on toward Vladivostok.⁶² On 27 May 1905, bottoms fouled by the accumulated sea growth of a long voyage, the Russian Baltic fleet met the Japanese navy at Tsushima Strait. The Russian formation included eight battleships and three armored cruisers along with smaller escorts; the Japanese turned out four battleships accompanied by eight cruisers. Utilizing his speed advantage and the long-range accuracy of his guns, Adm. Heihachiro Togo crossed the Russians' "T" and sank four battleships and sixteen other ships in the Russian formation.⁶³ The intermediate-size batteries on the Japanese ships barely got into the battle. The great British writer and strategist Sir Julian Corbett later referred to the confrontation as "the most decisive naval victory ever recorded," surpassing even Nelson's victory at Trafalgar.[64] Some, including the formidable Alfred T. Mahan, attempted to credit the victory to the volume of fire issued by the Japanese intermediate batteries. That assertion concerned Roosevelt, who temporarily became cautious about proceeding down the all-big-gun-battleship path.[65] Then Lt. Cdr. William Sims entered the fray and destroyed Mahan's premise. Sims' analysis demonstrated that rapidity of fire, not volume of fire, had been the key at Tsushima. Further, the effectiveness of the intermediate batteries had been the result not of the inaccuracy of the larger guns but of their relative lack on the Japanese warships.[66] The big guns present had had a disproportionate impact. In fact, the battle confirmed the concept of the all-big-gun battleship.[67] Roosevelt quickly ordered the secretary of the Navy to review the schedule for warships under construction in American shipyards and request a list of their proposed armament.[68]

The second event that altered Roosevelt's mind was the laying of the keel of HMS *Dreadnought* on 1 October 1905 at the Portsmouth Naval Yard in England. Its appearance rendered all previous battleships obsolete.[69] *Dreadnought* was the brainchild of Adm. Sir John Fisher, perhaps the most brilliant and driven man ever to occupy the office of First Sea Lord in Britain's long maritime history. "Jackie" Fisher's first act was to consign more than 150 ships whose design and age had rendered them less than useful to the scrap yards or to unmanned status in homeports. In one fell swoop, he freed men and money to be directed toward a new strategy. Great Britain would abandon its traditional aim to maintain a numerical advantage over its competitors at sea and would instead field fewer vessels but with a greater technological advantage over an enemy.[70] To accomplish this technological modernization he combined in one hull the many recent advances in propulsion, armor, and gun design. The result was the *Dreadnought*.

Built in complete secrecy and completed in just over a year, HMS *Dreadnought* was the first major warship to derive propulsion from turbine engines. Its space-saving turbines made the *Dreadnought* faster than any other ship afloat.[71] Roosevelt received inside information about the *Dreadnought*'s design and potential via a secret report from Sims, who had been granted permission to tour the ship by Admiral Fisher.[72] Sheathed in heavy armor, the new battleship bristled with ten 12-inch guns that gave it double the ballistic throw weight of its nearest competitor. T. R. commented that "ordinary ships will be absolutely powerless before these ships."[73] Britain's competitors, most notably Germany, were stunned. They did not find their wits for nearly a year, at which time they began building dreadnoughts of their own.[74] Roosevelt, who had earlier decided to stand down from battleship construction, was caught flatfooted himself.

His own words about scaling back naval appropriations uttered in his 5 December 1905 message to Congress came back to haunt him when he sought funds to build dreadnoughts for the U.S. Navy.[75] Even his best friend, Massachusetts senator Henry Cabot Lodge, had warned him that promises of fiscal scale-backs were hard to reverse. Nor was Congress particularly inclined to be helpful; Roosevelt's "big stick" domestic politics had antagonized a number of elected officials on Capitol Hill.[76] By exerting tremendous effort T. R. was able to secure authorization in 1906 to build one new ship along the lines of the breakthrough British vessel. The USS *Delaware* would displace 20,000 tons and would exceed 20 knots while sporting ten 12-inch guns from its turrets. It would be the last battleship built with a reciprocating engine. Roosevelt's battle was far from over, though. While Congress had authorized the new battleship, it had not appropriated money to begin construction.[77]

The president lowered himself to go hat in hand to Congressman George Foss, chairman of the House Naval Affairs Committee, and Senator Eugene Hale, chairman of the Senate Naval Committee, to ask for their assistance. Roosevelt explained his reasoning to these two powerful committee heads.

> I feel strongly that there should be two first-class battleships, of the maximum size and speed and with their primary battery of all twelve-inch guns. . . . In my judgment we are not to be excused if we build any battleship inferior to those now being built by other nations. . . . We cannot afford to fall behind and we shall fall behind if we fail to build first-class battleships ourselves. . . . Now that a high degree of skill has been developed in naval marksmanship, especially with heavy guns, future battle ranges will be so great (three or four miles) that small guns (six-inch, etc.) will be practically ineffective, especially against large vessels having all their guns and gun-crews in twelve-inch turrets, behind heavy armor.[78]

To speed the process along, Roosevelt released the contents of his private correspondence with the two committee chairs a few days later for publication in major newspapers.[79] The ensuing public debate created a maelstrom around the issue of battleship construction, effectively placing Roosevelt temporarily back in control of naval policy. Congress ruefully bowed to Roosevelt's tactical victory but limited his strategic march forward by authorizing only one additional battleship in 1907. A special board convened by Assistant Secretary of the Navy Truman Newberry reviewed twenty plans for the two new ships.[80] In the end, the *North Dakota* was built as a sister ship to the *Delaware,* nearly identical in every detail except for its turbine engine.[81]

The shipbuilding programs in Great Britain, France, and Germany threatened Roosevelt's goal of standing second only to England in terms of naval power, and Congress was not providing him with the assistance he desired. In a move to regain momentum, the president completely abandoned all moderation in his December 1907 message to Congress: "To build one battleship of the best and most advanced type a year would barely keep our fleet up to its present force. This is not enough. In my judgment, we should this year provide for four battle ships."[82]

In one of the first debates of its type during the twentieth century, leaders in Congress resisted, calling on the president and other heads of state to enter into arms limitation negotiations and asking the citizens of the United States to oppose the president's construction goals as a means to avoid future involvement in foreign wars.[83] Undeterred, Roosevelt fired back. In another well-publicized letter to leading members of Congress in January 1908, T. R. explained the error in his previous statements with regard to building only one capital ship per year. He had hoped that one or more of the leading nations of Europe and Asia might adopt some form of arms limitation,

> but actual experience showed . . . that it was impossible to obtain such an agreement for the limitation of armament among the various leading powers. . . . Coincidentally with this discovery occurred a radical change in the building of battle ships among the great military nations—a change in accordance with which the most modern battle ships have been or are being constructed, of a size and armament which doubles, or more probably trebles, their effectiveness. Every other great naval nation has or is building a number of ships of this kind; we have provided for but two and therefore the balance of power is now inching against us. . . . I earnestly advise that the congress now provide four battle ships of the most advanced type.[84]

The president's decision earlier in 1907 to send the American battle fleet around the tip of South America and on to visit U.S. Pacific Coast ports now proved fortuitous. The fleet's absence from the Atlantic seaboard even as the nations of Europe began building ships more powerful and efficient than those now sailing with gleaming white paint to the West Coast raised concerns among Atlantic Coast residents and their political representatives.[85] Only half-bowing to Roosevelt's ongoing public relations triumph, Congress authorized and appropriated funds for two new battleships, the *Florida* and *Utah*.

Although their design incorporated new technology, the *Delaware* and *North Dakota* still had material shortfalls that professionals such as William Sims and Roosevelt's naval aide, Cdr. Albert Key, did not hesitate to point out.[86] The journalist Henry Reuterdahl picked up on the dissension in the middle ranks of the Navy's officer corps surrounding the new vessels. His story "The Needs of Our Navy" appeared in the pages of the January 1908 edition of *McClure's Magazine*. Reuterdahl's article detailed shortcomings in armor placement, which was often 6 inches above the waterline, and poorly designed ammunition hoists that allowed open, uninterrupted access from the turrets down through the bowels of the ship to the vulnerable ammunition magazines.[87] The article, in the words of one historian, "dropped like a well-aimed bomb."[88] In combination with Sims' ongoing lobbying for better designs it stimulated President Roosevelt to call for a conference on ship design to be held at the Naval War College at Newport, Rhode Island, beginning on 22 July 1908.[89] Roosevelt had less than a year left in office to effect the changes he desired.

The senior members of the Board of Construction came to Newport confident that they would be able to dominate any discussion over future designs of U.S. Navy vessels. They were the senior officers; they would set the rules of discussion and decide what kind of ships would be built. They had not counted on the senior officer of the U.S. Navy attending, but the commander in chief decided to journey up from his home at Oyster Bay to preside over the opening of the conference.

Roosevelt's first decision with regard to the conference was to ensure that younger officers were included in the meeting's deliberations, adopting an idea the Germans had introduced.[90] Active commanding officers, executive officers, and department heads of ships of the line at sea possessed the type of experience that was needed to ensure that the most effective ships would be built for the Navy.[91] Having recently had a Navy bureau chief resign in protest when the president made a decision against the chief's recommendation, T. R. was thoroughly frustrated with the entrenched senior officer corps and meant to exert his will upon them.[92]

Roosevelt arrived in Newport aboard the *Mayflower* on the morning of the conference's opening day. Commander Sims, who now carried the title of naval aide to the president, met him at the pier. Also present was the president of the Naval War College, Rear Adm. John P. Merrell, who immediately attempted to convince T. R. to send away the younger "extra" officers and leave the decision making to the members of the General Board and the staff of the War College. Sims spoke to the president while Merrell was distracted and convinced him to retain the junior officers; he also requested that all decisions of the conference be made by recorded vote and reported to the secretary of the Navy.[93]

The conference was not a complete success for Roosevelt and his supporters, but he did manage to pry the power to design ships without outside guidance or overview from the hands of the entrenched bureau. Yet the president was disappointed by the final outcome with regard to the designs of the new battleships. He had hoped that the *Florida* and *Utah* would represent significant improvements on the designs of their predecessors. "I want them to mount fourteen-inch guns and to have heavier armor," he wrote to a subordinate, "although preserving the same general measurements and tactical properties, so that they can maneuver as units with the *North Dakota*."[94] The conference was a failure because it did not bring about meaningful adjustments to the *Delaware, North Dakota, Utah,* or *Florida.* The conference report recommended that the last two ships be built essentially as repeats of the *North Dakota* design, with some modifications to the placement of aft turrets and redesign of the ammunition hoists. The opportunity to equip the ships with 14-inch guns and to increase their armor belt by 12 percent passed by.[95]

After receiving the conference report from Assistant Secretary of the Navy Truman Newberry, Roosevelt felt compelled to follow its recommendations and directed that the two new ships be designed as it specified.[96] His interest in the situation did not end, however. He pored over the conference notes and the related correspondence. The more he read, the deeper his disquiet became. He communicated his concerns to the assistant secretary.

My Dear Mr. Newberry:

I am puzzled what to do about the papers that you submit. I call your attention to the statement of Mr. Alger [Phillip R. Alger, leader of those at the Newport conference opposed to placing 14-inch guns on the *Utah* and *Florida*] at the foot of page 4 where he says "to go to a larger caliber now is therefore to acknowledge that our former action was an error." This single sentence gives me hearty distrust of

Mr. Alger's whole judgment in this matter and of Admiral Mason's judgment so far as it is based on Alger's. If there is one thing more than any other which our bureau chiefs and technical experts need to learn it is that they must never for a moment consider the question of acknowledgement of error in judgment in the past as a factor in doing what is best possible in the present. . . . To refuse to accept any change until its advantages have been demonstrated by factual experience means that we must always be behind the times.

Moreover, Mr. Alger's paper shows that he is content to follow the example of other nations. I want us to lead other nations. . . . The Newport Conference recommended that we should proceed with the development of the 14-inch gun. Every effort should be made to proceed with this development.[97]

As was generally the case, the president's enthusiastic attention drew immediate results.

Roosevelt moved quickly to make use of the bureaucratic advantage he perceived within the Newport conference report. When Congress voted in early March, just days before Roosevelt left office, to authorize the building of two new battleships, he was prepared to present the design he desired.

Months earlier the president had convened a small group of young officers fresh from sea tours on the battleships then deployed and asked them to work together to design the ship of their own choosing. Roosevelt specifically requested "tentative plans of new battleships mounting fourteen-inch guns prepared as soon as possible. . . . I think it desirable that soon after Congress meets we should be prepared to ask for an appropriation for battleships of a well defined type, and that this type be very superior to anything produced or contemplated abroad."[98]

Engineers from the steel and armaments industry would convince the president that the United States was not ready yet to field a 14-inch gun, but the battleships *Wyoming* and *Arkansas* would put to sea with six turrets mounting two 12-inch guns apiece. At 26,000 tons displacement and capable of speeds just over 21 knots, they were the finest warships of their day—the summation of Roosevelt's efforts to "upbuild" a Navy capable of backing his activist foreign policy.[99] But battleships were not the only innovations he brought to the fleet.

Theodore Roosevelt had carved out a reputation as an agent for change from his earliest days in the Navy Department in 1897. Throughout his career he eagerly sought out technology that might help the United States to match or exceed its competitors in the international arena. He considered himself an innovator, and he worked to match his public image with his private one.[100] As early as 1893 Roosevelt was aware of the efforts of Samuel P. Langley to create a heavier-than-air flying machine.[101] In 1898 he had an opportunity to examine Dr. Langley's machine in order to ascertain whether it had a military application. Roosevelt recommended to Secretary Long "that you appoint two officers of scientific attainments and practical ability [to] examine . . . the flying machine, to inform us whether or not they think it could be duplicated on a large scale, to make recommendations as to its practicability and prepare estimates as to the cost. I think this is well worth doing."[102] The U.S. government invested $50,000 in Professor Langley's experiment, only to see the vehicle plow into the mud of the Potomac in 1903.[103] Regardless of that failure, Roosevelt's early initiative is largely responsible for beginning the Navy's long fascination with launching and recovering aircraft on ships at sea.

Roosevelt also championed shipbuilding design innovations as assistant secretary of the Navy. One of his favorite strategists, Lt. Cdr. William Wirt Kimball, served double duty as the leader of the first torpedo boat flotilla. The idea of using small, fast boats to attack much larger ships originated with the Jeune Ecole (young school), an innovative movement in France that sought to challenge Great Britain's domination of the high seas with new technology. The Jeune Ecole envisioned small torpedo boat squadrons flitting quickly in and out of formations of larger, heavier, and slower capital ships, delivering deadly torpedo strikes.[104] Roosevelt worked closely with Kimball, becoming the patron of this new technology and tactic, and taking a certain pride in ownership as well. In a letter to Henry Cabot Lodge, for instance, Roosevelt stated, "My torpedo-boat flotilla is in fine shape. Of course the six torpedo boats they have got [sic] only two with proper commanders, which is a real misfortune, but still, though I can't get the best work out [of] the flotilla, I shall get pretty good work."[105] He also championed the construction of the larger version of this type of combatant, the "destroyer." It was an enthusiasm, unlike some others, that would carry over into his presidency.[106]

The success of the Japanese torpedo boat attacks on the Russian Pacific fleet at Port Arthur had further cemented Roosevelt's view of the utility of the "torpedo destroyers." He was not quite satisfied with their design, however, for they were not yet "sea-going and sea-keeping" craft capable of going to sea "for weeks and, if necessary, for months at a time."[107] The U.S. Navy versions of these quick, nimble sea fighters were capable of carrying out combat operations for short periods in littoral waters, but they did not have the endurance or stability to be useful away from American shores, where they could act as "fast scouts."[108] Twenty destroyers were purchased during Roosevelt's administration to go with six experimental prototypes.[109]

Submarines also fascinated Theodore Roosevelt. On 25 August 1905, in the midst of the Japanese-Russian peace negotiations, he requested that one of the six new submarines in service be brought to Oyster Bay for him to board and tour. After rowing out to the small submersible, the USS *Plunger*, in heavy rain and gusting winds, the commander in chief scrambled on board and asked to be taken down into the depths of Long Island Sound. He watched fish swim by the craft's small watertight window, and even took the controls and maneuvered the small craft himself, broaching it stern first at one point.[110] On returning to the surface he pronounced the experience "very interesting."[111]

During his underwater journey, he spoke with the crew about the craft's potential and their own duties. He was intrigued by the strategic promise of the craft but incensed by the poor treatment of the crew. Writing to the secretary of the Navy three days later, he said,

> As to the second matter, I have become greatly interested in submarine boats. They are in no sense substitutes for above water torpedo boats, not to speak of battleships, cruisers and the like, but they may on certain occasions supplement other craft, and they should be developed. Now there are excellent old-style naval officers of the kind who drift into positions at Washington who absolutely decline to recognize this fact and who hamper the development of the submarine boat in every way. One of the ways they have done it has been by the absurd and worse than absurd ruling that the officers and men engaged in the very hazardous, delicate, difficult and responsible work of experimenting with these submarine boats are not to be considered as on sea duty.

Thanks to Roosevelt's efforts, sailors detailed to submarines received hazardous duty pay and special allowances for promotion to higher ranks.[112] He continued to champion the construction and improvement of submarines; twenty-seven were purchased during his administration.[113]

Roosevelt's support for naval innovations such as the torpedo destroyer and the submarine, as well as his early interest in the purchase of additional coaling ships, make it clear that he understood the U.S. Navy as a "fleet." He understood where each platform fit within a spectrum of warfare capabilities, and knew enough about Mahan's theories to understand that those capabilities interlocked to provide mutual support. Overall, however, his writings do not evince a clear fleet-based naval strategy.

Near the end of his presidency, Roosevelt returned to one of his earliest passions, the military potential of aviation. He had waited for the staffs of the Army and the Navy to pursue the promise of the new machine developed by the Wright brothers during his administration until he could wait no more. Finally, he took money from a discretionary fund allotted by Congress for national defense and challenged the War Department to purchase some aircraft for testing. The department advertised an offer to purchase and test three dissimilar designs. Only the Wright brothers showed up for the demonstration flights at Fort Myers across the Potomac River in Arlington, Virginia, in September 1908. The event opened well, with Orville setting a new record for time aloft, but turned disastrous a few days later when he crashed, killing an Army lieutenant who was flying with him as a passenger.[114] A few years later, during World War 1, Roosevelt gave aviation another push forward. Aviation "should be the fifth arm of our Army," he wrote to Augustus Post. "We should at once begin to prepare on the largest scale for warfare in the air, as one of the great features of the warfare of the future."[115] In the end, Roosevelt paid the highest price possible for his support of military aviation when his youngest son, Quentin, was shot down while piloting an Army Air Corps aircraft over France.[116]

Form and Function

Policy without structure is meaningless and impossible to execute. Had Theodore Roosevelt arrived in the presidency in 1880, when the Navy was in its doldrums, he would not have been able to pursue an activist foreign policy; the tools to back it up were simply not present, and they could not be created overnight. The work and effort of T. R. and many others during the twenty years leading up to his assumption of the presidency established the capabilities on which he built his "speak softly and carry a big stick" foreign policy. Yet, he was not satisfied merely to take what he had been given, or even to extend the nation's military along the lines of its natural progression. Roosevelt's grasp of the technological domain was such that he became a catalyst for change in the U.S. Navy to a degree that few other national leaders could claim in any field.

Modern military aircraft, submarine, and destroyer communities trace their inception back to Roosevelt's patronage. He arrived at his position of support for these platforms via a standard method: he noticed a gap in the Navy's spectrum of capabilities and took action to fill it. What is unique about Roosevelt, however, is that he took a special interest in the technological development of the platforms that issued forth from his actions and followed up with specific suggestions as to how to improve the product over several generations of platform evolution. Admiral Sims noted when commenting on his long history with Roosevelt that he would have difficulty imagining "any other president asking for information concerning a technical subject" with the precision Roosevelt brought to the conversation.[117]

Theodore Roosevelt's decisions with regard to the development of specific naval platforms were not without risk. For instance, his decisions first to pursue and later to dictate the construction of the all-big-gun battleship were based on an assumption of what the character of future naval battles would be. At the time the decisions were made, there was very little hard information on the topic.[118] The battles of the Spanish-American War and the Russo-Japanese War presented conflicting data, and the military technology and techniques employed were shifting monthly. Roosevelt struggled with his decisions, wavering at times, but finally settled on a course of action and doggedly pushed ahead.[119]

By the end of his administration Roosevelt had conquered doctrinal and bureaucratic resistance to create a modern Navy arrayed around a strategic centerpiece, the all-big-gun battleship.[120] The pattern of the *Wyoming* class, with its centerline placement of twelve identical large, rifled barrels; 1.5-foot belt armor; and steam-turbine engines, would remain intact for nearly eighty years. The guns would become larger and the turbines more efficient and capable of producing higher speeds, but the basic design did not change. Roosevelt sought power for the purpose of making his nation a decisive factor in international politics. Convinced that the ships of the U.S. Navy were the manifestation of that power, he dedicated himself to creating the finest, most efficient, and most powerful ships to serve as supports for his overall engagement strategy.[121] Ultimately he transformed the service he focused so much of his life's efforts on into a larger and much more capable force.

chapter seven

The Great White Fleet and the
Birth of the American Century

*Dear Will: One closing legacy. Under no circumstances divide
the battleship fleet between the Atlantic and Pacific Oceans
prior to the finishing of the Panama Canal.*

THEODORE ROOSEVELT TO WILLIAM TAFT

ON THE FINAL DAY OF HIS PRESIDENCY,

3 MARCH 1909

Theodore Roosevelt could not contain his enthusiasm as the long line of gleaming white battleships steamed past the presidential yacht *Mayflower* on 16 December 1907. The "Great White Fleet" owed its name to the natural cooling qualities of white paint, which lowered the internal temperature of ships operating in the tropics.[1] The plan of the day had called for the *Mayflower* to remain at anchor as the ships sailed by, with the president taking their salutes and tipping his hat in turn. Such was his joy, however, that he ordered the yacht's crew to raise anchor and race after the departing ships. This formation—sixteen battleships in one column and the flagship of the Navy's commander in chief steaming alongside like a parent following a young child on the first day of school—continued until Roosevelt reluctantly allowed the *Mayflower's* crew to turn back toward the Chesapeake Bay.[2] He had just over one year remaining in the White House and much yet to do.

Shortly after sailing out of sight of land, the fleet shifted formation into four columns of four ships sailing abreast. It was the fleet commander's intention to drill the fleet continuously in close formation to build up the abilities and confidence of his officers while keeping the ships close to enable him to communicate effectively via signal flags. Rear Adm. Robley Evans also had the ability to communicate through more modern means, and on the evening of 16 December he used wireless telegraphy to tell his ships the secret that Roosevelt had confided to him before their departure: they would be returning to the East Coast via the Suez Canal. Unfortunately, he transmitted this information uncoded, and antennas ashore picked up his signal. A denial from the White House quickly followed.[3]

Upholding the Monroe Doctrine

The fleet was scheduled to make several stops along the way to take on food, coal, and other supplies. In each port, the enlisted crew would take liberty in town while senior officers paid official calls on local leaders. The first such layover was at British-held Trinidad, where the fleet took on coal from contracted commercial ships. The British welcome for the visiting Americans was subdued. The lack of enthusiasm may have been an expression of resentment against the growing American naval power, but more likely it was a result of the tensions surrounding the response of the U.S. Navy to a massive earthquake near Jamaica in January 1907. On that occasion, an American battleship division commander had ruffled the feathers of the British governor-general when he had landed American sailors to render aide without first saluting the British flag and paying a courtesy visit to the governor's residence.[4] The fleet spent Christmas in Trinidad, then got under way on 29 December en route for Rio de Janeiro, Brazil.[5]

A rising tide of interest accompanied the fleet across the equator and into the South Atlantic. The American ships were expected to arrive in the mid-afternoon, but by mid-morning, thousands of people had gathered in the street overlooking Rio de Janeiro's harbor to welcome them. Private and commercial boats crowded the harbor where the fleet was to anchor. The town's leaders planned a program of events to entertain the American sailors that provided ample distraction and frivolity for each day the fleet was in port. The visit resulted in a wonderful upturn in relations between the United States and Brazil.[6] A few days later, coal bunkers filled to maximum capacity, the fleet left Rio with the intention of passing through the Strait of Magellan before making port calls in Chile and Peru. A diplomatic flap forced the alteration of that itinerary. Proud Argentina had been overlooked in the scheduling, and that would not do.

The American chargé d'affaires in Buenos Aires notified his superiors in Washington, D.C., that Argentina's foreign minister had summoned him to explain the favoritism shown to Brazil and the slight to Argentina. The fleet, the American chargé emphasized, *must* visit Argentina. Logistics and timelines be damned, the spectacle of the Great White Fleet was quickly becoming a phenomenon and a source of pride for the entire Western Hemisphere, and every nation desired port visits to allow its leaders to bask in the reflected glow. Because the port channel at Buenos Aires was not deep enough to take the battleships' draft, the ships were ordered to rendezvous with four Argentinean navy vessels off Cape Corrientos to exchange ceremonial salutes. The fleet's flotilla of torpedo boat destroyers, which drew less water, did make a port visit. The young lieutenants who commanded the small ships were fêted like admirals with honors and celebrations that rivaled those in Rio de Janeiro.[7] Hurt feelings were assuaged and U.S.-Argentinean relations continued unharmed.

Admiral Evans' fleet proceeded on to Puntas Arenas, Chile, at the southern tip of South America, to take on its next allotment of coal and supplies. Chile's president, anxious to reap diplomatic rewards like those bestowed on Brazil and Argentina, asked the fleet to visit Valparaiso as well, but the coal bunkers were full and there was no need for a port visit. At the personal urging of Secretary of State Elihu Root, Evans consented to parade the battleships through the harbor before continuing up the west coast of South America. The side trip to Valparaiso must have been a particularly satisfying sojourn down memory lane for "Fighting Bob" Evans. In 1891, as the commander of the USS *Yorktown,* he had nearly triggered a war when he chose to respond strongly to the murder of two American sailors in a Valparaiso bar. His refusal to back down had brought fame and honor to the U.S. Navy. In the end, however, the administration of President Benjamin Harrison had chosen to settle the issue with Chile diplomatically, largely owing to the relative superiority of the Chilean navy. Eighteen years later Evans must have felt immense satisfaction as he gazed across the water at the president of Chile standing on the deck of an antiquated Chilean cruiser receiving the twenty-one-gun salutes of sixteen modern American warships.[8] The honor paid to Chile was deemed sufficient, and the demonstration of American power was noted in diplomatic dispatches.[9]

As the cruise progressed, host nations attempted to outdo each other. Crowds increased in size, and welcoming celebrations and events grew ever more elaborate as the round-the-world voyage of the Atlantic Fleet transformed into the phenomenon known as the Great White Fleet. As the fleet proceeded with its circumnavigation of the South American continent en route to the port cities of California, it became increasingly clear that the reaction was more than just a response to large ships with brilliant white paint, gold bow fixtures, and large guns. It was the culmination of Theodore Roosevelt's foreign policies.

Roosevelt's muscular interpretation of the Monroe Doctrine, forbidding European interference in the internal affairs of the free nations on the American continents, led the way in this new dynamic. T. R. revised and extended the doctrine in 1904 when he declared that the United States had taken upon itself the responsibility of "policing" the hemisphere. While controversial and seemingly imperialistic in hindsight, the new doctrine immediately served notice to European nations that they could no longer use military force to gain redress for defaulted loans or other claims on behalf of their citizens. Aware of growing concerns among the Latin American republics that they might be exchanging an imperialistic Europe for an equally imperialistic United States, Roosevelt took action. He sent Secretary of State Elihu Root on a "goodwill tour" in 1906 to make it clear that the United States desired only to guarantee the independence and sovereignty of the Latin American republics.[10] Roosevelt viewed the United States as a protector—an intermediary between the smaller, weaker neighbors to the south and the larger, stronger powers of Europe. The fact that the United States now had a fleet capable of upholding these responsibilities reassured South American leaders that they could put to rest their enduring fears of colonial reconquest by European powers.

As the fleet left South America in its wake and drew steadily nearer to the United States, Admiral Evans began preparing for the gunnery exercise that served as the official justification for the battleships' voyage into the Pacific. Arriving at Magdalena Bay, Mexico, on 12 March, the fleet met two colliers dispatched from California. The circumstances surrounding the battleships' arrival were diplomatically awkward. Mexico's government had been eager to share in the glory surrounding the Great White Fleet's voyage and had asked the U.S. ambassador in Mexico City for the fleet's itinerary in order to prepare a welcome. The information available to the ambassador had the ships arriving at Magdalena on 17 March. Their arrival five days earlier than planned surprised everyone and left the Mexican government scrambling to get a local governor to sea to welcome the ships as protocol demanded. Admiral Evans cannot be blamed for the misunderstanding because he had informed the State Department of his updated schedule. For whatever reason, the State Department did not forward this information to Mexico City. Perhaps it was because the Navy and State departments were looking on this part of the voyage as a training period rather than time set aside for diplomatic engagement, but Mexican feelings were hurt nonetheless. Nearly simultaneous with the fleet's arrival in Mexico came the official announcement from Secretary of the Navy Victor Metcalf that the fleet would return to the Atlantic Coast by way of Australia and the Philippines. In other words, the Atlantic Fleet would completely circle the globe.[11]

The fleet gunnery exercises consumed the next month. For the first few days, the ships took on coal and prepared the targets that their large guns would eventually destroy. Then, beginning with the USS *Illinois* and progressing sequentially through the fleet, the ships raised their anchors and began steaming back and forth, taking careful aim and shooting for what was then called "record practice." Competition between the ships, and even between gun crews on the same vessel, was fierce. Additional bonus pay and prestige accrued to those who performed well.

When all of the ships had completed the gunnery exercise, they began mine-laying exercises. They ended their time in Magdalena Bay with naval infantry marching drills in preparation for the parades and celebrations that would dominate their time in West Coast ports.[12] Admiral Evans, who had been in ill health since December, was forced to seek medical attention at a facility near Santa Barbara. Bowing to the inevitable, he transmitted his request for retirement. As a favor for his long and distinguished service, he asked to meet the fleet when it arrived in San Francisco and have the formal retirement ceremony there. He was the last Civil War veteran on active duty in the Navy.[13]

Lobbying for Votes

The Atlantic Fleet arrived on the West Coast, not accidentally, just as the U.S. House of Representatives and Senate were taking up the naval appropriations bills. Theodore Roosevelt, as discussed in chapter 6, had done everything in his power to convince Congress to authorize the construction of four new battleships. The dispatch of the Great White Fleet was to some degree a domestic political strategy to accomplish this goal. It was Roosevelt's hope that the gleaming white battleships would encourage broader popular support for naval construction in a region of the country not known for its enthusiasm for the Navy. T. R. went so far as to hint to western representatives that if all four capital ships were funded, one of the new vessels would bear the name of their home state![14] The fleet did its best to excite the citizens of the cities visited. From San Diego in southern California to Port Angeles in the state of Washington, sailors and Marines marched in parades and interacted with local citizens, educating them on the importance of the U.S. Navy's mission in the world. The largest celebration in San Francisco included more than 8,000 sailors marching alongside soldiers and Marines in a parade viewed by 500,000 spectators. The monumental occasion heralded the Navy's progressive shift toward the Pacific.

Into the Pacific

At the beginning of the twentieth century, New Zealand and Australia, as members of the British Empire, relied on the Royal Navy to defend their coasts. When the First Lord of the Admiralty, Adm. Sir John Fisher, decided to concentrate British naval power in the waters surrounding the British islands to counter the growing German naval threat, Britain's Pacific colonies felt exposed and vulnerable.[15] British leaders tried unsuccessfully to assuage their concerns, pointing to a recently negotiated treaty between Britain and Japan, but Japan's recent military victories over China, Korea, and Russia represented an undeniable threat to other Pacific nations.[16]

The impending visit of the U.S. Atlantic Fleet was like a lifeline thrown to a drowning man. When the news of the fleet's voyage into the Pacific reached the two isolated British territories, both scrambled to issue invitations. That these invitations were issued without consulting the British colonial authorities or Foreign Office was a great source of embarrassment for the king's ministers. Local interest in the American battleships brought out a crowd of nearly 100,000 in Auckland, New Zealand. As the fleet came into Sydney, Australia, ten days later, American sailors saw between 500,000 and 650,000 people ringing the harbor.[17] The *New York Times* speculated that the United States might well be considering some form of alliance with the two British colonies.[18] Australia, for its part, decided shortly after the fleet's departure to pursue an independent navy of its own.[19] The relationships created during these port visits laid the foundation for the Australia–New Zealand–United States security arrangement that defined the early days of World War II in the Pacific and continues to this day.

The fleet then journeyed north, stopping briefly in the Philippines en route to Japan, the ostensible target of Theodore Roosevelt's order to send the fleet around the world. Japan began its preparations to host the American battleships in early April, when local civic associations as well as the Yale and Harvard alumni societies were asked to contribute to the forthcoming festivities. Japan's government wanted a visit that was in every aspect warmhearted and welcoming for the American sailors.[20] The preparations did not go completely smoothly. Count Shigenobu Okuma, a Japanese diplomat, caused some embarrassment when he suggested that Roosevelt's naval buildup had been directed at Japan, whose sudden arrival among the ranks of the Great Powers had alarmed the Western world.[21] Regardless of the controversy, Japan proceeded to put together a very detailed itinerary for the sixteen American ships and their crews, including a luncheon for the commanding admiral and his senior officers hosted by the emperor himself.[22]

On the morning of 16 October 1908 the American fleet appeared at the mouth of Yokohama Harbor escorted by sixteen warships of the Japanese fleet. Local trains had brought citizens from the countryside into the city throughout the previous night, and now they crowded every vantage point overlooking the bay.[23] Japanese children in small boats sailed alongside the white battleships singing an approximate rendition of "The Star-Spangled Banner."[24] Emperor Meiji told his American dinner guests that he hoped the visit would solidify the bonds between the United States and Japan.[25] The Japanese were perfect hosts, and the diplomatic results of the Great White Fleet's stop were immediately evident. Two days after the Americans left Japanese waters, Japan's ambassador in Washington suggested that the two great naval powers in the Pacific come to an accord with regard to their mutual interests in the Far East. Subsequent conversations resulted in the Root-Takahira Agreement, which recognized Japan's preponderant interests in China and Korea in return for Japan's promise of nonaggression in the Philippines.[26] This agreement placed relations between the two nations on a level playing field and perhaps pushed back the eventual conflict between the two countries by twenty years.

The Great White Fleet continued on its way, making stops in Amoy, China (the Chinese were humiliated that only half of the battleships stopped, when all of them had anchored in Japan), and Sri Lanka.[27] On clearing the Suez Canal and entering the Mediterranean the Atlantic Fleet demonstrated the unique advantages of a mobile and flexible force. Demands from virtually every country that bordered the Mediterranean forced the fleet to split up into small groups for port visits. The fleet commanders' desire to characterize these visits as "unofficial," thus offering their tired crews more rest and recreation, met disfavor from American diplomats in the various embassies and legations. These U.S. State Department representatives quickly pointed out the diverse collection of American interests that would be served by "official" visits, with the numerous receptions and court balls that accompanied this form of international exchange.[28]

A massive earthquake near Messina, Sicily, gave the fleet an opportunity to demonstrate the Navy's humanitarian aspects. All the ships contributed food, water, and medical supplies to the relief effort.[29] These materials along with six surgeons and other medical personnel were transferred to two ships that raced ahead to the scene of the calamity. Working parties unloaded the supplies and helped find survivors and recover the bodies of victims, including those of the American consul and his wife. Other ships transported equipment and personnel from surrounding countries.[30] After this operation, only the trip home remained on the itinerary.

The Return of the Fleet

The *Mayflower*, scene of so many important events of the Roosevelt administration, set out from the Washington Navy Yard at noon on 21 February 1909 carrying the commander in chief of the U.S. Navy on the last trip of his presidency. He would turn over the office to his handpicked successor, William H. Taft, on 4 March. The joy that filled Theodore Roosevelt's heart at the return of his treasured fleet was tempered by sorrow for the loss of his nephew Stewart, the son of his sister Corinne, dead from a freak fall from his sixth-floor dormitory window at Harvard the day before. He wished to be at his sister's side, but the Great White Fleet, the fleet he had created, was returning from its round-the-world cruise, and the exhilaration of that one final salute and celebration at the achievement could not be denied.[31]

On reaching Hampton Roads, where the waters of the Chesapeake Bay mix with those of the Atlantic Ocean, Roosevelt searched for the burst of white that would mark the return of his fleet. It had done its job. Relations with Latin America, Australia, and, perhaps most important, Japan had been significantly improved by the voyage and general show of goodwill. The cruise also represented a technological achievement unparalleled in modern naval history. The fleet had made the trip without one major breakdown, stranding, or need for a tow.[32] Just past eleven o'clock, a shout went up as the tops of the ship's masts emerged into view through the morning fog.

On a hoisted signal from the flagship *Connecticut*, the sixteen battleships and ten attendant screening ships of the Great White Fleet fired a simultaneous twenty-one-gun salute to their leader. Enormous battle flags fluttered in the wind as the ships steamed by the *Mayflower*, each firing a second, individual twenty-one-gun salute as it passed, and receiving a wave from Roosevelt in return. It was the ultimate moment of a career dedicated to the "upbuilding" of the American Navy.[33]

As the ships anchored, Roosevelt had his barge take him to the flagship of each of the fleet's divisions. Hoisted aboard, he quickly climbed up to stand on the turret housing that covered two of the ship's big guns. From this "Bully-ist" of pulpits he addressed the admiring throng of sailors. "Other nations may do as you have done, but they'll have to follow you," he proclaimed to their cheers. And that was the end. He returned to the *Mayflower*, and to the White House, to finish the business remaining to him. Only a few days earlier he had ordered Cdr. William Sims to command the new battleship *Minnesota*, protecting the young man from the revenge of those he had antagonized as the president's naval aide.[34] Sims was the most junior officer ever to command an American capital vessel; he was soon promoted to captain and eventually became a full four-star admiral.[35] The president also signed an instruction to have the fleet's white paint covered with tactical gray.[36] While in Japan, the fleet's officers had noted how impressive the Japanese fleet looked in its muted battle colors. There was also a realization that any sudden shift of paint schemes during a future crisis could significantly tip off U.S. intentions.[37] The gilding that had adorned the ships' bows was also removed. The Great White Fleet was a battle fleet now.[38]

Less than two weeks later, on his last full day in office, Roosevelt sat down to write his final letter as his nation's president. It was to his successor, and it contained his final thoughts, advice, and one last request: that William Taft not divide the battleship fleet until the Panama Canal was finished.[39] A few weeks later he left for a hunting trip in Africa. Roosevelt's friends, including Henry Cabot Lodge, advised him that Taft could not emerge from his shadow so long as he was on the North American continent. Hunting lions would be tame compared with the tasks he had undertaken during his presidency. In his autobiography, published in 1912, T. R. would record, "In my own judgment the most important service that I rendered to peace was the voyage of the battle-fleet around the world." Theodore Roosevelt died eleven years later. His eulogists spoke of his achievements as a historian, legislator, cattle rancher, civil service commissioner, police commissioner, assistant secretary of the Navy, Army colonel, governor, vice president, and president. By any standard of historical objectivity, the sixty years allotted him by his maker represented a remarkably full life.

The Birth of the American Century

At the dawn of the twentieth century the Royal Navy still maintained its policy of having more ships than its next two competitors combined, but Great Britain knew that its days of dominance were nearly at an end. On 21 November 1902 the British Colonial Office forwarded a memorandum on the defense of British possessions in the Caribbean Sea and the western Atlantic to the British War Office and Admiralty for comment. The War Office's reply, titled "Strategic Conditions in Event of War with the United States," was thorough in its analysis and stunning in its conclusions.

After first expressing doubt that Britain possessed "a sufficient naval force to maintain sea supremacy" in the Caribbean and the western Atlantic, the secret memorandum went on to detail how the U.S. Navy operating with a concentrated force in its local waters could cut off Britain's grain supply, which originated largely in Canada, Argentina, and the United States itself. The memorandum went on to point out that most of the British Empire's colonial possessions in the Western Hemisphere were indefensible in the event of a war with the United States. The report ended by emphasizing "the necessity of our preserving good relations with the United States" and concluded, "Should we ever find ourselves in the very awkward position of being threatened by the United States and a strong maritime naval power at the same time, it would be well . . . to resort to diplomatic agency to get us out of it."[40]

The report did not indicate a belief on the part of British policy makers that an attack from the United States was imminent. After all, the United States was also considering a number of wartime scenarios against different nations that posed no current threat. All nations did that. The report did, however, reflect recognition on the part of the British Empire that if it did not face an enemy in the United States, it at least looked across the table at a peer. America's place in the world, a position of leadership it would occupy for the remainder of the twentieth century, owed to Theodore Roosevelt's step-by-step effort to establish the country as a Great Power on the international stage.

A Cohesive Foreign Policy

Nineteenth-century U.S. foreign policy was largely the product of domestic politics, not an overall combination of the young republic's permanent interests, refuting Lord Palmerston's well-known law for at least the time being.

Throughout the first century of American constitutional government, the Federalists, Democratic-Republicans, Whigs, and Republicans each took their turn pandering to the domestic political interest groups of the day and used Europe's Great Powers and other nations of the Western Hemisphere as convenient bogeymen to cast in front of the electorate in order to bring out voters. By the start of the twentieth century, America's inconsistency had caused most foreign nations to regard the upstart democracy with disdain and to ignore most of its statements. Theodore Roosevelt changed this particular aspect of American diplomacy forever.

Long before Roosevelt arrived in the White House as an "accidental president," he had believed that the United States could, and indeed must, become a Great Power ranked among the imperial nations of Europe. He also held a sophisticated view that Great Power status derived from a careful balance of military power, diplomatic outreach, and economic interests. His philosophical vehicle for repositioning American power was the Monroe Doctrine. While the doctrine itself had never really faded from the international landscape, its influence had risen and fallen with the changes of American presidential administrations. Roosevelt, however, fixed on it as the ideal justification for American economic, diplomatic, and military dominance in North and South America and beat a steady drumbeat for its adoption as the centerpiece of U.S. foreign policy throughout his early governmental career. By the time he arrived in the White House in late 1901, he possessed a coherent vision of his nation's place in the world but faced an international system that did not take American rhetoric seriously. Roosevelt's bruisingly clear statements regarding the Monroe Doctrine and his adroit actions during the Venezuelan Crisis of 1902–3 erased all confusion on the part of Europe's leaders regarding American foreign policy. In addition, his efforts to improve and enlarge the American Navy and open foreign markets to American products produced a balanced approach to the world that firmly established the United States in the upper strata of Great Powers, a position it occupied for the remainder of the twentieth century.

Today the United States occupies a unique position as the lone superpower within the international system, but its ongoing internal domestic debate has produced a foreign policy that is discordant and confusing. There are those who believe that the United States must continue to work within the array of international entities that it helped to create after World War II, institutions that characterized the ensuing forty years of Cold War. Opposing this faction are those who believe that the country must take the lead in creating a new order centered on the permanent leadership of the United States and its political, economic, and military interests. This group does not seek an American territorial empire in the sense of Rome or Great Britain at the height of their power, but instead harkens back to Jefferson's "Empire of Liberty" wherein the philosophical values of the American Revolution become the cultural norms of the international system. While we cannot put words in a dead man's mouth, we can say that Theodore Roosevelt, throughout his life, enunciated a foreign policy that promoted a strong position based on America's interests within a robust international system.

Consistent American Interests

A constant tug-of-war between American interests and American values has characterized the history of the republic. The American Revolution had been very much about philosophical concepts such as freedom, representative democracy, individual liberties, and human rights. Throughout the nineteenth century, with the nation dominated by the unsettled question surrounding slavery in the South, these ideas found a place in the statements of leading American politicians. As the United States transitioned from Jeffersonian agrarianism into the industrial age, however, with the attendant search for foreign markets, a new set of leaders emerged for whom American *economic interests* predominated over the republic's *philosophical values*. These interests included access to foreign markers for American manufacturers predicated on open access to the sea-lanes on which most international commerce flowed.

These concepts of free trade with its attendant access to foreign markets and protected sea-lanes characterized the foundation of British imperial power throughout the eighteenth and nineteenth centuries. England's colonial possessions became the source of its wealth, and the Royal Navy was their guarantor. When the American frontier closed in the 1880s and the nation's collective expansionist mind began to express itself outward, it found a ready partner in a business community that was eager to find overseas markets for the products that flowed from its rapidly expanding industrial base. The national interests, both domestic and foreign, consistently voiced during this period can be paraphrased as "whatever is good for the U.S. economy is good for the United States." In the last two decades of the nineteenth century it was well understood that what was good for the U.S. economy was the shipment of the nation's goods on the world's sea-lanes of commerce.

Theodore Roosevelt understood that economic power was intrinsic to Great Power status, and he also understood that the United States did not need colonies to provide its mills, foundries, and factories with raw materials. The relatively untapped North American continent supplied those needs. But he did desire the same level of access to foreign markets already enjoyed by the nations of Europe. While it may appear to current observers that T. R. reveled in naval power for its own sake, a closer reading of his letters and books reveals a sophisticated understanding of the supporting position played by naval power in the international competition of the day.

Competition also drove another initiative with great traction in the policy circles that surrounded Theodore Roosevelt throughout his presidency: international institutions. During this ascendant period of American military and naval power, a movement emerged that sought to level the playing field and establish fair play among the nations of the world. International institutions such as the Permanent Court for Arbitration at The Hague came into being. Designed to be a peaceful alternative to the catch-and-grab minor wars of colonial conquest that dominated the era, the arbitration court was the first of the international institutions that dominated the diplomatic landscape during the twentieth century. The United States in general and Theodore Roosevelt in particular eagerly and consistently supported these institutions both as an avenue for expanding the rule of law that served as a philosophical bulwark of the then-revolutionary American political system and as a means to mitigate the overwhelming military power of nations such as Germany, France, and Great Britain. Roosevelt, however, understood better than anyone that no nation could rest its entire foreign policy on an embryonic international system and the good intentions of well-armed competitors.

Theodore Roosevelt supported the idea of a permanent international congress of nations throughout his presidency and afterward. When his political archrival, Woodrow Wilson, announced a similar proposal, however, Roosevelt rapidly reversed course. Nevertheless, his early support for international arbitration later found fruition first in Wilson's ill-fated League of Nations and then ultimately in institutions such as the United Nations and the World Court. Other economic organizations such as the World Bank and the International Monetary Fund sprang up in response to various challenges throughout the twentieth century. More recently, nongovernmental groups with a global vision have championed issues surrounding the environment and resource sustainability. All during this time, the United States supported a shift from a "might makes right" perspective to a democratic form of international consensus.

Roosevelt would be pleased, but he would also expect Americans participating in these forums to leverage American power—be it economic, diplomatic, or military—to support American interests.

The Rise of American Coercive Diplomacy

Nearly seventy years after Theodore Roosevelt left office, the noted scholar Alexander L. George introduced the term "coercive diplomacy" into the modern lexicon of international relations. George defined coercive diplomacy as a defensive strategy employed to cause an opponent "to stop or reverse an action." George's checklist for successful coercive diplomacy includes carefully creating a demand of the opponent; creating a sense of urgency for compliance; determining what punishment to threaten for noncompliance; and, finally, making the demand potent and credible. Coercive diplomacy within the modern school of international relations represents an advanced, enlightened strategy for relations among nation-states under difficult circumstances in that it "seeks to make force a much more flexible, refined psychological instrument of policy in contrast to the 'quick, decisive' military strategy, which uses force as a blunt instrument."[41] Force as a blunt instrument was typical of classic imperial diplomacy, as evidenced by Great Britain and Germany's actions with regard to Venezuela, while Roosevelt's actions throughout that crisis—and, in fact, throughout the remainder of his administration—clearly foreshadow George's strategic construct.

Beginning with his speech at the Naval War College titled "Washington's Forgotten Maxim," Theodore Roosevelt consistently promoted robust naval power not as an instrument of war but as the surest guarantor of peace. It is odd, on reflection, to consider that T. R., who is thought to be among the most belligerent chief executives to occupy the White House, managed to pass through his entire term of office without having to fire a shot in anger. This is not to say that he did not have opportunity. Each of the crises delineated within the previous pages could have sparked into a limited or worldwide conflict. The challenge to Britain and Germany's combined naval blockade of Venezuela could have easily backfired, given the power and prestige of those countries. The colonial powers of Europe could have taken umbrage with Roosevelt's precipitous recognition of Panama, and the kidnapping of Ion Perdicaris in Tangiers could have gone very wrong in very many ways.

Things did not go wrong because Roosevelt quickly and clearly stated his basic foreign policy tenet of establishing and upholding a U.S. sphere of influence in the Western Hemisphere in keeping with the language of the Monroe Doctrine and then backed it up by positioning the U.S. Navy in the Caribbean as a demonstration of American resolve. The Great Powers of Europe swiftly understood that Roosevelt's foreign policy was not demagogery directed at his domestic political audience but was instead a concise statement of U.S. interests directed at them. This clarity, when buttressed by his reorganization of the Navy's various squadrons into an effective battle fleet and his aggressive naval construction plan, gave his statements increased credibility within the international community. The operational record shows that T. R.'s "big stick" was not a bluff, and those who mistook it for one soon realized their error.

These early steps—the enunciation of a clear policy; the construction of a newer, larger Navy; its reorganization into a more effective force; and its evolving assignments as a forward-presence force—provided Theodore Roosevelt with the tools to carry out diplomacy with the sure and subtle promise that if America's prestige was insulted or its interests infringed upon, there would be a price and it could be a steep one. Under Roosevelt's coercive diplomacy German thoughts of expansion into the Caribbean and South America were reversed and Japanese plans for possible expansion into the Pacific were, for a time, halted. To use the classic phrase that evokes the American Wild West that he loved so much, Theodore Roosevelt was a man with a gun, and he was not afraid to use it.

The key advantage of Roosevelt's chief "gun," the U.S. naval services (the Navy and the Marine Corps), was their deployment in theaters where American interests were threatened. Their mobility, versatility, and lethality allow the naval services to bring pressure to bear where and when it is needed. From the time of the Venezuelan Crisis onward throughout the twentieth century, the Navy and Marine Corps have moved around the globe at the bidding of the commander in chief to uphold the interests of the United States. Coercion does not always work, as was the case in Vietnam, where nationalist desire on the part of North Vietnam and the inept application of American power failed to uphold American interests. Political shortsightedness has sometimes underfunded the military—including the naval services—compromising its ability to dissuade others from attacking American interests and reducing its ability, in Roosevelt's words, to serve as "the surest guaranty for peace." By and large, however, the timeline of the twentieth century is a roadmap dotted with incidents wherein conflict was avoided by a judicial application of force just shy of actual conflict.

Some of these incidents, such as the Cuban Missile Crisis, are well-known, but most have escaped public notice and serve only as objects for the curiosity of historians. It is clear, however, that Roosevelt's form of naval coercion remains a favorite tool of American foreign policy in the post-9/11 world.

The Scalability of Response

Probably the most obvious advantage of naval forces is their scalability; that is, their ability to "right-size" themselves to the scope of the situation they were dispatched to confront. Roosevelt's actions throughout his administration demonstrated his instinctive grasp of this characteristic, marking him as one of the earliest statesmen of the modern political age to aquire a nuanced understanding of the implications of postindustrial naval power. Winston Churchill, under the tutelage of Adm. Jackie Fisher, would quickly follow. Many would argue that the Venezuelan Crisis, when Roosevelt flooded the Caribbean basin with nearly the entirety of American naval power against a relatively small British and German force, runs counter to the scalability argument; and taken in isolation, they would be correct. But when the scope of historical review is broadened to take into account Roosevelt's reponse in Panama, we arrive at a different appraisal.

When the crisis occurred in Venezuela, Roosevelt was a new, and very young, president. No one in Europe took the United States—let alone Roosevelt—seriously when it came to stating a foreign policy and sticking to it. Additionally, the action he contemplated, namely coercing Great Britian and Germany to back down in their efforts to recover lost loans and possibly aquire territory as compensation from Venezuela, was fraught with danger for the United States. These were two of the most powerful nations on the planet, and each alone could overwhelm the United States in terms of naval power; combined, they were literally awesome. Roosevelt's strategy with regard to these two powers depended on two variables: magnitude and timing. He brought together nearly all of the ships of the Atlantic fleet in one location in order to create an overwhelming force within a confined battlespace—the Caribbean—and then issued his ultimatum with an established deadline that allowed only a limited time for the British and German home governments to consider it. Roosevelt's gamble provided for two outcomes: (1) arbitration and (2) a battle in which the combined Atlantic Fleet would destroy the smaller British and German squadrons before they could be reinforced from their home fleets. Even then, Germany and, more important, Britain would have had to decide whether to pursue armed conflict and risk their other interests in the Western Hemisphere (Canada in Britain's case) or sue for an arbitrated peace. Roosevelt's successful use of naval power at the upper end of the engagement scale was a good gamble, and it established his bona fides within the international community.

When the situation in Panama reared its head one year later, Roosevelt could have repeated his performance but did not. Instead, paying homage to the sensitivities of European governments who were willing, but not happy, to see the United States establish suzerainty over the proposed isthmusian canal, he chose to apply the minimal amount of force necessary to accomplish the goal of establishing Panama as an independent republic. At the onset of the Panamanian revolution only small auxiliary cruisers were positioned to maintain order—and Panama's independence—in the two ports on the Pacific and Caribbean coasts of the small country. When these cruisers did not dissuade the Colombians from landing troops to recover their runaway province, a troopship carrying five hundred Marines appeared over the horizon and did the trick. Had this proved inadequate, however, there remained a whole line of American battleships stationed at strategic intervals over the horizon, ready to appear in increments to bring about the desired outcome. Marines also played their part, arriving in force in Panama under the leadership of the commandant with a plan to invade Colombia itself in order to dictate new diplomatic terms should it be necessary.

That invasion was not necessary, but Theodore Roosevelt demonstrated his understanding of the inherent ability of the naval services to be separated and reassembled in new combinations of power to meet emergent contingencies, be they small or large. This ability was exploited with increasing assurance throughout the twentieth century and became a hallmark of American engagement around the world, from a response to a massive earthquake near Messina, Sicily, in 1908 to the movement of Task Force 58 into Camp Rhino, Afghanistan, in 2001. The U.S. Navy and Marine Corps maintain their ability to provide tailored force packages within newly revamped Expeditionary Strike Groups (ESGs), which combine the littoral capabilities of amphibious ships and the diverse responses inherent in a Marine Expeditionary Unit (MEU) with the strategic striking power of Tomahawk cruise missile–equipped *Ticonderoga-* and *Arleigh Burke*–class cruisers and destroyers. These forces give the United States the ability to respond to emergent crises—be it humanitarian assistance to tsunami victims in 2005–6 or full-scale combat operations in the Middle East—with a precise application of power. Theodore Roosevelt would have admired the naval forces of today and recognized their evolutionary development as a response to numerous technological "gaps" present in his day.

Seamless Spectrum of Military Power

When Theodore Roosevelt began his study of the application of naval power during the War of 1812, he quickly discerned the technological lead that the United States enjoyed over its British counterpart with regard to the superior design and construction of its frigates. These sturdy yet swift forty-four-gun vessels could outgun all ships of their own class and could outrun anything more powerful than themselves, giving them the ability to choose their engagements with care and to mount up a quick tally of victories. T. R. also found, however, that American power was limited to one specific band in the spectrum of engagement. While it excelled in frigate engagements, the early American Navy lacked the capability to meet ships of the line in squadron-style engagements and had little to no ability to protect American commerce over the seas with open-ocean cruisers. Further, its riverine and coastal defense boats were poorly designed and ineffective.

As Roosevelt's understanding broadened with experience and began to focus on the modern Navy of his day, he saw that while American naval influence had expanded, there still remained broad seams where the United States could exert little to no influence. His sponsorship of and interest in new innovations such as Samuel Langley's flying experiments, John Holland's submarines, and the torpedo-boat destroyer reflected his seach for answers to these perceived shortcomings. Simultaneously, he promoted movements within the Navy to refine existing capabilities to their most effective form, as evidenced by his leading role in the evolution of the all-big-gun battleship. Throughout Roosevelt's presidency the U.S. Navy expanded its capabilities and deepened its experience within its existing force structures, creating a climate that was to some degree open to technological change. I say "to some degree" because conservative forces beholden to old technologies and old tactics remained at work throughout this period. The underlying proto-American inclination toward innovation survived these forces, however, and forged ahead with change.

As the century progressed, this openness to change fostered new technologies that forever changed the face of the U.S. Navy. The aircraft carrier, deep strike aviation, nuclear power, and nuclear warhead–tipped ballistic missiles each expanded the influence of the Navy even as the rapidly evolving amphibious capabilities of the Marine Corps deepened the naval services' ability to influence events ashore. Some of these technologies, such as the ballistic missile submarine with its implied ability to survive a nuclear first strike, caused whole generations of treaties and defense agreements to be set aside and new arrangements negotiated.

Along with progress came imbalance. While the U.S. Navy did improve its ability to cover nearly the entire spectrum of engagement, shrinking budgets and the rise of a military industrial complex placed disproportionate emphasis on big-budget items such as nuclear aircraft carriers and their supporting Aegis-class cruisers and destroyers, which occupied the upper limit of the engagement scale. Carrier strike groups were designed to meet the threats of the twentieth century—first the Japanese Imperial Navy and later a massive naval force from the Soviet Union—in gigantic battles at sea. Twenty-first-century challenges of terrorism and piracy at sea would be much better served by a broader, more numerically superior force that is able to provide security in a number of theaters simultaneously and continuously, something the U.S. Navy is currently unable to do with its eleven carrier strike groups and current deployment schedules. Where the Navy does attempt to meet the current challenges, its operations represent the type of overkill that is illustrated by the old saying, "when all you have is a hammer, everything looks like a nail." Maintaining power and influence in the present and future international climates will require careful analyis of that environment and investment in technologies that will best support American interests. Failure to pursue the proper balance will quickly bring the United States face to face with the limits of naval power.

The Limits of Naval Power

When Theodore Roosevelt dispatched two squadrons of American cruisers to Tangiers to effect the recovery of Ion Perdicaris from his kidnappers, he had little appreciation for the diplomatic quicksand he was entering. The Moroccan government was so ineffective and so riddled with corruption that the show of naval power, while terrifying, could not move it to do any more that it was already doing. The U.S. naval force, for its part, was so top-heavy and so lacking in local intelligence resources that it could not field the type of small-unit search-and-recovery operations that would have been required to find Perdicaris on its own. But Roosevelt had committed the prestige of the United States to the situation. Withdrawal prior to the return of the kidnap victim would have struck a humiliating blow to America's reputation. The incident disrupted the summer cruise schedule of the ships involved and their diplomatic commitments throughout Europe, Asia, and Africa.

The naval services of the United States spent much of the twentieth century developing the sort of skill sets necessary to execute Perdicaris-type rescue operations in parallel with diplomatic efforts that sought to limit the requirement for such actions through strengthening state actors and international agreements. What remains unchangeable, however, is the tyranny of distance. In blue-water, littoral, and riverine environments, the U.S. Navy can establish and maintain maritime dominance at will. Inland for tens of miles, the Marine Corps can establish and hold local land dominance until relieved by larger, more sustainable Army forces. But a logistical string can be stretched only so far until it breaks, and that is the limit of hard naval power. Theodore Roosevelt could easily have followed the argument presented up to this point, but he lacked the tools to navigate within the framework that follows.

Another set of limits has arisen in the post-9/11 world, and these involve the concepts of "soft power" and the "war of ideas." U.S. naval forces are well positioned, for example, to fight a Soviet Surface Action Group steaming through the Greenland–Iceland–United Kingdom gap. The Navy has trained for this type of game plan since the early 1970s. Al-Qaida's attacks on 11 September 2001 fundamentally changed the strategic landscape, and the Navy has been struggling to adjust its playbook ever since. The Marine Corps has had less of a struggle. Its "Four Block War" concept, originated before 9/11, has been more than adequate for adapting to the modern strategic climate.

Al-Qaida has no carrier strike groups; it does not even have a country. It is a movement organized on an international scale that operates wherever ignorance, economic strife, and disease create an opening. Al-Qaida and similar movements such as Hamas and Hezbollah take up residence in areas that lack an effective local government and provide order, schools, services, and a constant drumbeat of propaganda against the West. Aircraft carriers cannot bomb al-Qaida out of existence. Aegis-class cruisers cannot, by their mere presence, "shield" local populations from Hamas hate-speech. This is a limit of hard naval power.

It is possible to stop wars before they begin, however—to deny terrorists fertile ground in which to plant their radical Islamic seeds of discontent.

Expeditionary Strike Groups with their light amphibious aircraft carriers, heavy-lift helicopters, and plentiful Marines are organized to engage the backwater regions of the oceanic Pacific, eastern Africa, and southern Asia where terrorism is making its greatest inroads. In these places, U.S. government agencies and nongovernmental organizations can construct schools and hospitals and can drill wells to provide clean drinking water. It is capabilities such as these, at the lower end of the engagement scale, that are needed today to fight this most modern and most ancient war.

Conclusion

The voice of Theodore Roosevelt has not grown faint in the ninety years since his death. If anything, it has grown louder and more strident as the pressures of superpower status have reached ever-higher levels. He created the core policies, structures, and precedents that established the twentieth century as "the American Century." Now, at the dawn of the twenty-first century, in the face of the challenges of a "Clash of Civilizations," a crumbling domestic national consensus, and declining international institutions, the United States needs to "recalibrate" its national compass and face some truths. First, Americans must put aside their idealistic hope that military intervention could become an anachronism and accept that diplomacy and military power (including the ever-elastic naval power) are two parts of one continuous spectrum of influence. They cannot ignore one and expect the other to be effective. Next, the citizens of the United States must put aside their domestic political differences and formulate a cohesive foreign policy, based on American interests, that seeks a proper mixture of economic, diplomatic, and military influence in the world. U.S. military strategy should place its forces forward and present in the world while also maintaining a scalability of response to meet emergent crises. Lastly, the United States should understand that all power has its limits and should seek to avoid the danger of hubris.

Some would claim that Theodore Roosevelt was an imperialist, and they would be correct. However, Roosevelt's imperialism differed from its European cousin in that it was not a philosophy centered on the color of a person's skin. Instead he saw the American brand of imperialism as a benevolent force that set about to free the individuals and nations it encountered to pursue the uniquely American dream of "the strenuous life" wherein individuals would be free to throw off constricting categories of race or social class to pursue their maximum potential. With his children Theodore Roosevelt played a cross-country hiking game called "over, under, or through," in which participants were not allowed to avoid obstacles by going around them. T. R. abhorred weakness in his children, himself, and his country. He felt that the United States, as an entity coexisting with other countries, should always confront obstacles head-on and pursue a "strenuous life" for itself, competing for a place not only among the nations of his day, but also among the great nations of history. He cited the Monroe Doctrine to justify his decision to take the United States into the maelstrom of international competition, used the U.S. Navy and U.S. Marine Corps as the tools of his trade, and bequeathed the twentieth century as his legacy. His voice has not grown silent. He speaks to us still, and we should listen to him.

Notes

Prologue: The Sailing of the Great White Fleet

Epigraph from Charles W. Freeman Jr., *The Diplomat's Dictionary* (Washington, D.C.: Peace Institute, 1997), 228.

1. Kenneth Wimmel, *Theodore Roosevelt and the Great White Fleet* (Washington, D.C.: Brassey's, 1998), xiv–xv.
2. Ibid., xi.
3. "World Cruise of the Great White Fleet," *U.S. Naval Institute Proceedings* 84, no. 10 (1958): 89.
4. Roosevelt to Harrison Otis, 8 January 1907; Roosevelt to Gov. James Gillett; 14 March 1907; Roosevelt to Kentaro Kaneko, 23 May 1907; Roosevelt to Henry Cabot Lodge, 10 July 1907, in Theodore Roosevelt and Elting Elmore Morison, *The Letters of Theodore Roosevelt* (Cambridge: Harvard University Press, 1951) [henceforth *TLTR*], 1:541–542, 618–619, 671–672, 709–710.
5. Roosevelt to Kaneko, 23 May 1907, *TLTR*, 5:671.
6. Richard H. Collin, "Gentlemen's Agreements," in *Encyclopedia of U.S. Foreign Relations*, ed. Bruce W. Jentleson and Thomas G. Paterson (New York: Oxford University Press, 1997), 212–213.
7. Claude A. Buss, *Asia in the Modern World* (New York: Macmillan, 1964), 296–297.
8. Julius W. Pratt, *A History of United States Foreign Policy* (Englewood Cliffs, N.J.: Prentice-Hall, 1955), 446.
9. Randolph G. Adams, *The Foreign Policy of the United States* (New York: Macmillan, 1925), 347–349.
10. Roosevelt to Ambassador Kogoro Takahira, 28 April 1907, *TLTR*, 5:656–657.
11. Arthur P. Dudden, *The American Pacific* (New York: Oxford University Press, 1992), 136–148.
12. Pratt, *History of U.S. Foreign Policy*, 445.
13. Roosevelt to Kermit Roosevelt, 13 June 1907, *TLTR*, 5:688–689.
14. Roosevelt to Charles Joseph Bonaparte, 10 August 1906, *TLTR*, 5:353.
15. Akira Iriye, *Pacific Estrangement: Japanese and American Expansion, 1897–1911* (Cambridge: Harvard University Press, 1972), 163.
16. Roosevelt to Rear Adm. Alfred T. Mahan, 12 January 1907, *TLTR*, 5:550–551.
17. Wimmel, *Theodore Roosevelt and the Great White Fleet,* 221.
18. Acting Secretary of State diplomatic mutatis mutandis, 31 August 1907, *Papers Relating to the Foreign Relations of the United States, 1907* (Washington, D.C.: Government Printing Office, 1908).
19. Henry F. Pringle, *Theodore Roosevelt, a Biography* (New York: Smithmark, 1995), 196.

Chapter One. Roosevelt, Navalism, and
the Monroe Doctrine

Epigraph from Owen Wister, *Roosevelt, the
Story of a Friendship*, 1880–1919 (New York:
Macmillan, 1930), 24. Portions of this chap-
ter appeared previously in "Roosevelt's
Naval Thinking prior to Mahan," in
*Theodore Roosevelt, the U.S. Navy and the
Spanish American War* (New York: Palgrave
Press, 2001); and "Fulcrum of Greatness,"
Naval History Magazine (December 2002).

1. Henry Adams, *The Education of Henry
   Adams* (New York: Random House,
   1931), 417.
2. Edmund Morris, " 'A Matter
   of Extreme Urgency': Theodore
   Roosevelt, Wilhelm II, and the
   Venezuela Crisis of 1902," *Naval War
   College Review* 55, no. 2 (2002): 73.
3. H. W. Brands, *T. R.: The Last Romantic*
   (New York: Basic Books, 1997), 62–63;
   Theodore Roosevelt, *The Naval War
   of 1812*, vol. 2 of *The Works of Theodore
   Roosevelt*, National Edition (New York:
   Scribner's, 1926), xi.
4. Morris, "A Matter of Extreme
   Urgency," 73.
5. "Theodore Roosevelt: The Winning of
   the West," C-SPAN American Writers,
   http://www.americanwriters.org/writ-
   ers/Roosevelt.asp.
6. Theodore Roosevelt, *Theodore
   Roosevelt, an Autobiography*, vol. 20
   of *The Works of Theodore Roosevelt*,
   National Edition (New York:
   Scribner's, 1926), 3.
7. Pringle, *Theodore Roosevelt*, 6–7.
8. Brands, *T. R.*, 19; David McCullogh,
   Mornings on Horseback (New York:
   Simon and Schuster, 1981) 57; Nathan
   Miller, *Theodore Roosevelt, a Life*
   (New York: William Morrow, 1992),
   33; Edmund Morris, *The Rise of
   Theodore Roosevelt* (New York: Coward,

McCann and Geoghegan, 1979),
39–40; Edward J. Renehan, *The Lion's
Pride* (New York: Oxford University
Press, 1998), 24–25.
9. Morris, *The Rise of Theodore Roosevelt*,
   38–39.
10. James D. Bulloch, *The Secret Service
    of the Confederate States in Europe*
    (London: Bentley and Son, 1883), 4.
11. Roosevelt, *Autobiography*, 14–15.
12. Bulloch, *Secret Service of the
    Confederate States in Europe*, 7–17.
13. William R. Thayer, *Theodore Roosevelt*
    (New York: Grosset and Dunlap,
    1919), 6.
14. Morris, *The Rise of Theodore Roosevelt*, 43.
15. F. C. Iglehart, *Theodore Roosevelt:
    The Man as I Knew Him* (New York:
    Christian Herald, 1919), 121–122.
16. There is a common misperception that
    Theodore Roosevelt routinely went
    by the nickname "Teddy." This is not
    true. Family and close friends called
    him "Teedie" or "Tee" (Morris, *The
    Rise of Theodore Roosevelt*, 331).
17. Roosevelt, *Autobiography*, 18.
18. William S. Dudley, "Naval Historians
    and the War of 1812," *Naval History* 4
    (Spring 1990): 53.
19. Roosevelt, *Autobiography*, ix.
20. Theodore Roosevelt to Anna
    Roosevelt, 21 August 1881, *TLTR*, 1:50.
21. Theodore Roosevelt to Martha
    Roosevelt, 14 September 1881, *TLTR*,
    1:52.
22. Roosevelt, *Autobiography*, 24.
23. Wister, *Roosevelt, the Story of a
    Friendship*, 24.
24. Frederick Merk, *Manifest Destiny
    and Mission in American History: A
    Reinterpretation* (New York: Alfred A.
    Knopf, 1963), 228–265.
25. Pratt, *History of U.S. Foreign Policy*,
    219–242.

26. Walter LaFeber, *The New Empire: An Interpretation of American Expansion, 1860–1898* (Ithaca, N.Y.: Cornell University Press, 1963).

27. Morris, *The Rise of Theodore Roosevelt,* 773–774.

28. Peter Karsten, "The Nature of 'Influence,' " *American Quarterly* 23 (Fall 1971): 588.

29. Capt. Edward L. Beach, *The United States Navy* (New York: Henry Holt, 1986), 330.

30. Capt. W. D. Puleston, *Mahan: The Life and Work of Captain Alfred T. Mahan, USN* (New Haven: Yale University Press, 1939), 69.

31. Karsten, "The Nature of Influence," 587–588.

32. Warren Zimmermann, *First Great Triumph: How Five Americans Made Their Country a World Power* (New York: Farrar, Straus and Giroux, 2002), 197.

33. Theodore Roosevelt, *Thomas Hart Benton. Gouverneur Morris,* vol. 7 in *The Works of Theodore Roosevelt,* National Edition (New York: Scribner's, 1926), 423.

34. Elbert B. Smith, *Magnificent Missourian: Thomas Hart Benton* (Philadelphia: Lippincott, 1957), 225–227.

35. Ibid., 174–175.

36. Roosevelt, *The Naval War of 1812,* 405–406.

37. Roosevelt to Henry Cabot Lodge, 22 January 1888, in Henry C. Lodge and Theodore Roosevelt, *Selections from the Correspondence of Theodore Roosevelt and Henry Cabot Lodge* (New York: Scribner's, 1925), 63 [henceforth *SCTRHL*].

38. Guy Cane, "Sea Power—Teddy's Big Stick," *U.S. Naval Institute Proceedings* 102, no. 8 (1976): 41.

39. Zimmermann, *First Great Triumph,* 89.

40. Harold Sprout and Margaret Sprout, *The Rise of American Naval Power, 1776–1918* (Princeton: Princeton University Press, 1939), 202–203.

41. Roosevelt to Mahan, 12 May 1890, *TLTR,* 1:222.

42. William L. Langer, *The Diplomacy of Imperialism* (New York: Alfred A. Knopf, 1951), 419.

43. Roosevelt to James S. Clarkson, 22 April 1893, *TLTR,* 1:313.

44. Zimmermann, *First Great Triumph,* 155–162.

45. Ernest R. May, *American Imperialism* (New York: Atheneum, 1968), 27.

46. Morris, *The Rise of Theodore Roosevelt,* 259.

47. William C. Widenor, *Henry Cabot Lodge and the Search for an American Foreign Policy* (Berkeley: University of California Press, 1980), 88.

48. Pratt, *History of U.S. Foreign Policy,* 223.

49. Zimmermann, *First Great Triumph,* 150–151.

50. Roosevelt to Clarkson, 22 April 1893, *TLTR,* 1:313.

51. Roosevelt to the editors of the *Harvard Crimson,* 2 January 1896, *TLTR,* 1:505–506.

52. Theodore Roosevelt, *American Ideals and Other Essays, Social and Political* (New York: Scribner's, 1906), 50.

53. LaFeber, *The New Empire,* 195.

54. Roosevelt, *The Naval War of 1812,* 143–144.

55. Ibid.

56. Roosevelt, *Autobiography,* 133, 173.

57. Mrs. Bellamy Storer, "How Theodore Roosevelt Was Appointed Assistant Secretary of the Navy," *Harper's Magazine,* 1901, Theodore Roosevelt Collection, Harvard University [henceforth TRC].

58. Lodge to Roosevelt, 2 December 1896, *SCTRHL*, 240–241.

59. Zimmermann, *First Great Triumph*, 238.

60. *Review of Reviews* 15, no. 5 (1897): 518.

61. Roosevelt to Lodge, 23 March 1897, *TLTR*, 1:590.

62. Roosevelt to Capt. Bowman McCalla, 19 April 1897, *TLTR*, 1:599.

63. Wendell D. Garrett, "John Davis Long, Secretary of the Navy, 1897–1902: A Study in Changing Political Alignments," *New England Quarterly* 31, no. 3 (1958): 295.

64. John Long, *The Journal of John D. Long*, ed. Margaret Long (Ringe, N.H.: Richard R. Smith, 1956), 209.

65. Roosevelt to Cecil Spring Rice, 28 April 1897, *TLTR*, 1:604.

66. Long, 21 April 1897, *Journal*.

67. Roosevelt to John D. Long, 26 April 1897, *TLTR*, 1:603–604.

68. "Armed or Unarmed Peace," *Harper's Weekly* 41, no. 2113 (19 June 1897): 603.

69. Theodore Roosevelt, *American Ideals. The Strenuous Life. Realizable Ideals*, vol. 13 in *The Works of Theodore Roosevelt*, National Edition (New York: Scribner's, 1926), 182–199.

70. May, *American Imperialism*, 192–230.

71. Morris, *The Rise of Theodore Roosevelt*, 571–572.

72. Roosevelt to Senator Cushman Davis, 13 August 1897, *TLTR*, 1:649.

73. Roosevelt to Long, 18 June 1897, *TLTR*, 1:628.

74. Roosevelt to Lodge, 17 August 1897, *SCTRHL*, 1:272.

75. Roosevelt to Bellamy Storer, 19 August 1897, *TLTR*, 1:655.

76. Roosevelt to Mahan, 3 May 1897, *TLTR*, 1:607.

77. Roosevelt to Capt. Henry Taylor, 24 May 1897, *TLTR*, 1:617.

78. Clark G. Reynolds, *Famous American Admirals* (Annapolis: Naval Institute Press, 1978), 173–174.

79. Roosevelt to Mahan, 9 June 1897, *TLTR*, 1:622–623.

80. Roosevelt to McCalla, 3 August 1897, *TLTR*, 1:636.

81. Roosevelt to Lodge, 29 September 1897, *SCTRHL*, 1:284.

82. Roosevelt to Long, 30 September 1897, *TLTR*, 1:695–696.

83. Long, 13 January 1898, *Journal*, 212–213.

84. Roosevelt to William McKinley, 26 April 1897, *TLTR*, 1:602–603.

85. Roosevelt to Lodge, 21 September 1897, *SCTRHL*, 1:278.

86. Roosevelt to Lodge, 15 September 1897, *TLTR*, 1:676–677.

87. Roosevelt to Adm. Montgomery Sicard, 17 June 1897, *TLTR*, 1:626–627.

88. Roosevelt to Lodge, 21 September 1897, *SCTRHL*, 1:278.

89. Roosevelt to Long, 14 January 1898, *TLTR*, 1:759–762.

90. Roosevelt to Lodge, 21 September 1897, *SCTRHL*, 1:278.

91. Roosevelt to Long, 14 January 1898, *TLTR*, 1:759–762.

92. Roosevelt to Capt. William Cowles, 5 April 1896; Roosevelt to Cowles, 20 June 1896; Roosevelt to Richard Dana, 8 May 1897; Roosevelt to Long, 30 September 1897, *TLTR*, 1:524, 544, 609–610, 695–696.

93. Roosevelt to Charles A. Boutelle, 22 June 1897, *TLTR*, 1:629.

94. Roosevelt to Long, 18 February 1898, *TLTR*, 1:778–779.

95. Roosevelt to Cowles, 3 August 1897, *TLTR*, 1:637.

96. Roosevelt to Long, 30 September 1897, *TLTR*, 1:695–696.

97. Roosevelt to Boutelle, 21 August 1897; Roosevelt to William Bigelow,

29 October 1897; Roosevelt to Capt.
Arent Crowninshield, 24 November
1897, *TLTR,* 1:656, 702, 720.

98. Roosevelt to Long, 30 September
1897, *TLTR,* 1:695–696.

99. Roosevelt to Cowles, 3 August 1897,
TLTR, 1:637.

100. Roosevelt to Long, 9 August 1897,
TLTR, 1:642.

101. Roosevelt to Long, 13 August 1897,
TLTR, 1:650.

102. Roosevelt to Lodge, 21 September
1897, *SCTRHL,* 1:278.

103. Long, *Journal,* 216.

104. Roosevelt to Commo. George Dewey,
25 February 1898, *TLTR,* 1:784–785.

105. The original letter books from which
these orders were extracted are located
in Record Group [henceforth RG]
80, Records of the Department of the
Navy, National Archives [henceforth
NARA], Washington, D.C.

106. Long, *Journal,* 216–217.

107. Roosevelt to Gen. Whitney
Tillinghast, 25 February 1898, *TLTR,*
1:784.

108. *TLTR,* 2:1495.

109. Walter LaFeber, *The Cambridge
History of American Foreign Policy*
(Cambridge, Mass.: Cambridge
University Press, 1993), 2:192.

110. Thayer, *Theodore Roosevelt,* 180.

111. Roosevelt to John Hay, 18 February
1900, *TLTR,* 2:1192.

112. James D. Richardson, ed.,
*Compilation of the Messages and Papers
of the Presidents,* (New York: Bureau
of National Literature and Art, 1920),
14:6522–6523.

**Chapter Two. Overwhelming Force and
the Venezuelan Crisis of 1902–1903**

Epigraph, Roosevelt to Cecil Spring Rice, 1
November 1905, *TLTR,* 5:61–64.

1. Roosevelt to Whitelaw Reid, 27 June
1906; Roosevelt to Henry White,
14 August 1906, *TLTR,* 5:318–320,
357–359.

2. William R. Thayer, *Life and
Letters of John Hay* (Boston: Houghton
Mifflin, 1915), 284–295.

3. Howard C. Hill, *Roosevelt and
the Caribbean* (Chicago: University of
Chicago Press, 1927), 106–141; Pringle,
Theodore Roosevelt, 197–203.

4. Nancy Mitchell, "The Height of
the German Challenge: The Venezuela
Blockade, 1902–03," *Diplomatic
History* 20, no. 2 (1996): 185–209.

5. Seward Livermore, "Theodore
Roosevelt, the American Navy, and
the Venezuelan Crisis of 1902–03,"
American Historical Review 51, no. 1
(1945): 452–471.

6. Morris, "A Matter of Extreme
Urgency," 74.

7. Edmund Morris, *Theodore Rex* (New
York: Random House, 2001), 632–635.

8. Donald L. Herman, "Democratic
and Authoritarian Traditions," in
*Democracy in Latin America: Colombia
and Venezuela* (New York: Praeger,
1988), 5.

9. Judith Ewell, *Venezuela: A Century of
Change* (Stanford: Stanford University
Press, 1984), 23–28.

10. Ruhl J. Bartlett, ed., *The Record of
American Diplomacy,* (New York:
Alfred A. Knopf, 1964), 341–354.

11. Brian S. McBeth, *Gunboats,
Corruption, and Claims: Foreign
Investment in Venezuela, 1899–1908*
(Westport, Conn.: Greenwood Press,
2001), 15–21.

12. Herbert W. Bowen, *Recollections Diplomatic and Undiplomatic* (New York: Grafton Press, 1926), 252.

13. Ibid., 248–251.

14. McBeth, *Gunboats, Corruption, and Claims,* 82–83.

15. Sheldon B. Liss, *Diplomacy and Dependency: Venezuela, the United States, and the Americas* (Salisbury, N.C.: Documentary Publications, 1978), 27–30.

16. Richardson, *Compilation of the Messages and Papers of the Presidents,* 2:787–788.

17. LaFeber, *Cambridge History of American Foreign Policy,* 60–61.

18. Ibid., 121–125.

19. Edward Wagenknecht, *The Seven Worlds of Theodore Roosevelt* (New York: Longman, Green, 1958), 119.

20. Howard K. Beale, *Theodore Roosevelt and the Rise of America to World Power* (Baltimore: Johns Hopkins University Press, 1956), 395–431.

21. Roosevelt to Cecil Spring Rice, 6 July 1901, *TLTR,* 3:107–109.

22. Ronald Spector, *Admiral of the New Empire* (Baton Rouge: Louisiana State University Press, 1974), 126–127.

23. Report of the General Board, 27 March 1902, Dewey Collection, Library of Congress [henceforth DCLOC], box 43, folder 7, Records of the General Board of the Navy, Washington, D.C.

24. Roosevelt to Ambassador Joseph H. Choate, 3 February 1902, *TLTR,* 3:225.

25. Richard H. Collin, *Theodore Roosevelt, Culture, Diplomacy, and Expansion: A New View of American Imperialism* (Baton Rouge: Louisiana State University Press, 1985), 156.

26. Frederick W. Marks, *Velvet on Iron* (Lincoln: University of Nebraska Press, 1979), 37–70.

27. Hill, *Roosevelt and the Caribbean,* 141–146.

28. William Hard, "How Roosevelt Kept the Peace," *Metropolitan Magazine* (May 1916): 5, TRC.

29. Holger H. Herwig, *Politics of Frustration: The United States in German Naval Planning, 1889–1941* (Boston: Little, Brown), 1976, 94.

30. Henry Taylor to Roosevelt, late November 1902, Theodore Roosevelt Collection, Library of Congress [henceforth TRLOC], box 57, Military Correspondence of the President.

31. Ronald Spector, "Roosevelt, the Navy, and the Venezuela Controversy: 1902–1903," *American Neptune* 32, no. 4 (1972): 259–260.

32. General Board Memorandum, 25 June 1901, DCLOC, box 43, folder 7, Records of the General Board of the Navy.

33. *Annual Reports of the Navy Department, 1902* (Washington D.C.: Government Printing Office, 1902), 976.

34. "Puerto Rico, Study of Theater Operations," Geographical Files, Puerto Rico Folder, USMC Historical Center, Washington Navy Yard.

35. Beale, *Theodore Roosevelt and the Rise of America,* 356–357.

36. *Annual Reports of the Secretary of the Navy, 1902,* 977.

37. Colby M. Chester, "Diplomacy on the Quarter Deck," *American Journal of International Law* 8, no. 3 (1914): 443–476.

38. Lt. Cdr. Nathan Sargent to Secretary of the Navy William Moody, 28 February 1901, NARA, RG 45, box 671, VI, Venezuela Situation.

39. Cdr. T. C. McLean, Commanding Officer, USS *Cincinnati,* to Secretary of the Navy Moody, 26 July 1902;

Cdr. John Nickles, Commanding Officer, USS *Topeka,* to Secretary of the Navy Moody, 23 July 1902, both in NARA, RG 45, box 671, VI, Venezuela Situation.

40. Memorandum of the General Board, 28 May 1901, DCLOC, box 43, folder 7, Records of the General Board of the Navy.

41. Memorandum of the General Board, 2 November 1901, DCLOC, box 43, folder 7, Records of the General Board of the Navy.

42. Herwig, *Politics of Frustration,* 69.

43. Thomas A. Bailey, "Dewey and the Germans at Manila Bay," *American Historical Review* 45, no. 1 (1939): 63–70.

44. Terrell D. Gottschall, *By Order of the Kaiser* (Annapolis: Naval Institute Press, 2003), 206–211.

45. Herwig, *Politics of Frustration,* 47.

46. Holger H. Herwig, *Germany's Version of Empire in Venezuela* (Princeton: Princeton University Press, 1986), 196.

47. "The German Emperor and the Monroe Doctrine," *Harper's Weekly,* 31 January 1903, TRC.

48. See "Progress of the World," *American Review of Reviews* (April 1902), TRC.

49. Isaac F. Marcosson, "Attorney-General Moody and His Work," *World's Work* (November 1906): 8191.

50. Paul T. Heffron, "Secretary Moody and Naval Administration Reform: 1902–1904," *American Neptune* 29 (January 1969): 33.

51. Spector, *Admiral of the New Empire,* 139.

52. Roosevelt to Adm. George Dewey, 14 June 1902, DCLOC, box 13, General Correspondence.

53. Mildred Dewey Diary, DCLOC, box 73, General Correspondence, 71.

54. Marks, *Velvet on Iron,* 50.

55. Roosevelt to William H. Moody, 20 September 1902, DCLOC, box 13, General Correspondence.

56. Memorandum dated 24 April 1902, DCLOC, box 13, General Correspondence.

57. Heffron, "Secretary Moody and Naval Administration Reform," 33.

58. William H. Moody memorandum, 24 July 1902, DCLOC, box 13, General Correspondence.

59. Translations of Messages Sent in Cipher, October 1888–January 1910, vol. 4, p. 289, NARA, RG 45, Naval Records Collection, Office of the Secretary of the Navy, General Records.

60. Order dated 23 September 1902 signed by Acting Commandant, Col. Reid, NARA, RG 127, U.S. Marines Overseas Brigades, Battalions, Regiments, Panama, box 4.

61. Record of Percival Clarence Pope, USMC, Biographical Facts, Percival C. Pope Folder, USMC Historical Center, Washington Navy Yard.

62. *Annual Reports of the Navy Department, 1903,* 1232.

63. Col. P. C. Pope to Commandant, 15 October 1902, NARA, RG 127, U.S. Marines Overseas Brigades, Battalions, Regiments, Panama, box 4.

64. *Annual Reports of the Navy Department, 1903,* 1233.

65. Allan Nevins, *Henry White: Thirty Years of American Diplomacy* (New York: Harper and Brothers, 1930), 209.

66. Leonard Wood Diary, 10 September 1902, Leonard Wood Papers, Library of Congress, Washington, D.C.

67. Alfred P. Dennis, *Adventures in American Diplomacy, 1896–1906* (New York: E. P. Dutton, 1928), 287.

68. Edmund Morris, "A Few Pregnant Days," *Theodore Roosevelt Association Journal* 15, no. 1 (1987): 10.
69. Ibid.
70. Bailey, "Dewey and the Germans at Manila Bay," 62–63.
71. George Dewey, *Autobiography of George Dewey* (Annapolis: Naval Institute Press, 1987), 220–231; Mildred Dewey Diary, DCLOC, box 73, General Correspondence, p. 93.
72. Iestyn Adams, *Brothers across the Ocean: British Foreign Policy and the Origins of the Anglo-American "Special Relationship" 1900–1905* (London: Tauris Academic Studies, 2005), 39; memorandum for communication to the German ambassador, 22 October 1902, British National Archives, Foreign Office [henceforth BNA, FO] 115/1241, "From Foreign Office."
73. Marquess of Lansdowne to Sir F. Lascelles, 22 October 1902, BNA, FO 115/1241.
74. W. L. Penfield, "Anglo-German Intervention in Venezuela," *North American Review* 177 (July 1903): 96.
75. Warren G. Kneer, *Great Britain and the Caribbean* (East Lansing: Michigan State University Press, 1975), 22.
76. Ibid., 26.
77. Mildred Dewey Diary, 86. Dewey had previously served in the American Civil War and the Spanish-American War without receiving a wound.
78. McBeth, *Gunboats, Corruption, and Claims,* 88.
79. Liss, *Diplomacy and Dependency,* 38.
80. McBeth, *Gunboats, Corruption, and Claims,* 88.
81. Richard H. Collin, *Theodore Roosevelt's Caribbean* (Baton Rouge: Louisiana State University Press, 1990), 95.
82. Herwig, *Politics of Frustration,* 79.
83. Ewell, *Venezuela,* 40.
84. *Papers Relating to the Foreign Relations of the United States, 1903* (Washington, D.C.: Government Printing Office, 1904), 420–422.
85. Margaret Robinson, *Arbitration and the Hague Peace Conferences* (Philadelphia, 1936), 24, 70.
86. Beale, *Theodore Roosevelt and the Rise of America,* 419.
87. "May 23, 1916, George Dewey letter to Henry A. Wise," *New York Herald Tribune,* September 27, 1925, 9.
88. Morris, "A Matter of Extreme Urgency," 79.
89. *Annual Reports of the Navy Department, 1903,* 647.
90. Secretary Moody to Naval Attachés, 4 December 1904, NARA, RG 45, General Records, Translations of Messages Sent in Cipher, October 1888–January 1910, vol. 4.
91. *Mayflower* Letter Book, DCLOC, box 44, p. 39.
92. Ibid., 41.
93. Ibid., 55.
94. Ibid., 139.
95. Elting E. Morison, *Admiral Sims and the Modern American Navy* (Boston: Houghton Mifflin, 1942), 132.
96. Hill, *Roosevelt and the Caribbean,* 133.
97. Ronald Reter, "The Real versus Rhetorical Theodore Roosevelt in Foreign Policy Making," Ph.D. diss., University of Georgia, 1973, 42–44.
98. Adm. George Dewey to George Dewey Jr., 14 December 1902 (63–291–LB), Dewey Papers, Personal Letters, Naval Archives, Naval Historical Center [henceforth DPNHC], Washington Navy Yard.
99. Morris, "A Few Pregnant Days," 3.
100. Moody to Dewey; Moody to Commandant, Naval Station,

San Juan, Puerto Rico, 15 December 1902, NARA, RG 45, General Records, Translations of Messages Sent in Cipher, October 1888–January 1910, vol. 4.

101. Journal of the Commander in Chief, DCLOC, box 44, p. 39.

102. Albert Gleaves, *The Admiral* (Pasadena, Calif.: Hope Publishing, 1985).

103. *Annual Reports of the Navy Department, 1903*, 1249.

104. Ibid., 647–648.

105. Journal of the Commander in Chief, DCLOC, box 44, p. 43; Dewey to Moody, 16 December 1902, NARA, microfiche M625, roll 261, Area File of Naval Collection, 1775–1910, Area 8, December 1902–January 1903.

106. Commanding Officer, USS *Marietta*, to Secretary Moody, copy to Admiral Dewey, 16 December 1902, NARA, RG 45, box 671, Venezuela Situation, p. 4.

107. *Mayflower* Letter Book, DCLOC, box 44, pp. 146–147.

108. Ibid., 148.

109. Reter, "The Real versus Rhetorical Theodore Roosevelt," 45.

110. *Mayflower* Letter Book, DCLOC, box 44, p. 44.

111. British Ambassador to British Foreign Minister, 16 December 1902, BNA, FO 115/1244.

112. Sir Michael Herbert to Lansdowne, Cipher Telegram, 13 December 1902, BNA, FO 115/1244.

113. Kneer, *Great Britain and the Caribbean*, 35.

114. Ibid., 38.

115. Iestyn Adams, *Brothers across the Ocean*, 50–51.

116. Collin, *Theodore Roosevelt's Caribbean*, 106–107.

117. Morris, "A Few Pregnant Days," 11.

118. Morris, "A Matter of Extreme Urgency," 82–84.

119. Burton J. Hendrick, "Historic Crises in American Diplomacy," *World's Work* (June 1916): 186.

120. Henry Mann, "The Monroe Doctrine," *Harmsworth Self-Educator* (July 1907): 1556.

121. NARA, Microfiche M625, roll 261, Area File of Naval Collection, 1775–1910, Area 8, December 1902–January 1903.

122. Gleaves, *The Admiral*, 106.

123. Admiral Dewey to George Dewey Jr., 4 January 1903 (63–291–MH), DPNHC.

124. Dudley W. Knox, *A History of the United States Navy* (New York: G. P. Putnam's Sons, 1936), 375.

125. Morris, "A Few Pregnant Days," 3.

126. Dennis, *Adventures in American Diplomacy*, 291–292.

127. Admiral Dewey to George Dewey Jr., 21 December 1902 (63–291–MH), DPNHC.

128. "Roosevelt and Venezuela," *New York Herald Tribune*, 27 September 1925, p. 26, TRC.

129. Roosevelt to Lodge, 27 March 1901, *TLTR*, 3:31–32.

130. Roosevelt to Cecil Spring Rice, 3 July 1901, *TLTR*, 3:107–109.

131. "Caribbean Sea and Western Atlantic: Strategic Conditions in Event of War with the United States," BNA, Admiralty Group (ADM) 1/8875, 21 January 1903.

132. Tilchin, *Theodore Roosevelt and the British Empire*, 102–105.

Chapter Three. Scalable Response in Defense of the Panamanian Revolution
Epigraph from James F. Vivian, "The 'Taking' of the Panama Canal Zone: Myth and Reality," *Diplomatic History* 4 (1980): 95–100.

1. *Papers Relating to the Foreign Relations of the United States, 1903*, 133.
2. Robert W. Sellen, "The Just Man Armed: Theodore Roosevelt on War," *Military Review* 39 (May 1959): 38.
3. Hill, *Roosevelt and the Caribbean*, 61; Pringle, *Theodore Roosevelt*, 229; Marks, *Velvet on Iron*, 101–103; Collins, *Theodore Roosevelt, Culture, Diplomacy, and Expansion*, 8–10; Morris, *Theodore Rex*, 278–289.
4. Marks, *Velvet on Iron*, 99–100.
5. *Papers Relating to the Foreign Relations of the United States, 1903*, 154–155.
6. Capt. Chauncey B. Humphrey, "History of the Revolution of Panama," unpublished manuscript, 1923, p. 5, in author's private collection.
7. Bernard A. Weisberger, "The Strange Affair of the Taking of the Panama Canal Zone," *American Heritage* 27, no. 6 (1976): 70; *Papers Relating to the Foreign Relations of the United States, 1903*, 156.
8. *Papers Relating to the Foreign Relations of the United States, 1903*, 146.
9. Ibid., 151–152.
10. Ibid., 157.
11. Ibid., 158.
12. Ibid., 163.
13. Bruce W. Jentleson and Thomas G. Paterson, eds., *Encyclopedia of U.S. Foreign Relations* (New York: Oxford University Press, 1997), 3:353.
14. *Papers Relating to the Foreign Relations of the United States, 1903*, 166.
15. Ibid., 172–173.
16. Ibid., 191.
17. Ibid., 168.
18. C. Mallet to British Foreign Secretary, 30 September 1902, BNA, FO 115/1241, "From Foreign Office."
19. Roosevelt to John Hay, 19 August 1903, *TLTR*, 3:566–567.
20. Pratt, *History of U.S. Foreign Policy*, 287.
21. Lewis M. Haupt, "Why Is an Isthmian Canal Not Built?" *North American Review* 178 (1902): 3–11, TRC.
22. Roosevelt to Hay, 19 August 1903, *TLTR*, 3:567–568.
23. E. Taylor Parks, *Colombia and the United States, 1765–1934* (Durham, N.C.: Duke University Press, 1935), 219–234.
24. Roosevelt, *Autobiography*, 503–507.
25. Ibid., 514; Roosevelt to Albert Shaw, 10 October 1903, *TLTR*, 3628.
26. Philippe Bunau-Varilla, *Panama: The Creation, Destruction, and Resurrection* (New York: McBride, Nast, 1914), 311.
27. Thomas Schoonover, "Research Note: Max Farrand's Memorandum on the U.S. Role in the Panamanian Revolution of 1903," *Diplomatic History* 12 (Fall 1988): 505.
28. Bunau-Varilla, *Panama: Creation, Destruction, and Resurrection*, 312.
29. Weisberger, "The Strange Affair of the Taking of the Panama Canal Zone," 72.
30. Philippe Bunau-Varilla, *The Great Adventure of Panama* (New York: Doubleday, 1920), 147–148.
31. Pringle, *Theodore Roosevelt*, 221–222.
32. *New York Times* obituaries for Col. Chauncey Benton Humphrey, 6 January 1958, p. 39; and Col. Grayson M. P. Murphy, 19 October 1937, p. 25.
33. Humphrey, *History of the Revolution of Panama*, 7–9.
34. Ibid., 10–11.
35. Ibid., 11.
36. Ibid., 12–13.
37. Ibid., 14.

38. Ibid., 18.
39. Ibid., 19.
40. Lt. Cdr. Miles Du Val, "The Canal Zone," unpublished manuscript dated 1937, Washington Navy Yard, Washington, D.C., 112.
41. Schoonover, "Research Note," 507.
42. Bunau-Varilla, *Panama: Creation, Destruction, and Resurrection,* 319.
43. Secretary of the Navy William H. Moody to the Commander in Chief of the Atlantic Fleet, 6 November 1903, NARA, RG 45, Subject File: U.S. Navy 1775–1910, box 473, Operations North Atlantic Squadron.
44. Ibid.
45. Commander in Chief, Pacific Squadron, to Secretary of the Navy, 4 November 1903, NARA, RG 45, Office of the Secretary of the Navy, General Records, 1798–1910, Confidential Letters Sent September 1893–June 1904, vol. 3 of 6, p. 394.
46. Acting Secretary of the Navy to Commander in Chief, Atlantic Fleet, 4 September 1903, NARA, RG 45, Confidential Letters Sent September 1893–June 1904, vol. 3 of 6, p. 368.
47. Bunau-Varilla, *Panama: Creation, Destruction, and Resurrection,* 318.
48. Weisberger, "The Strange Affair of the Taking of the Panama Canal Zone," 68–77.
49. Schoonover, "Research Note," 504.
50. Weisberger, "The Strange Affair of the Taking of the Panama Canal Zone," 71.
51. Bunau-Varilla, *Panama: Creation, Destruction, and Resurrection,* 336.
52. Historicus, "The Fifty Mile Order," *North American Review* 179 (February 1904): 235, TRC.
53. Chester, "Diplomacy on the Quarter Deck," 474–475.
54. Secretary of the Navy to Secretary of State John Hay, 5 November 1903, quoting message from Commanding Officer, USS *Nashville,* dated 8:57 PM, 3 November 1901, NARA, RG 45, Confidential Letters Sent, September 1893–June 1904, vol. 3 of 6, p. 395.
55. Cdr. John Hubbard, Commanding Officer, USS *Nashville,* to the Secretary of the Navy, 3 November 1903, NARA, RG 45, Translations of Messages Received in Cipher, vol. 2 of 6, p. 330.
56. Telegram from American Consul, Panama, to Commanding Officer, USS *Nashville,* 3 November 1903, NARA, RG 45, Microfiche Section M625, roll 264.
57. RG 45, Confidential Letters Sent, September 1893–June 1904, vol. 3 of 6, p. 398.
58. Commanding Officer, USS *Nashville,* to Secretary of the Navy, 4 November 1903, NARA, RG 45, Translations of Messages Received in Cipher, vol. 2 of 6, p. 326.
59. Bunau-Varilla, *Panama: Creation, Destruction, and Resurrection,* 347.
60. RG 45, Confidential Letters Sent September 1893–June 1904, vol. 3 of 6, p. 391.
61. RG 127, U.S. Marines Overseas Brigades, Battalions, Regiments, Panama, box 4.
62. Hubbard to Secretary of the Navy, 8 November 1903, NARA, RG 127, box 4.
63. RG 45, Confidential Letters Sent, September 1893–June 1904, vol. 3 of 6, p. 397.
64. Ibid., 392.
65. Hubbard to Secretary of the Navy, 8 November 1903, NARA, RG 127, box 4.
66. "Forty Cool Marines Defied Five Hundred," *Detroit Evening Press,* 26 December 1903, p. 8, TRC.
67. RG 45, Confidential Letters Sent, September 1893–June 1904, vol. 3 of 6, p. 401.

68. Cdr. Francis Delano to Secretary of the Navy, 6 November 1903, NARA, RG 45, Translations of Messages Received in Cipher, May 1899–25 December 1904, vol. 2 of 6, p. 333.

69. Delano to Secretary of the Navy, 10 November 1903, NARA, RG 127, box 4.

70. Hubbard to Secretary of the Navy, 5 November 1903, NARA, RG 127, box 4.

71. Telegram from Beaupré to Secretary of State John Hay, 4 November 1903, *Diplomatic History of the Panama Canal* (Washington, D.C.: U.S. Department of State, 1914), 474.

72. Rear Adm. Henry Glass to Senior U.S. Naval Officer Present, Colón, 10 November 1903, NARA, RG 127, box 4.

73. *Annual Reports of the Navy Department, 1904* (Washington, D.C.: Government Printing Office, 1904), 550; Glass to Commanding Officer, USS *Concord*, 10 November 1903, NARA, RG 127, box 4.

74. RG 45, Translations of Messages Sent in Cipher, 1 June 1898–16 September 1906, vol. 4 of 10, pp. 328–329.

75. Telegram from Beaupré to Secretary of State Hay, 6 November 1903, *Papers Relating to the Foreign Relations of the United States, 1903*, 225.

76. Telegram from Beaupré to Secretary of State Hay, 6 November 1903, *Diplomatic History of the Panama Canal*, 474.

77. Secretary of State Hay to Felix Ehrman, Acting Consul General, Panama, 6 November 1903, NARA, RG 127, box 4.

78. *Papers Relating to the Foreign Relations of the United States, 1903*, 226–227.

79. Ibid., 229.

80. *Messages and Papers of the Presidents*, 14:6756.

81. Ibid., 6816–6823.

82. Glass to Rear Adm. J. B. Coghlan, 14 November 1903, NARA, RG 127, box 4.

83. Ehrman to Glass, 13 November 1903, NARA, RG 127, box 4.

84. Glass to Ehrman, 14 November 1903, NARA, RG 127, box 4.

85. *Annual Reports of the Navy Department, 1904*, 532.

86. Coghlan to Secretary of the Navy, 23 November 1903, NARA, RG 45, Microfiche Section M625, roll 264.

87. Ibid.

88. General Order from Gen. Daniel Ortiz, General in Charge of the General Staff of the Army of Colombia, 23 November 1903, NARA, RG 45, Microfiche Section 625, roll 264.

89. *Papers Related to the Foreign Relations of the United States, 1903*, 228–230.

90. The noted diplomatic historian Randolph Greenfield Adams pointed out that many Caribbean and Latin American nations had to wait years for formal recognition, while Panama, owing to its peculiar circumstance, was recognized in less than a week. See Adams, *History of the Foreign Relations of the United States* (New York: Macmillan, 1925), 288.

91. Secretary of the Navy to Glass, 9 November 1903, NARA, RG 45, Translations of Messages Sent in Cipher, p. 330.

92. Ibid., 341.

93. Edward Garcynski to Secretary of the Navy Moody, 11 December 1903, Papers of William H. Moody, Library of Congress, Manuscript Division, container 17, folder 1, Correspondence 1896–1903.

94. Captain Diehl, Commanding Officer, USS *Boston*, to Secretary of the Navy, 9 November 1903, NARA, RG 45, Translations of Messages received in

Cipher, May 1899–25 December 1904, vol. 2 of 6, p. 337.

95. Glass to Secretary of the Navy Moody, 16 November 1903, NARA, RG 127, box 4.

96. Glass to Secretary of the Navy, 9 November 1903, NARA, RG 45, Translations of Messages received in Cipher, May 1899–25 December 1904, vol. 2 of 6, p. 339.

97. Glass to Commanding Officer, USS *Concord,* 10 November 1903, NARA, RG 127, box 4.

98. Glass to Commanding Officer, USS *Boston,* 12 November 1903, NARA, RG 127, box 4.

99. Glass to Secretary of the Navy, 16 November 1903, NARA, RG 127, box 4.

100. Glass to Ehrman, 11 November 1903, NARA, RG 127, box 4.

101. Rear Admiral Walker to Secretary of the Navy, 6 December 1903, NARA, RG 45, Translations of Messages Received in Cipher, vol. 2 of 6, May 1899–25 December 1904, p. 355.

102. Secretary of the Navy to Glass, 9 December 1903, NARA, RG 45, Translations of Messages sent in Cipher, vol. 4 of 10, p. 343.

103. Glass to Secretary of the Navy, 9 November 1903, NARA, RG 45, Translations of Messages received in Cipher, vol. 2 of 6, May 1899–25 December 1904, p. 362.

104. Glass to Secretary of the Navy, 10 December 1903, NARA, RG 45, Translations of Messages Received in Cipher, vol. 2 of 6, p. 358.

105. Glass to Commanding Officer, USS *Boston,* 7 December 1903, NARA, RG 127, box 4.

106. Confidential memorandum between Glass and Commanding Officer, USS

Wyoming, undated, NARA, RG 127, box 4.

107. Glass to Secretary of the Navy, 11 December 1903, NARA, RG 45, Translations of Messages received in Cipher, vol. 2 of 6, 344.

108. Ibid., 9 December 1903, p. 342; 12 December 1903, p. 346.

109. Glass to Commanding Officer, USS *Boston,* 14 December 1903, NARA, RG 127, box 4.

110. Cdr. W. H. Turner to Coghlan, 16 December 1903, NARA, RG 127, box 4.

111. Glass to Lt. W. G. Miller, 14 December 1903, NARA, RG 127, box 4.

112. Glass to Secretary of the Navy, 13 December 1903, NARA, RG 45, Confidential Letters Sent, September 1893–June 1904, vol. 3 of 6, p. 407.

113. Secretary of the Navy to Glass, 10 December 1903, NARA, RG 45, Translations of Messages sent in Cipher, vol. 4 of 10, p. 352.

114. Ibid., 11 December 1903, p. 345.

115. Ibid., 17 December 1903, p. 349.

116. Ibid., 18 December 1903, p. 351.

117. Brig. Gen. G. F. Elliott to Assistant Secretary of the Navy, 11 January 1904, NARA, RG 127, box 4.

118. John A. Lejeune, *The Reminiscences of a Marine* (Philadelphia: Dorrance, 1930), 159–160; Geographical Files, Panama Folder, USMC Historical Center, Quantico, Va.

119. Secretary of the Navy to Elliott, 18 December 1903, NARA, RG 45, Confidential Letters Sent, September 1893–October 1908, vol. 3 of 6, p. 409.

120. Lejeune, *Reminiscences of a Marine,* 161.

121. George F. Elliott Folder, Biographical Files, USMC Historical Center, Washington Navy Yard, Washington, D.C.

122. Elliott to Commanding Officer, Marine Barracks, Washington, D.C.,

19 December 1903, NARA, RG 127, box 4.

123. Harry A. Ellsworth, *One Hundred Eighty Landings of United States Marines: 1800–1934* (Washington, D.C.: History and Museums Division, Headquarters, USMC, 1974), 136.

124. Lejeune, *Reminiscences of a Marine,* 160; Panama Folder, Geographical Files, USMC Historical Center, Washington Navy Yard, 123.

125. Panama, American Intervention Folder, USMC Historical Center, Washington Navy Yard.

126. Coghlan to Secretary of the Navy, 5 January 1904, NARA, RG 127, box 4.

127. Panama, American Intervention Folder, USMC Historical Center, Washington Navy Yard.

128. Ibid.

129. Ibid.

130. Strength, distribution, and commanding officers of Marines in Panama summarized in Panama, American Intervention Folder, USMC Historical Center, Washington Navy Yard.

131. Elliott to Assistant Secretary of the Navy, 11 January 1904, NARA, RG 127, box 4.

132. Secretary of the Navy to Commander, Caribbean Squadron, undated, NARA, RG 45, Confidential Letters Sent, September 1893–October 1908, vol. 3 of 6, p. 410.

133. Richard W. Turk, "The United States Navy and the 'Taking' of Panama, 1901–1903," *Military Affairs* 38, no. 3 (1974): 94–95.

134. Elliott to Assistant Secretary of the Navy, 11 January 1904, NARA, RG 127, box 4.

135. Geographical Files, Panama Folder, USMC Historical Center, Washington Navy Yard.

136. *Annual Reports of the Navy Department, 1904,* 1110.

137. Elliott to Assistant Secretary of the Navy, 21 January 1904, NARA, RG 127, box 4.

138. Glass to Elliott, 23 January 1904, NARA, RG 127, box 4.

139. Secretary of the Navy to Elliott, 4 January 1904, NARA, RG 45, Confidential Letters Sent, September 1893–October 1908, vol. 3 of 6, pp. 419–420.

140. "Politics in the Panama Question," *Progress of the World, American Review of Reviews* 26 (February 1904): 144, TRC.

141. John Hay memorandum, 11 January 1904, John Hay Papers, Manuscript Division, Library of Congress [henceforth HPLOC], vol. 5.

142. Hay to Gen. Rafael Reyes, 11 December 1903, HPLOC, vol. 5.

143. Lodge, *SCTRHL,* 72.

144. "Politics in the Panama Question," 142.

145. Geographical Files, Panama Folder, USMC Historical Center, Washington Navy Yard.

146. Clyde H. Metcalf, *History of the U.S. Marine Corps* (New York: G. P. Putnam's Sons, 1939), 295–296.

147. Rear Adm. Henry Taylor to Secretary of the Navy, undated [but early February as reflected by letters catalogued before and after it], NARA, RG 45, Confidential Letters Sent, September 1893–October 1908, vol. 3 of 6, p. 438.

148. Commander in Chief, North Atlantic Fleet, to Commandant of the Marine Corps, 22 April 1904, NARA, RG 45, Confidential Letters Sent, September 1893–October 1908, vol. 3 of 6, p. 460.

149. Secretary of the Navy to Commander of the Caribbean Squadron, 5 May 1904, NARA, RG 45, Confidential

Letters Sent, September 1893–October 1908, vol. 3 of 6, p. 463.

150. Facsimile of *London Times* article attached to 23 November 1903 note from John Hay to Roosevelt, HPLOC, vol. 5.

151. Phillip C. Jessup, *Elihu Root* (New York: Dodd, Mead, 1938), 1:404–405.

Chapter Four. Morocco and the Limits of Naval Power

Epigraph, Roosevelt to John Hay, 2 May 1903, *TLTR,* 3:473.

1. Roosevelt to Lodge, 11 May 1904; Roosevelt to Cornelius Bliss, 12 May 1904, *TLTR,* 4:796–797.

2. Lodge to Roosevelt, 27 May 1904; Roosevelt to Lodge, 28 May 1904, *SCTRHL,* 2:79–81.

3. Pringle, *Theodore Roosevelt,* 253.

4. Dumas Malone, *Dictionary of American Biography* (New York: Scribner's, 1961), 3:50; William J. Hourihan, "Roosevelt and the Sultans: The United States in the Mediterranean, 1904," Ph.D. diss., University of Massachusetts, 1975, 51.

5. S. R. Gummeré to Hon. David J. Hill, 4 April 1899, NARA, RG 45, U.S. Navy Subject File VI, International Relations and Politics, box 666, Correspondence related to Morocco, folder 4 [henceforth Correspondence related to Morocco].

6. Diary of Edward J. Dorn, 31 May 1904, Edward J. Dorn Collection, Manuscript Division, Library of Congress, Washington D.C. [henceforth Dorn Diary]; Gummeré to Loomis, 20 May 1904, General Records of the Department of State, NARA, RG 59, Dispatches from U.S. Consuls in Tangier, 1797–1906 [henceforth Dispatches/Tangier].

7. Barbara W. Tuchman, "Perdicaris Alive or Raisuli Dead," *American Heritage* 10, no. 5 (1959): 100.

8. Ibid., 100; David Woolman, "Did Theodore Roosevelt Overreact When an American Was Kidnapped in Morocco?" *Military History* 13 (October 1997): 16, 79.

9. Moody to Hay, 20 February 1904, Naval Records Collection, NARA, RG 45, Area Files of the Naval Records Collection, Geographical Area 4, 1903–1905 [henceforth Area File 4].

10. John B. Brebner, *The North Atlantic Triangle* (New Haven: Yale University Press, 1945), 262.

11. Seward W. Livermore, "The American Navy as a Factor in World Politics, 1903–1913," *American Historical Review* 63 (July 1958): 865–869.

12. Hourihan, "Roosevelt and the Sultans," 22–23.

13. Ibid., 53.

14. Albert Hourani, *A History of the Arab Peoples* (London: Faber and Faber, 1991), 41.

15. Gavin Maxwell, *Lords of the Atlas* (London: Arrow Books, 1991), 86–88.

16. Rosita Forbes, *El Raisuli, the Sultan of the Mountains* (London: Thornton Butterworth, 1924), 66.

17. C. R. Pennell, *Morocco since 1830, a History* (New York: New York University Press, 2000), 127.

18. Edmund Burke III, *Prelude to Protectorate in Morocco* (Chicago: University of Chicago Press, 1976), 66.

19. Hourihan, "Roosevelt and the Sultans," 48.

20. Ion Perdicaris, "In Raisuli's Hands: The Story of My Captivity and Deliverance, May 18th to June 26, 1904," *Leslie's Monthly Magazine* 7 (May 1906): 511.

21. Ion Perdicaris, "Morocco, the Land of the Extreme West and the Story of My Captivity," *National Geographic Magazine* 17 (March 1906): 142.

22. Perdicaris, "In Raisuli's Hands," 513.

23. Morris, *Theodore Rex,* 324.

24. William J. Hourihan, "Marlinspike Diplomacy," *U.S. Naval Institute Proceedings* 105 (January 1979), 45; Hay to Roosevelt, 18 May 1904, HPLOC, vol. 5.

25. Hourihan, "Roosevelt and the Sultans," 69.

26. Tuchman, "Perdicaris Alive or Raisuli Dead," 19.

27. Assistant Secretary of the Navy Charles Darling to Rear Adm. French E. Chadwick, 19 May 1904, Office of the Secretary of the Navy, NARA, RG 45, General Records, Confidential Letters Sent, September 1893–October 1908, vol. 4 of 6.

28. Hourihan, "Roosevelt and the Sultans," 41.

29. USS *Brooklyn* Cruising Report, Quarter ending 30 June 1904, Bureau of Navigation, 1813–1911, NARA, RG 45, Cruising Reports of Vessels of the United States Navy, January 1895–June 1910, vol. 8 of 14.

30. Roosevelt to Theodore Roosevelt Jr., 28 May 1904, *TLTR,* 4:807.

31. Roosevelt to Root, 20 May 1904, *TLTR,* 4:801.

32. Chadwick to Secretary of the Navy, 27 May 1904, Adm. French E. Chadwick Collection, Operational Archives, Washington Navy Yard [henceforth FECC].

33. *Annual Reports of the Navy Department, 1904,* 542.

34. Morris, *Theodore Rex,* 329.

35. Peter Larsen, "Theodore Roosevelt and the Moroccan Crisis, 1904–1906," Ph.D. diss., Princeton University, 1984, 3.

36. Woolman, "Did Theodore Roosevelt Overreact?" 79.

37. William B. Cogar, *Dictionary of Admirals of the U.S. Navy* (Annapolis: Naval Institute Press, 1991), 2:41–42.

38. Hourihan, "Roosevelt and the Sultans," 40.

39. Reynolds, *Famous American Admirals,* 65–66.

40. Beach, *The U.S. Navy,* 364–365.

41. Chadwick to Secretary of the Navy, 31 May 1904, FECC.

42. Burke, *Prelude to Protectorate in Morocco,* 66.

43. Maxwell, *Lords of the Atlas,* 87.

44. Larsen, "Theodore Roosevelt and the Moroccan Crisis," 6–7.

45. Gummeré to Loomis, 31 May 1904, Dispatches/Tangier.

46. Maxwell, *Lords of the Atlas,* 87.

47. J. M. Macheod to Sir Arthur Nicholson, 2 June 1904, BNA, FO 174/265, "From Fez Consulate."

48. Secretary of State to Secretary of the Navy, 10 February 1903, NARA, RG 45, Correspondence related to Morocco.

49. Gummeré to Hay, 25 May 1904, Dispatches/Tangier.

50. John Hay Diary, 28 May 1904, HPLOC, vols. 1 and 2.

51. Hourihan, "Marlinspike Diplomacy," 46.

52. Albert S. Barker, *Everyday Life in the Navy* (Boston: Gotham Press, 1932), 400.

53. Morris, *Theodore Rex,* 329.

54. Chadwick to Secretary of the Navy, 31 May 1904, NARA, RG 45, Translations of Messages Received in Cipher, vol. 2 of 6, p. 450.

55. John Hay Diary, 1 June 1904, HPLOC, vols. 1 and 2.

56. Ibid., 31 May 1904.

57. Roosevelt to Leonard Wood, 4 June

1904; Roosevelt to Theodore Roosevelt Jr., 5 June 1904, *TLTR*, 4:820–821.

58. Morris, *Theodore Rex*, 329.

59. Hourihan, "Roosevelt and the Sultans," 99–103.

60. Larsen, "Theodore Roosevelt and the Moroccan Crisis," 64–65.

61. Hourihan, "Roosevelt and the Sultans," 86.

62. Chadwick to Secretary of the Navy, 3 June 1904, NARA, RG 45, Translations of Messages Received in Cipher, vol. 2 of 6, p. 451.

63. "Muster Roll of Officers, Noncommissioned Officers, Drummers, Trumpeters, and Privates of the USMC stationed onboard USS *Brooklyn*, from the first to the thirty-first day of May 1904 inclusive," Geographical Files, Morocco Folder, USMC Historical Center, Washington Navy Yard [henceforth Morocco Folder, USMC].

64. Ellsworth, *One Hundred Eighty Landings of U.S. Marines*, 8.

65. Hourihan, "Roosevelt and the Sultans," 85.

66. Chadwick to Secretary of the Navy, 4 June 1904, FECC.

67. Chadwick to Secretary of the Navy, 9 June 1904, NARA, RG 45, Translations of Messages Received in Cipher, vol. 2 of 6, p. 459.

68. Tuchman, "Perdicaris Alive or Raisuli Dead," 21; "Muster Roll of the U.S. Marines stationed onboard the USS *Brooklyn* from the first to the 13th day of June, 1904," Morocco Folder, USMC.

69. Hourihan, "Roosevelt and the Sultans," 105.

70. Chadwick to Secretary of the Navy, 4 June 1904, NARA, RG 45, Translations of Messages Received in Cipher, vol. 2 of 6, p. 453.

71. Hourihan, "Marlinspike Diplomacy," 46.

72. The others had been destroyed in Manila Bay and off Santiago, Cuba, during the 1898 war. H. W. Wilson, *The Downfall of Spain: A Naval History of the Spanish American War* (London: Low, Marston, 1900), 60.

73. Burke, *Prelude to Protectorate in Morocco*, 44.

74. Hourihan, "Roosevelt and the Sultans," 53.

75. Luella Hall, *The United States and Morocco, 1776–1956* (Metuchen, N.J.: Scarecrow, 1971), 381.

76. Thomas H. Etzold, "Protection or Politics?" *Historian* 37 (February 1975): 300.

77. Dorn Diary, 8 June 1904.

78. Hourihan, "Roosevelt and the Sultans," 66.

79. Chadwick to Secretary of the Navy, 6 June 1904, NARA, RG 45, Translations of Messages Received in Cipher, vol. 2 of 6.

80. *Papers Relating to the Foreign Relations of the United States, 1905* (Washington, D.C.: Government Printing Office, 1906), 499.

81. J. M. Macheod to Sir Arthur Nicholson, 2 June 1904, BNA, FO 174/265, "From Fez Consulate."

82. Chadwick to Secretary of the Navy, 8 June 1904, NARA, RG 45, Translations of Messages Received in Cipher, vol. 2 of 6, p. 458.

83. Dorn Diary, 7 June 1904.

84. *Papers Relating to the Foreign Relations of the United States, 1905*, 500.

85. Chadwick to Secretary of the Navy, 10 June 1904, NARA, RG 45, Translations of Messages Received in Cipher, vol. 2 of 6, p. 462.

86. Chadwick to Secretary of the Navy, 12 June 1904, FECC.

87. Gummeré to Hay, 15 June 1904, *Papers Relating to the Foreign Relations of the United States, 1905,* 500.

88. John Hay Diary, 15 June 1904, HPLOC, vols. 1 and 2.

89. Nicolson to Lansdowne, 15 June 1904, TNA FO 99/415, "General Correspondence, Morocco."

90. Chadwick to Secretary of the Navy, 16 June 1904, NARA, RG 45, Translations of Messages Received in Cipher, vol. 2 of 6, p. 465.

91. Etzold, "Protection or Politics?" 300.

92. Chadwick to Secretary of the Navy, 16 June 1904, FECC.

93. Gummeré to Hay, 15 June 1904, *Papers Relating to the Foreign Relations of the United States, 1905,* 501.

94. Hay to Roosevelt, 15 June 1904, HPLOC, vol. 5.

95. Roosevelt to Hay, 15 June 1904, TRLOC, microfiche reel 334, "Outgoing Correspondence."

96. Tuchman, "Perdicaris Alive or Raisuli Dead," 99.

97. Chadwick to Southerland, Morrell, and Dorn, 16 June 1904, FECC.

98. Ellsworth, *One Hundred Eighty Landings of U.S. Marines,* 8.

99. "Biography of Lieutenant General John T. Myers, USMC (Deceased)," Biographical Files, John T. Myers Folder, USMC Historical Center, Washington Navy Yard.

100. Hourihan, "Marlinspike Diplomacy," 47.

101. Gummeré to Hay, 17 June 1904, *Papers Relating to the Foreign Relations of the United States, 1905,* 501–502.

102. John Hay Diary, 18 June 1904, HPLOC, vols. 1 and 2.

103. Chadwick to Secretary of the Navy, 19 June 1904, NARA, RG 45, Translations of Messages Received in Cipher, vol. 2 of 6, p. 466.

104. Dorn Diary, 19 June 1904.

105. Gummeré to Hay, 20 June 1904, *Papers Relating to the Foreign Relations of the United States, 1905,* 502.

106. Ibid., 503–504.

107. Gummeré to Hay, 21 June 1904, Dispatches/Tangier.

108. Gummeré to Hay, 22 June 1904, *Papers Relating to the Foreign Relations of the United States, 1905,* 503.

109. Dorn Diary, 21 June 1904.

110. Ibid.

111. Ibid.

112. Ibid.

113. Chadwick to Secretary of the Navy, 22 June 1904, NARA, RG 45, Translations of Messages Received in Cipher, vol. 2 of 6, p. 467.

114. Larsen, "Theodore Roosevelt and the Moroccan Crisis," 64–65.

115. Morris, *Theodore Rex,* 334.

116. Hay to Gummeré, 22 June 1904, *Papers Relating to the Foreign Relations of the United States, 1905,* 503.

117. Ibid., 23 June 1904, 503–504.

118. Tuchman, "Perdicaris Alive or Raisuli Dead," 101.

119. John Hay Diary, 27 June 1904, HPLOC, vols. 1 and 2.

120. Woolman, "Did Theodore Roosevelt Overreact?" 79.

121. Etzold, "Protection or Politics?" 303.

122. Tuchman, "Perdicaris Alive or Raisuli Dead," 100.

123. Chadwick to Secretary of the Navy, 25 June 1904, FECC.

124. USS *Brooklyn* Cruising Report, Quarter ending 30 June 1904.

125. Darling to Chadwick, 24 June 1904, NARA, RG 45, Confidential Letters Sent September 1893–October 1908, vol. 4 of 6.

126. Chadwick to Secretary of the Navy, 25 June 1904, NARA, RG 45,

Translations of Messages Received in Cipher, vol. 2 of 6, p. 471.

127. Hourihan, "Marlinspike Diplomacy," 49.

128. Cogar, *Dictionary of Admirals*, 2:42.

129. Hay to Gummeré, 25 June 1904, *Papers Relating to the Foreign Relations of the United States, 1905*, 504.

130. Serge Ricard, "Roosevelt Style Personal Diplomacy," in *Artists of Power: Theodore Roosevelt, Woodrow Wilson, and Their Enduring Impact on U.S. Foreign Policy*, ed. William N. Tilchin and Charles E. Neu (Westport, Conn.: Greenwood Press, 2006), 17–22.

131. H. W. Brands, *T. R., the Last Romantic* (New York: Basic Books, 1997), 576–578.

132. Woolman, "Did Theodore Roosevelt Overreact?" 79.

133. Letter dated 25 June 1904, FECC.

134. Pennell, *Morocco since 1830*, 132–133.

135. Tuchman, "Perdicaris Alive or Raisuli Dead," 101.

136. John Hay Diary, 23 June 1904, HPLOC, vols. 1 and 2.

Chapter Five. The Unlikely Location: Making Peace at the Portsmouth Navy Yard

Epigraph from Roosevelt, *Autobiography*, 528. Portions of this chapter appeared previously in "An Unlikely Location," *Naval History Magazine* 19 (August 2005): 37–41; and " 'I am having my hair turn gray . . .': Roosevelt's Backchannel Diplomacy and the Salvaging of the Portsmouth Peace Treaty Negotiations," *Theodore Roosevelt Journal* 27, no. 1 (2005): 12– 14, 17– 20.

1. Morinosuke Kajima, *The Diplomacy of Japan* (Tokyo: Kajima Institute of International Peace, 1978), 2:201; Roosevelt to Kentaro Kaneko, 31 May 1905; Roosevelt to William Howard Taft, 31 May 1905, *TLTR*, 4:1198.

2. Kajima, *Diplomacy of Japan*, 180–183.

3. Pringle, *Theodore Roosevelt*, 196; Thayer, *Theodore Roosevelt*, 203.

4. Wagenknecht, *Seven Worlds of Theodore Roosevelt*, 267; Peter Randall, *There Are No Victors Here* (Portsmouth, N.H.: Portsmouth Marine Society, 2002), 54.

5. Volume 8 of Ian Nish's *The Russo-Japanese War, 1904–5* (London: Global Oriental, 2003) is a notable exception to this statement.

6. Roosevelt to Oscar Solomon, 9 February 1904, *TLTR*, 4:721.

7. Roosevelt to Theodore Roosevelt Jr., 10 February 1904, *TLTR*, 4:724.

8. Roosevelt to Cecil Spring Rice, 13 June 1904, *TLTR*, 4:831.

9. Roosevelt to George von Lengerke Meyer, 26 December 1904, *TLTR*, 4:1078.

10. Roosevelt to George Otto Trevelyan, 9 March 1905, *TLTR*, 4:1134.

11. Roosevelt to John Albert Tiffin Hull, 16 March 1905, *TLTR*, 4:1141.

12. Komura to Takahira, 31 May 1905, in Kajima, *Diplomacy of Japan*, 218–219.

13. Letters from Sir H. M. Durand to Lord Lansdowne, 2 and 5 June 1905, BNA, FO 115/1359.

14. Durand to Lansdowne, 8 June 1905, BNA, FO 115/1359.

15. Telegram from Ambassador Meyer to Secretary of State, 7 June 1905, TRLOC 1/55.

16. Telegram from State Department to Ambassador Meyer, 8 June 1905, *Papers Relating to the Foreign Relations of the United States, 1905*, 807.

17. Roosevelt to Oscar Strauss, 15 June 1905, TRLOC 2/338.

18. Ambassador Meyer to Roosevelt, 18 June 1905; Minister Griscom to Secretary of State, 18 June 1905, *Foreign Relations of the United States, 1905*, 811–812.

19. Letter received at White House from unknown writer, possibly Kaneko, 14 June 1905, TRLOC 1/55.
20. Roosevelt to Kogoro Takahira, 15 June 1905, *TLTR,* 4:1226.
21. Ibid.
22. Henry Cabot Lodge to Roosevelt, 24 October 1901, *SCTRHL,* 1:508.
23. *TLTR,* 4:3, 183.
24. Eugene P. Trani, "The Treaty of Portsmouth: An Adventure in Rooseveltian Diplomacy," Ph.D. diss., University of Indiana, Bloomington, 1966, 74–75.
25. Edward N. Pearson, Secretary of the State of New Hampshire, to Herbert H. D. Peirce, 3 July 1905, TRLOC, 1/55.
26. Kajima, *Diplomacy of Japan,* 235.
27. Randall, *There Are No Victors Here,* 11–12.
28. Statement made by the president to the Russian ambassador at the White House, 15 June 1905, TRLOC 2/338; Ambassador Meyer to Secretary of State, 20 June 1905, TRLOC 1/55.
29. Tatsuji Takeuchi, *War and Diplomacy in the Japanese Empire* (New York: Doubleday, 1935), 151.
30. Lansdowne to Durand, 22 June 1905, BNA, FO 115/1353.
31. Ibid., 24 June 1905, BNA, FO 115/1353.
32. Ibid., 1 July 1905, BNA, FO 115/1353.
33. Assistant Secretary of State William Loeb to Roosevelt, 13 July 1905, TRLOC 1/56.
34. Tyler Dennett, *Roosevelt and the Russo-Japanese War* (Glouster, Mass.: Peter Smith, 1959), 236.
35. J. J. Korostovetz, *Pre-war Diplomacy: The Russo-Japanese Problem* (London: British Periodicals, 1920), 11.
36. Cecil Spring Rice to Lansdowne, 24 May 1905, BNA, FO 115/1353.
37. T. H. Titherington, "The Great Peace Conference," *Munsey's Magazine* 33, no. 6 (1905): 642.
38. *Foreign Relations of the United States, 1905,* 808–809.
39. Ibid., 810.
40. Durand to Lansdowne, 14 June 1905, BNA, FO 115/1359; Kaneko to Assistant Secretary of State Loomis, 14 June 1905, TRLOC 1/58.
41. Dennett, *Roosevelt and the Russo-Japanese War,* 236.
42. Lansdowne to Durand, 20 June 1905, BNA, FO 115/1353.
43. Memorandum for the Japanese government, given by the president to Minister Takahira, 15 June 1905, TRLOC 2/338.
44. Assistant Secretary of State Rudolph Forster to Ambassador Takahira, 13 July 1905, TRPLOC 1/56.
45. Navy Department to Rear Adm. William W. Mead, 10 July 1905, Portsmouth Navy Yard General Correspondence, folder 127, National Archives Annex, Waltham, Mass. (NARA–WM), RG 181; Cogar, *Dictionary of Admirals,* 2:189–190.
46. Telegram, Mrs. John Hay to Roosevelt, 1 July 1905, TRLOC 1/55.
47. Jessup, *Elihu Root,* 454–455.
48. Charles Bonaparte to Roosevelt, 29 July 1905, TRLOC 1/57.
49. Navy Department to Mead, 10 July 1905, RG 181, Portsmouth Navy Yard General Correspondence, folder 127.
50. Korostovetz, *Pre-war Diplomacy,* 44.
51. Assistant Secretary of State Herbert Peirce to Roosevelt, 6 July 1905, TRLOC, 1/56.
52. Rear Adm. George Mead to Commandant George Elliott, 20 July 1905, RG 181, Portsmouth Navy Yard, Letters and Endorsements Sent to the

Commandant, USMC (1902–1911),
1:84.

53. Elliott to Mead, 24 July 1905, RG
181, Portsmouth Navy Yard, General
Correspondence, folder 127.

54. Mead to J. J. Haring, 1 August
1905, RG 181.3.10, Records of the
Portsmouth Navy Yard, Miscellaneous
Letters Sent (Press Copies) 1899–1907,
17:418.

55. Rear Adm. William Mead, Special
Order, 2 August 1905, RG 181,
Portsmouth Navy Yard, Orders,
Memorandums and Circulars issued
by Commandant, 1898–1911, p. 166.

56. Mead to Secretary of the Navy
Charles Bonaparte, 8 August 1905, RG
181, Portsmouth Navy Yard, General
Correspondence, folder 127, pp. 33–34.

57. E. B. Pillsbury to Mead, 28 July
1905, RG 181, Portsmouth Navy Yard,
Telegrams Sent, 1901–1911, 7:461.

58. Mead to Assistant Secretary of the
Navy Charles Darling, 10 August 1905,
RG 181, Portsmouth Navy Shipyard,
General Correspondence, folder 55,
pp. 264–265.

59. Trani, "The Treaty of Portsmouth,"
75–76.

60. Susan J. Douglass, "The Navy Adopts
Radio," in Military Enterprise and
Technological Change, ed. Merritt Roe
(Cambridge, Mass.: MIT Press, 1985),
133–151.

61. Christopher Andrew, For the
President's Eyes Only (New York:
Harper Collins, 1995), 25–29.

62. Secretary of the Navy to Mead, 26
July 1905, Portsmouth Navy Yard,
folder 127, General Correspondence,
p. 17.

63. Mead to C. F. Ames, 4 August 1905,
Portsmouth Navy Yard, folder 127,
General Correspondence.

64. Mead to Chief of Navigation Bureau,
24 July 1905, RG 181, Portsmouth Navy
Yard, General Correspondence, folder
127; Mead to Bureau of Equipment
and Recruiting, 4 August 1905, RG 181,
Portsmouth Navy Yard, Letters Sent to
Bureau of Equipment and Recruiting
(1862–1910), 12:336.

65. Mead to Chief of the Bureau of
Navigation, 29 July 1905, RG 181,
Portsmouth Navy Yard, General
Correspondence, folder 127, p. 40.

66. Mead to Rear Adm. Henry Manney,
29 July 1905, RG 181, Portsmouth Navy
Yard, Commandants' Letter Books
(1891–1909), 2:190.

67. Bureau of Navigation to Mead, 31 July
1905, RG 181, Portsmouth Navy Yard,
General Correspondence (1900–1911),
folder 127.

68. Peirce to William Loeb, 22 July 1905,
TRLOC 1/57.

69. Peirce to Roosevelt, 6 July 1905,
TRPLOC 1/56.

70. Peirce to Benjamin F. Barnes, 1 August
1905, TRLOC 1/57.

71. Kajima, Diplomacy of Japan, 237;
Korostovetz, Pre-war Diplomacy, 31–32.

72. Kaneko Dan to Bei Daitoryo to
no Kaiken shimatsu, Kaneko reel
MT 804, Japanese Foreign Ministry
Archives; Korostovetz, Pre war
Diplomacy, 31.

73. Peirce to Barnes, 29 July 1905, TRLOC
1/57.

74. In Roosevelt's defense, Witte thought
nearly everyone in America was crass;
see Serge I. Witte, "Memoirs: My Visit
to America," World's Work (March
1921): 487, TRC.

75. Raymond A. Esthus, Double Eagle and
the Rising Sun (Durham, N.C.: Duke
University Press, 1988), 76.

76. Witte, "Memoirs," 488–489.

77. Korostovetz, *Pre-war Diplomacy,* 36.

78. Roman Rosen, *Forty Years of Diplomacy* (New York: Alfred A. Knopf, 1922), 1:265.

79. Korostovetz, *Pre-war Diplomacy,* 37.

80. Esthus, *Double Eagle and the Rising Sun,* 77.

81. RG 181, Portsmouth Navy Yard, General Correspondence, folder 93, Special Order, 4 August 1905.

82. Mead to Manney, RG 181, Portsmouth Navy Yard, Letters Sent to Bureau of Equipment and Recruiting (1862–1910), 12:339.

83. Korostovetz, *Pre-war Diplomacy,* 45.

84. Dennett, *Roosevelt and the Russo-Japanese War,* 244; Kajima, *Diplomacy of Japan,* 240–241.

85. Peirce to Roosevelt, 9 August 1905, TRLOC 1/58.

86. Imperial Japanese Cabinet decision of 21 April 1905, sanctioned by the emperor; Kajima, *Diplomacy of Japan,* 232.

87. Durand to Lansdowne, 5 June 1905, BNA, FO 115/1359.

88. Ibid., 2 June 1905.

89. Secret memorandum of Mr. O'Beirne, circa 5 June 1905, BNA, FO 115/1359.

90. Lansdowne to Durand, 13 June 1905, BNA, FO 115/1353; Durand to Lansdowne, 4 August 1905, BNA, FO 115/1360.

91. Kajima, *Diplomacy of Japan,* 240.

92. Korostovetz, *Pre-war Diplomacy,* 51.

93. Oliver Warner, *Great Sea Battles* (New York: Macmillan, 1963), 244–248.

94. Dennett, *Roosevelt and the Russo-Japanese War,* 231–232.

95. Korostovetz, *Pre-war Diplomacy,* 53.

96. Kajima, *Diplomacy of Japan,* 248, 253–254.

97. Trani, "The Treaty of Portsmouth," 155.

98. Korostovetz, *Pre-war Diplomacy,* 54–56.

99. Ibid., 66.

100. Ibid., 60.

101. John C. O'Laughlin to Roosevelt, 13 August 1905, TRLOC, 1/58.

102. O'Laughlin to Roosevelt, 14 August 1905, TRLOC, 1/58.

103. Witte, "Memoirs," 494.

104. Kajima, *Diplomacy of Japan,* 210–212, 214, 219–221.

105. Mead to Commanding Officers, USS *Mayflower* and USS *Dolphin,* 17 August 1905, RG 181, Portsmouth Navy Yard, folder 127, General Correspondence (1900–1911).

106. Kajima, *Diplomacy of Japan,* 321.

107. Oscar S. Straus to Roosevelt, 15 August 1905, TRLOC 1/58.

108. Roosevelt to Hermann Von Sternberg, 21 August 1905; Roosevelt to Jean Jusserand, 21 August 1905; Roosevelt to Kaneko, 22 August 1905, *TLTR,* 4:1306–1308.

109. Randall, *There Are No Victors Here,* 51.

110. Rosen, *Forty Years of Diplomacy,* 2:269–271.

111. Kajima, *Diplomacy of Japan,* 330–331.

112. Witte to Roosevelt, 22 August 1905, TRLOC 1/58.

113. Roosevelt to Von Sternberg, 21 August 1905, *TLTR,* 4:1306–1307.

114. Kajima, *Diplomacy of Japan,* 322.

115. Rudolph Forester to B. F. Barnes, 23 August 1905, TRLOC 1/58.

116. O'Laughlin to Roosevelt, 23 August 1905, TRLOC 1/58.

117. Forester to Barnes, 24 August 1905, TRLOC 1/58.

118. Kajima, *Diplomacy of Japan,* 336.

119. Roosevelt to Kaneko, 23 August 1905, *TLTR,* 4:1312–1313.

120. Durand to Lansdowne, 24 August 1905, BNA, FO 115/1360.

121. Kaneko to Roosevelt, 27 August 1905, TRLOC 1/58.

122. O'Laughlin to Roosevelt, 27 August 1905, TRLOC 1/58.

123. Kajima, *Diplomacy of Japan,* 345.

124. Meyer to Roosevelt, 28 August 1905, TRLOC 1/58.

125. Kaneko to Roosevelt, 27 August 1905; Komura to Roosevelt, 28 August 1905, TRLOC 1/58.

126. Memorandum, Oyster Bay, 27 August 1905, TRLOC 1/58.

127. Peirce to Barnes, 28 August 1905, TRLOC 1/58.

128. Kajima, *Diplomacy of Japan,* 350.

129. Peirce to Roosevelt, 27 August 1905, TRLOC 1/58.

130. Kaneko to Roosevelt, 29 August 1905, TRLOC 1/58.

131. Peirce to Roosevelt, 29 August 1905, 11:25 AM, TRLOC 1/58.

132. Ibid., 1:20 PM, TRLOC 1/58.

133. Ibid., 5:40 PM, TRLOC 1/58.

134. Kaneko to Roosevelt, 29 August 1905, TRLOC 1/58.

135. Randall, *There Are No Victors Here,* 54–55.

136. Gunnar Knudsen, Presentation Speech, Nobel Peace Prize 1906, http://nobelprize.org/peace/laureates/1906/press.html.

137. *TLTR,* 4:1163.

138. Roosevelt to Clara Hay, 1 July 1905, *TLTR,* 3:1258.

139. Jessup, *Elihu Root,* 454.

140. *TLTR,* vol. 4, 1299–1301.

141. Roosevelt to Hermann Von Sternberg, 21 August 1905; Roosevelt to Jean Jules Jusserand, 21 August 1905; Roosevelt to Kaneko, 22 August 1905; Roosevelt to Peirce, 23 August 1905; Roosevelt to Kaneko, 23 August 1905, *TLTR,* 4:1306–1312.

Chapter Six. T. R., Technology, and Transformation

Epigraph, Roosevelt to Sims, 5 October 1904, *TLTR,* 4:973.

1. Matthew M. Oyos, "Theodore Roosevelt and the Implements of War," *Journal of Military History* 60, no. 4 (1996): 633.

2. William H. Thiesen, *Industrializing American Shipbuilding: The Transformation of Ship Design and Construction, 1820–1920* (Gainesville: University Press of Florida, 2006), 26–43.

3. Zimmermann, *First Great Triumph,* 85–122, 171–184, 215–229.

4. Wimmel, *Theodore Roosevelt and the Great White Fleet,* 4–5.

5. Beach, *The United States Navy,* 321–322; Thiesen, *Industrializing American Shipbuilding,* 153–156.

6. Zimmermann, *First Great Triumph,* 94.

7. Norman Friedman, *U.S. Battleships: An Illustrated Design History* (Annapolis: Naval Institute Press, 1985), 418.

8. Sprout and Sprout, *The Rise of American Naval Power,* 190.

9. George W. Baer, *The U.S. Navy, 1890–1990: One Hundred Years of Sea Power* (Stanford: Stanford University Press, 1993), 18–19.

10. Walter LaFeber, *The New Empire: An Interpretation of American Expansion, 1860–1898* (Ithaca, N.Y.: Cornell University Press, 1963), 124–126.

11. Friedman, *U.S. Battleships,* 425.

12. Ibid., 24–26.

13. Baer, *The U.S. Navy, 1890–1990,* 21–22.

14. Wimmel, *Theodore Roosevelt and the Great White Fleet,* 77.

15. William S. Sims, "Roosevelt and the Navy, part 2," *McClure's Magazine,* 54, no. 10 (1922): 56.

16. William S. Sims, "Roosevelt and the Navy, part 1," *McClure's Magazine*, 54, no. 9 (1922): 41. Sims cited his earlier correspondence with Roosevelt throughout these postmortem salutes to his former commander in chief.

17. Gordon Carpenter O'Gara, *Theodore Roosevelt and the Rise of the Modern Navy* (Princeton: Princeton University Press, 1943), 41.

18. Roosevelt to Capt. Hendry McCalla, 19 April 1897, *TLTR*, 1:599.

19. Roosevelt to McKinley, 26 April 1897, *TLTR*, 1:602–603.

20. Roosevelt to Mahan, 3 May 1897, *TLTR*, 1:608.

21. *Messages and Papers of the Presidents*, 13:6268–6269.

22. Roosevelt to Richard Henry Dana, 8 May 1897, *TLTR*, 1:609–610.

23. Ibid., 21 May 1897, *TLTR*, 1:616–617.

24. Roosevelt to Lodge, 11 September 1897, *TLTR*, 1:672–673.

25. Roosevelt to William Bigelow, 29 October 1897, *TLTR*, 1:702.

26. Morison, *Admiral Sims and the Modern American Navy.*

27. Friedman, *U.S. Battleships*, 44.

28. Morison, *Admiral Sims and the Modern American Navy*, 84–85.

29. Roosevelt to Cowles, 12 December 1901, *TLTR*, 3:206–207.

30. Brayton Harris, *The Age of the Battleship* (New York: Franklin Watts, 1965), 122–123.

31. Roosevelt to Sims, 27 December 1901, *TLTR*, 3:212.

32. Roosevelt to Rear Adm. Henry Taylor, 18 December 1901, *TLTR*, 3:212.

33. Ibid., 22 April 1902, *TLTR*, 3:253–254.

34. Harris, *The Age of the Battleship*, 122–123.

35. Roosevelt to William H. Moody, 4 August 1902, *TLTR*, 3:308.

36. Ibid., 13 May 1903, *TLTR*, 3:475.

37. Roosevelt to Albert Gleaves, 7 August 1902, *TLTR*, 3:310–311.

38. Roosevelt to Charles Darling, 14 March 1903, *TLTR*, 3:446.

39. Roosevelt to Taylor, 15 September 1903, *TLTR*, 3:601.

40. Ibid., 2 October 1903, *TLTR*, 3:609.

41. Roosevelt to Lawrence Abbott, 14 March 1904; Roosevelt to Moody, 1 April 1904, *TLTR*, 4:751–752, 766.

42. Roosevelt to Moody, 10 May 1904, *TLTR*, 4:793.

43. Friedman, *U.S. Battleships*, 52.

44. Wimmel, *Theodore Roosevelt and the Great White Fleet*, 180.

45. Homer C. Poundstone, "Size of Battleships for U.S. Navy," *U.S. Naval Institute Proceedings* 29, no. 1 (1903): 169–174.

46. Homer C. Poundstone, "Proposed Armament for Type Battleship of U.S. Navy, with Some Suggestions Relative to Armor Protection," *U.S. Naval Institute Proceedings* 29, no. 2 (1903): 404–407.

47. O'Gara, *Theodore Roosevelt and the Rise of the Modern Navy*, 65.

48. George T. Davis, *A Navy Second to None* (New York: Harcourt, Brace, 1940), 165–166.

49. Wimmel, *Theodore Roosevelt and the Great White Fleet*, 176.

50. Beach, *The United States Navy*, 405; Puleston, *Mahan*, 273–274.

51. Wimmel, *Theodore Roosevelt and the Great White Fleet*, 191.

52. Sims to Roosevelt, 6 October 1904, NARA, RG 80, file 18711.

53. Roosevelt to Secretary of the Navy Paul Morton, 6 October 1904, *TLTR*, 4:974.

54. Note, *TLTR*, 4:973.

55. Friedman, *U.S. Battleships*, 52–55.

56. Wimmel, *Theodore Roosevelt and the Great White Fleet*, 181–182.
57. Note, *TLTR*, 3:441.
58. *Messages and Papers of the Presidents*, 15:692.
59. Wimmel, *Theodore Roosevelt and the Great White Fleet*, 188–189.
60. Friedman, *U.S. Battleships*, 55–63.
61. Roosevelt to Maj. Gen. Leonard Wood, 9 March 1905, *TLTR*, 4:1136.
62. E. B. Potter and Chester Nimitz, eds., *Sea Power: A Naval History* (Englewood Cliffs, N.J.: Prentice-Hall, 1960), 356–360.
63. S. S. Robison and Mary Robison, *A History of Naval Tactics from 1530 to 1930* (Annapolis: Naval Institute Press, 1942), 788–794.
64. Julian S. Corbett, *Some Principles of Maritime Strategy* (Annapolis: Naval Institute Press, 1988), 38.
65. Roosevelt to George Converse, 10 September 1906, *TLTR*, 5:403.
66. Roosevelt to Sims, 27 September 1906, *TLTR*, 5:427.
67. Stephen Howarth, *To Shining Sea: A History of the United States Navy 1775–1998* (Norman: University of Oklahoma Press, 1991), 284.
68. Roosevelt to Paul Morton, 20 February 1905, *TLTR*, 4:1123.
69. Wimmel, *Theodore Roosevelt and the Great White Fleet*, 186.
70. Jon T. Sumida, *In Defence of Naval Supremacy: Finance, Technology, and British Naval Policy, 1889–1914* (Boston: Unwin Hyman, 1989), 26–27; Nicolas Lambert, *Sir John Fisher's Naval Revolution* (Columbia: University of South Carolina Press, 1999), 7–10.
71. Sumida, *In Defence of Naval Supremacy*, 37–42.
72. Sims, "Roosevelt and the Navy, part 1," 62.
73. Roosevelt to Sims, 13 October 1906, *TLTR*, 5:455.
74. Robert K. Massie, *Dreadnought* (New York: Random House, 1991), 485–486.
75. *Messages and Papers of the Presidents*, 15:7001–7002.
76. Sprout, and Sprout, *The Rise of American Naval Power*, 262.
77. O'Gara, *Theodore Roosevelt and the Rise of the Modern Navy*, 67.
78. Roosevelt to George Edmund Foss, 11 January 1907, *TLTR*, 5:545–549.
79. Sims, "Theodore Roosevelt at Work," 66.
80. Morison, *Admiral Sims and the Modern American Navy*, 201.
81. Friedman, *U.S. Battleships*, 69.
82. *Messages and Papers of the Presidents*, 15:7114.
83. Sprout and Sprout, *The Rise of American Naval Power*, 265.
84. *Messages and Papers of the Presidents*, 15:7147–7148.
85. William R. Braisted, *United States Navy in the Pacific, 1909–1922* (Annapolis: U.S. Naval Institute, 1971), 212–213.
86. O'Gara, *Theodore Roosevelt and the Rise of the Modern Navy*, 68.
87. Henry Reuterdahl, "The Needs of Our Navy," *McClure's Magazine*, 30, no. 3 (1908): 251–263.
88. Morison, *Admiral Sims and the Modern American Navy*, 183.
89. Sims, "Roosevelt at Work," 97.
90. Morison, *Admiral Sims and the Modern American Navy*, 203.
91. Oyos, "Theodore Roosevelt and the Implements of War," 651.
92. Roosevelt to Secretary of the Navy Metcalf, 2 January 1908, *TLTR*, 6:891.
93. James R. Reckner, *Teddy Roosevelt's Great White Fleet* (Annapolis: Naval Institute Press, 1988), 128–129.
94. Roosevelt to Truman Newberry, 10 August 1908, *TLTR*, 6:1165–1166.

95. Sims, "Theodore Roosevelt at Work," 99–100.

96. Roosevelt to Newberry, 28 August 1908, *TLTR,* 6:1199.

97. Ibid., 25 November 1908, *TLTR,* 6:1379–130. Phillip R. Alger, ballistics expert and member of the Board of Naval Ordnance, had led those at the Newport conference opposed to placing 14-inch guns on the *Utah* and *Florida.*

98. Roosevelt to Newberry, 15 September 1908, *TLTR,* 6:1237.

99. Roosevelt to Cdr. Albert Key, 8 January 1909, *TLTR,* 6:1469–1470; Friedman, *U.S. Battleships,* 435–436.

100. Oyos, "Theodore Roosevelt and the Implements of War," 634.

101. Roosevelt to Anna Roosevelt, 31 December 1893, *TLTR,* 1:344.

102. Roosevelt to Long, 25 March 1898, *TLTR,* 1:799.

103. Oyos, "Theodore Roosevelt and the Implements of War," 640.

104. Erik J. Dahl, "Net-centric before Its Time: The Jeune Ecole and Its Lessons for Today," *Naval War College Review* 58 (2005): 109–135; Roosevelt to Long, 9 August 1897, 13 August 1897, *TLTR,* 1:642–643, 649–650.

105. Roosevelt to Lodge, 17 August 1897, *TLTR,* 1:654.

106. Oyos, "Theodore Roosevelt and the Implements of War," 634.

107. *Messages and Papers of the Presidents,* 15:692; Roosevelt to Secretary of the Navy Charles Bonaparte, 20 December 1905, *TLTR,* 5:120.

108. Roosevelt to George E. Foss, 11 January 1907, *TLTR,* 5:545–549.

109. Norman Friedman, *U.S. Destroyers,* rev. ed. (Annapolis: Naval Institute Press, 2004), 14–25, 488–489.

110. Morris, *Theodore Rex,* 413.

111. Roosevelt to Kermit Roosevelt, 25 August 1905, *TLTR,* 4:1316.

112. Roosevelt to Bonaparte, 28 August 1905, *TLTR,* 4:1323–1325.

113. Roosevelt to George Ross, 11 January 1907, *TLTR,* 5:545–549; Harris, *The Age of the Battleship,* 114.

114. Oyos, "Theodore Roosevelt and the Implements of War," 640–641.

115. Roosevelt to Augustus Post, 27 July 1917, *TLTR,* 8:1213–1214.

116. *TLTR,* 8:1495.

117. William S. Sims, notation on correspondence file, 1905, Sims Papers, box 96, folder 4, Library of Congress.

118. Oyos, "Theodore Roosevelt and the Implements of War," 645.

119. Roosevelt to Bonaparte, 20 December 1905, *TLTR,* 5:120.

120. Oyos, "Theodore Roosevelt and the Implements of War," 634.

121. Arthur M. Johnson, "Theodore Roosevelt and the Navy," *U.S. Naval Institute Proceedings* 84, no. 10 (1958): 76; Oyos, "Theodore Roosevelt and the Implements of War," 635.

Chapter Seven. The Great White Fleet and the Birth of the American Century

Epigraph, Roosevelt to William H. Taft, 3 March 1909, *TLTR,* 6:1543.

1. Frank Uhlig Jr., "The Great White Fleet," *American Heritage* 15, no. 2 (1964): 30–43, 103–106.

2. Reckner, *Teddy Roosevelt's Great White Fleet,* 24.

3. Ibid., 26–27.

4. Tilchin, *Theodore Roosevelt and the British Empire,* 117–127.

5. Wimmel, *Theodore Roosevelt and the Great White Fleet,* 225.

6. "The Voyage of the Fleet," *Army and Navy Register,* 25 January 1908.

7. *Annual Reports of the Navy Department, 1908*, 331.

8. Zimmermann, *First Great Triumph*, 5.

9. *Papers Relating to the Foreign Relations of the United States, 1908*, 58–59.

10. James R. Holmes, *Theodore Roosevelt and World Order* (Washington, D.C.: Potomac Books, 2007), 190–191.

11. Braisted, *U.S. Navy in the Pacific*, 228.

12. Reckner, *Teddy Roosevelt's Great White Fleet*, 51–52.

13. Wimmel, *Theodore Roosevelt and the Great White Fleet*, 230.

14. Roosevelt to Senator Frances Warren, 18 April 1908, *TLTR*, 6:1011.

15. "Big Stick Afloat," *New York Times*, 21 August 1908.

16. "The British Race Issue," *New York Times*, 23 September 1908; "London, August 22, the Daily Telegraph," reported in *New York Times*, 22 August 1908.

17. "American Fleet Reaches Auckland," *New York Times*, 9 August 1908; "500,000 Welcome Fleet at Sydney," *New York Times*, 20 August 1908.

18. "Talk of an Alliance," *New York Times*, 16 August 1908.

19. "Flotilla for Australia," *New York Times*, 25 September 1908.

20. "Japan Prepares Welcome for Fleet," *New York Times*, 5 April 1908.

21. "Count Okuma Stirs Americans in Japan," *New York Times*, 15 August 1908.

22. "Japan's Reception Plans," *New York Times*, 5 September 1908.

23. "Yokohama Greets America's Fleet," *New York Times*, 18 October 1908.

24. Arthur Dudden, "Japan," in *Encyclopedia of U.S. Foreign Relations*, ed. Bruce Jentleson and Thomas Paterson (New York: Oxford University Press, 1997), 450–451.

25. Braisted, *U.S. Navy in the Pacific*, 231.

26. Ruhl J. Bartlett, *The Record of American Diplomacy* (New York: Alfred A. Knopf, 1964), 414.

27. "China Humiliated; Only Half a Fleet," *New York Times*, 5 November 1908.

28. Reckner, *Teddy Roosevelt's Great White Fleet*, 144–145.

29. "Atlantic Fleet Is Now at Suez," *New York Times*, 4 January 1909.

30. "Yankton Off for Messina," *New York Times*, 6 January 1909.

31. Roosevelt to Douglass and Corinne Robinson, 21 February 1909, *TLTR*, 6:1533.

32. Wimmel, *Theodore Roosevelt and the Great White Fleet*, 243.

33. Reckner, *Teddy Roosevelt's Great White Fleet*, 154–155.

34. Roosevelt to Secretary of the Navy Newberry, 16 February 1909, *TLTR*, 6:1524.

35. Roosevelt to Capt. Cameron Winslow, 16 February 1909, *TLTR*, 6:1523.

36. Roosevelt to Rear Adm. Charles Sperry, 5 December 1908, *TLTR*, 6:1411.

37. Uhlig, "The Great White Fleet."

38. Wimmel, *Theodore Roosevelt and the Great White Fleet*, 243–244.

39. Roosevelt to William H. Taft, 3 March 1909, *TLTR*, 6:1543.

40. "Caribbean Sea and Western Atlantic: Strategic Conditions in Event of War with the United States."

41. Alexander George and William Simons, *The Limits of Coercive Diplomacy* (San Francisco: Westview Press, 1994), 7–16. For a description of the use of naval forces to influence foreign policy, see Ken Booth, *Navies and Foreign Policy* (New York: Holmes and Miers, 1979), 85–109.

Bibliography

Primary Source Materials

ARCHIVAL SOURCES

British National Archives, Kew Gardens, U.K.

Admiralty Group

Folder 1, series 8875. Caribbean Sea and Western Atlantic: Strategic Conditions in Event of War with the United States.

Foreign Office Group

Folder 99, series 415. General Correspondance, Morocco.

Folder 115, series 1241 and 1353. From Foreign Office.

Folder 115, series 1244. To Foreign Office.

Folder 115, series 1359 and 1360. Washington, D.C., Embassy to Foreign Office.

Folder 174, series 265. From Fez Consulate.

U.S. National Archives

Record Group 45, Naval Records Collection

Bureau of Navigation, 1813–1911. Cruising Reports of Vessels of the United States Navy, January 1895–June 1910. Vol. 8 of 14.

Office of the Secretary of the Navy. General Records. Translations of Messages Received in Cipher May 1899–25 December 1904. Vol. 2 of 6.

Office of the Secretary of the Navy. General Records 1798–1910. Confidential Letters Sent September 1893–October 1908. Vols. 3 and 4 of 6.

Office of the Secretary of the Navy. General Records. Translations of Messages Sent in Cipher, 1 June 1898–16 September 1906. Vol. 4 of 10.

U.S. Navy Subject Files, 1775–1910. Box 473, Operations North Atlantic Squadron, Microfiche section M625, roll 264. Box 671, folder VI, Venezuela Situation.

U.S. Navy Subject File VI. International Relations and Politics.
Box 666, folder 4, Correspondence related to Morocco.

Area Files of the Naval Records Collection. Geographical Area 4,
1903–1905.

Record Group 59. General Records of the Department of State. Dispatches
from U.S. Consuls in Tangier, 1797–1906.

Record Group 127. U.S. Marines Overseas Brigades, Battalions, Regiments,
Panama. Box 4.

Record Group 181. National Archives Annex, Waltham, Massachusetts.
Folder 55. Portsmouth Navy Yard to the Secretary of the Navy.
Folder 93. Special Orders.
Folder 127. Portsmouth Navy Yard General Correspondence,
1900–1911.
Commandants' Letter Books (1891–1909). Vol. 2.
Letters Sent (Press Copies) (1899–1907). Vol. 17.
Orders, Memoranda, and Circulars Issued by Commandant,
1898–1911.
Letters and Endorsements Sent to the Commandant, USMC
(1902–1911). Vol. 1.
Letters Sent to Bureau of Equipment and Recruiting 1862–1910.
Vol. 12.
Portsmouth Navy Yard. Telegrams Sent, 1901–1911. Vol. 7.
Area File of Naval Collections, 1775–1910. Microfiche M625.
Roll 261, Area 8, December 1902–January 1903. Roll 264,
Area 8, December 1904–January 1905.

PRIVATE CORRESPONDENCE, DIARIES, AND MEMORANDA

Manuscripts Division, Library of Congress, Washington, D.C.
George Dewey Collection.
Edward J. Dorn Collection.
John Hay Collection.
Stephen Luce Collection.
William H. Moody Collection.
Theodore Roosevelt Collection.
William S. Sims Collection.
Leonard Wood Collection.

Operational Archives, Naval Historical Center, Washington Navy Yard,
      Washington, D.C.
      Admiral French E. Chadwick Papers.
      Admiral of the Navy George Dewey Papers.
U.S. Marine Corps Historical Center, Washington Navy Yard, Washington,
      D.C.
      Biographical Files
            Biography of Major General Commandant George F.
            Elliot, USMC (deceased).
            Biography of Lieutenant General John T. Myers, USMC
               (deceased).
            Biography of Colonel Percival Clarence Pope, USMC
               (deceased).
      Geographical Files, Morocco Folder
            Muster Roll of Officers, Noncommissioned Officers,
            Drummers, Trumpeters, and Privates of the U.S. Marine
            Corps stationed onboard USS *Brooklyn* from the first to
            the thirty-first day of May 1904 inclusive.
            Muster Roll of the U.S. Marines stationed onboard the
            USS *Brooklyn* from the first to the 13th day of June 1904.
      Geographical Files, Panama Folder
            American Intervention Folder.
      Geographical Files, Puerto Rico Folder
            Puerto Rico, Study of Theater Operations.
Diplomatic History of the Panama Canal. Washington, D.C.: Government
      Printing Office, 1914.
Du Val, Lt. Cdr. Miles. "The Canal Zone." Unpublished manuscript dated
            1937. Navy Library, Naval Historical Center, Washington Navy Yard.
Humphrey, Capt. Chauncey B. "History of the Revolution of Panama."
      Unpublished manuscript dated 1923. Author's private collection.

OFFICIAL DOCUMENTS AND OTHER GOVERNMENT PUBLICATIONS

Annual Reports of the Navy Department, 1902. Washington D.C.: Government
      Printing Office, 1902.
Annual Reports of the Navy Department, 1903. Washington D.C.: Government
      Printing Office, 1903.

Annual Reports of the Navy Department, 1904. Washington D.C.: Government
  Printing Office, 1904.
A Compilation of the Messages and Papers of the Presidents. 20 vols. Ed. James D.
  Richardson. New York: Bureau of National Literature and Art, 1920.
England, Gordon, Vernon Clark, and James Jones. *Naval Power 21 . . . a
  Naval Vision.* Department of the Navy White Paper, October 2002.
National Military Strategy of the United States of America, 2004. Washington,
  D.C.: Government Printing Office, 2004.
Papers Relating to the Foreign Affairs of the United States, 1903. Washington,
  D.C.: Government Printing Office, 1904.
Papers Relating to the Foreign Affairs of the United States, 1905. Washington,
  D.C.: Government Printing Office, 1906.
Papers Relating to the Foreign Affairs of the United States, 1907. Washington,
  D.C.: Government Printing Office, 1908

PUBLISHED PRIMARY SOURCES

Adams, Henry. *The Education of Henry Adams.* New York: Random House, 1931.
Barker, Albert S. *Everyday Life in the Navy.* Boston: Gotham Press, 1932.
Bowen, Herbert W. *Recollections Diplomatic and Undiplomatic.* New York:
  Grafton Press, 1926.
Bulloch, James D. *The Secret Service of the Confederate States in Europe.*
  London: Bentley and Son, 1883.
Bunau-Varilla, Philippe. *The Great Adventure of Panama.* New York:
  Doubleday, 1920.
———. *Panama: The Creation, Destruction and Resurrection.* New York:
  McBride, Nast, 1914.
Dennis, Alfred P. *Adventures in American Diplomacy, 1896–1906.* New York:
  E. P. Dutton, 1928.
Dewey, George. *Autobiography of George Dewey.* Annapolis: Naval Institute
  Press, 1987.
Ellsworth, Capt. Harry A. *One Hundred Eighty Landings of United States
  Marines 1800–1934.* Washington, D.C.: Government Printing
  Office, 1974.
Gleaves, Albert. *The Admiral.* Pasadena, Calif.: Hope Publishing, 1985.
Iriye, Akira. *Pacific Estrangement: Japanese and American Expansion, 1897–
  1911.* Cambridge, Mass.: Harvard University Press, 1972.

Korostovetz, J. J. *Pre-war Diplomacy: The Russo-Japanese Problem.* London: British Periodicals, 1920.

Lejeune, John A. *The Reminiscences of a Marine.* Philadelphia: Dorrance, 1930.

Lodge, Henry Cabot, and Theodore Roosevelt. *Selections from the Correspondence of Theodore Roosevelt and Henry Cabot Lodge.* New York: Scribner's, 1925.

Long, John. *The Journal of John D. Long.* Ed. Margaret Long. Ringe, N.H.: Richard R. Smith, 1956.

Roosevelt, Theodore. *American Ideals and Other Essays, Social and Political.* New York: Scribner's, 1906.

———. *Fear God and Take Your Own Part.* New York: George H. Doran, 1916.

———. *The Letters of Theodore Roosevelt.* 8 vols. Ed. Elting E. Morison. Cambridge, Mass.: Harvard University Press, 1951–1954.

———. *Theodore Roosevelt, an Autobiography.* Vol. 20 of *The Works of Theodore Roosevelt,* National Edition. New York: Scribner's, 1926.

Secondary Sources

Adams, Iestyn. *Brothers across the Ocean: British Foreign Policy and the Origins of the Anglo-American "Special Relationship" 1900–1905.* London: Tauris Academic Studies, 2005.

Adams, Randolph Greenfield. *History of the Foreign Relations of the United States.* New York: Macmillan, 1925.

Andrew, Christopher M. *For the President's Eyes Only.* New York: Harper Collins, 1995.

"Arbitration of the Venezuela Case." *Gunton's Magazine* (February 1903): 175–176. Theodore Roosevelt Collection, Harvard University.

"Armed or Unarmed Peace." *Harper's Weekly,* 19 June 1897, 603.

Baer, George W. *One Hundred Years of Sea Power: The U.S. Navy, 1890–1990.* Stanford, Calif.: Stanford University Press, 1993.

Bailey, Thomas A. "Dewey and the Germans at Manila Bay." *American Historical Review* 45, no. 1 (1939): 63–70.

Barnett, Thomas P. M. *The Pentagon's New Map.* New York: G. P. Putnam's Sons, 2004.

Bartlett, Ruhl J., ed. *The Record of American Democracy.* New York: Alfred A. Knopf, 1964.

Beach, Edward L., Jr. *The United States Navy.* New York: Henry Holt, 1986.

Beale, Howard K. *Theodore Roosevelt and the Rise of America to World Power.* Baltimore, Md.: Johns Hopkins University Press, 1956.

Blind, Karl. "The Transvaal War and European Opinion." In *Briton and Boer: Both Sides of the South African Question*, 133–163. New York: Harper and Brothers, 1900.

Booth, Ken. *Navies and Foreign Policy.* New York: Holmes and Miers, 1979.

Brands, H. W. *T. R., the Last Romantic.* New York: Basic Books, 1997.

Bratton, Patrick C. "When Is Coercion Successful?" *Naval War College Review* 58, no. 3 (2005): 99–115.

Brebner, John B. *The North Atlantic Triangle.* New Haven, Conn.: Yale University Press, 1945.

Bryce, James, Sydney Brooks, F. V. Engelenburg, Karl Blind, Andrew Carnegie, Francis C. Harmes, Demetrius Boulger, and Max S. Nordau. *Briton and Boer: Both Sides of the South African Question.* New York: Harper and Brothers, 1900.

Burke, Edmund III. *Prelude to Protectorate in Morocco.* Chicago: University of Chicago Press, 1976.

Cane, Guy. "Sea Power—Teddy's Big Stick." *U.S. Naval Institute Proceedings* 102, no. 8 (1976): 40–48.

Charmes, Frances. "Will the Powers Intervene?" In *Briton and Boer: Both Sides of the South African Question*, 177–197. New York: Harper and Brothers, 1900.

Chester, Colby M. "Diplomacy on the Quarter Deck." *American Journal of International Law* 8, no. 3 (1914): 443–476.

Cogar, William B. *Dictionary of Admirals of the U.S. Navy.* Vol. 2. Annapolis: Naval Institute Press, 1991.

Cohen, Eliot A. *Supreme Command.* New York: Free Press, 2002.

Collin, Richard H. "The Image of Theodore Roosevelt in American History and Thought 1885–1965." Ph.D. diss., New York University, 1966.

———. *Theodore Roosevelt, Culture, Diplomacy and Expansion: A New View of American Imperialism.* Baton Rouge: Louisiana State University Press, 1985.

———. *Theodore Roosevelt's Caribbean.* Baton Rouge: Louisiana State University Press, 1990.

Cooper, John M. *The Warrior and Priest: Woodrow Wilson and Theodore Roosevelt.* New York: Daedalus Books, 1983.

Corbett, Julian S. *Some Principles of Maritime Strategy.* Annapolis: Naval Institute Press, 1988.

Davis, George T. *A Navy Second to None.* New York: Harcourt, Brace, 1940.

Dennett, Tyler. *Roosevelt and the Russo-Japanese War.* Gloucester, Mass.: P. Smith, 1959.

Dennis, Alfred P. *Adventures in American Diplomacy, 1896–1906.* New York: E. P. Dutton, 1928.

Diplomat. "A Vindication of the Boers." In *Briton and Boer: Both Sides of the South African Question,* 133–163. New York: Harper and Brothers, 1900.

Douglass, Susan J. "The Navy Adopts Radio." In *Military Enterprise and Technological Change,* ed. Merritt Poe, 117–173. Cambridge, Mass.: MIT Press, 1985.

Dudden, Arthur P. *The American Pacific.* New York: Oxford University Press, 1992.

Dudley, William. "Naval Historians and the War of 1812." *Naval History* 4, no. 2 (1990): 54–55.

Esthus, Raymond A. *Double Eagle and the Rising Sun.* Durham, N.C.: Duke University Press, 1988.

———. *TR and the International Rivalries.* Waltham, Mass.: Ginn-Blaisdell, 1970.

Etzold, Thomas H. "Protection or Politics?" *Historian* 37 (February 1975): 300.

Ewell, Judith. *Venezuela: A Century of Change.* Stanford, Calif.: Stanford University Press, 1984.

Forbes, Rosita. *El Raisuli, the Sultan of the Mountains.* London: Thornton Butterworth, 1924.

Freeman, Charles W., Jr. *The Diplomat's Dictionary.* Washington, D.C.: Peace Institute, 1997.

Friedman, Norman. *U.S. Battleships: An Illustrated Design History.* Annapolis: Naval Institute Press, 1985.

———. *U.S. Destroyers.* Rev. ed. Annapolis: Naval Institute Press, 2004.

Gable, John A. *The Bull Moose Years: Theodore Roosevelt and the Progressive Party.* Port Washington, N.Y.: Kennikat Press, 1978.

Garrett, Wendell D. "John Davis Long, Secretary of the Navy, 1897–1902: A Study in Changing Political Alignments." *New England Quarterly* 31, no. 3 (1958): 291–311.

George, Alexander, and William Simons. *The Limits of Coercive Diplomacy.* San Francisco: Westview Press, 1994.

"The German Emperor and the Monroe Doctrine." *Harper's Weekly,* January 31, 1903, 187–188. Theodore Roosevelt Collection, Harvard University.

Gottschall, Terrell D. *By Order of the Kaiser.* Annapolis: Naval Institute Press, 2003.

Hall, Luella. *The United States and Morocco, 1776–1956.* Metuchen, N.J.: Scarecrow, 1971.

Hard, William. "How Roosevelt Kept the Peace." *Metropolitan Magazine,* May 1916,: 19–23. Theodore Roosevelt Collection, Harvard University.

Harris, Brayton. *The Age of the Battleship.* New York: Franklin Watts, 1965.

Haupt, Lewis M. "Why Is an Isthmian Canal Not Built?" *North American Review* 178 (1902): 3–11.

Heffron, Paul T. "Secretary Moody and Naval Administration Reform: 1902–1904." *American Neptune* 29 (January 1969): 31–35. Theodore Roosevelt Collection, Harvard University.

Hendrick, Burton J. "Historic Crises in American Diplomacy." *World's Work* (June 1916). Theodore Roosevelt Collection, Harvard University.

Herman, Donald L. "Democratic and Authoritarian Traditions." In *Democracy in Latin America: Colombia and Venezuela,* 1–15. New York: Praeger, 1988.

Herwig, Holger H. *Germany's Version of Empire in Venezuela.* Princeton, N.J.: Princeton University Press, 1986.

———. *Politics of Frustration: The United States in German Naval Planning, 1889–1941.* Boston: Little, Brown, 1976.

Hill, Howard C. *Roosevelt and the Caribbean.* Chicago: University of Chicago Press, 1927.

"Historians Rank Presidential Leadership in New C-SPAN Survey." CSPAN News release, 21 February 2000. http://www.americanpresidents. org/survey/amp022100.asp.

Historicus. "The Fifty Mile Order." *North American Review* 179 (February 1904): 235. Theodore Roosevelt Collection, Harvard University.

Hobsbawm, Eric. *The Age of Empire, 1875–1914.* New York: Vintage Books, 1989.

Holmstrum, Vladimir. "Great Britain on the War Path." In *Briton and Boer: Both Sides of the South African Question,* 269–286. New York: Harper and Brothers, 1900.

Hourani, Albert. *A History of the Arab Peoples.* London: Faber and Faber, 1991.

Hourihan, William J. "Marlinspike Diplomacy." *U.S. Naval Institute Proceedings* 105 (January 1979): 42–47.

———. "Roosevelt and the Sultans: The United States in the Mediterranean, 1904." Ph.D. diss., University of Massachusetts, 1975.

Howarth, Stephen. *To Shining Sea: A History of the United States Navy 1775–1998*. Norman: University of Oklahoma Press, 1991.

Iglehart, F. C. *Theodore Roosevelt: The Man as I Knew Him*. New York: Christian Herald, 1919.

James, William. *A Full and Correct Account of the Chief Naval Occurrences of the Late War between Great Britain and the United States of America; Preceded by a Cursory Examination of the American Accounts of Their Naval Actions Fought Previous to That Period: To Which Is Added an Appendix; with Plates*. London: T. Egerton, 1817.

Jentleson, Bruce W., and Thomas G. Paterson, eds. *Encyclopedia of U.S. Foreign Relations*. Vol. 3. New York: Oxford University Press, 1997.

Jessup, Philip C. *Elihu Root*. New York: Dodd, Mead, 1938.

Johnson, Arthur. "Theodore Roosevelt and the Navy." *U.S. Naval Institute Proceedings* 84, no. 10 (1958): 76–82.

Judd, Denis. *Balfour and the British Empire: A Study in Imperial Evolution*. New York: St. Martin's Press, 1968.

Judd, Denis, and Keith Surridge. *The Boer War*. London: John Murray, 2002.

Kajima, Morinosuke. *The Diplomacy of Japan*. Vol. 2. Tokyo: Kajima Institute of International Peace, 1978.

Karsten, Peter. "The Nature of 'Influence.'" *American Quarterly* 23 (Fall 1971): 89–97.

Keegan, John. *The Price of Admiralty*. New York: Viking Press, 1989.

Kennedy, Paul. "The Kaiser and German Weltpolitik." In *Kaiser Wilhelm II: New Interpretations: The Corfu Papers*, ed. John C. G. Röhl and Nicolaus Sombart, 143–168. Cambridge: Cambridge University Press, 1982.

———. *The Rise and Fall of Great Powers*. New York: Random House, 1987.

Kissinger, Henry. *Diplomacy*. New York: Simon & Schuster, 1994.

Kneer, Warren G. *Great Britain and the Caribbean*. East Lansing: Michigan State University Press, 1975.

Knox, Dudley W. *A History of the United States Navy*. New York: G. P. Putnam's Sons, 1936.

Kohut, Thomas A. "Kaiser Wilhelm II and His Parents." In *Kaiser Wilhelm II: New Interpretations: The Corfu Papers*, ed. John C. G. Röhl and Nicolaus Sombart, 63–89. Cambridge: Cambridge University Press.

LaFeber, Walter. *The American Age*. New York: W. W. Norton, 1989.

———. *The Cambridge History of American Foreign Policy*. Vol. 2. Cambridge, Mass.: Cambridge University Press, 1993.

―――. *The New Empire: An Interpretation of American Expansion, 1860–1898*. Ithaca, N.Y.: Cornell University Press, 1963.

Lambert, Nicholas A. *Sir John Fisher's Naval Revolution*. Columbia: University of South Carolina Press, 1999.

Langer, William L. *The Diplomacy of Imperialism, 1890–1902*. New York: Alfred A. Knopf, 1951.

Larsen, Peter. "Theodore Roosevelt and the Moroccan Crisis, 1904–1906." Ph.D. diss., Princeton University, 1984.

Liss, Sheldon B. *Diplomacy and Dependency: Venezuela, the United States, and the Americas*. Salisbury, N.C.: Documentary Publications, 1978.

Livermore, Seward. "The American Navy as a Factor in World Politics, 1903–1913." *American Historical Review* 63 (July 1958): 863–879.

―――. "Theodore Roosevelt, the American Navy, and the Venezuelan Crisis of 1902–03." *American Historical Review* 51 (October 1945): 452–471.

Mahan, Alfred T. *The Influence of Sea Power upon History, 1660–1783*. New York: Dover, 1987.

Malone, Dumas. *Dictionary of American Biography*. Vol. 3. New York, Scribner's, 1961.

Mann, Henry. "The Monroe Doctrine." *Harmsworth Self-Educator*, July 1907. Theodore Roosevelt Collection, Harvard University.

Marcosson, Isaac F. "Attorney-General Moody and His Work." *World's Work*, November 1906. Theodore Roosevelt Collection, Harvard University.

Marks, Frederick W. *Velvet on Iron*. Lincoln: University of Nebraska Press, 1979.

Massie, Robert K. *Dreadnought*. New York: Random House, 1991.

Maxwell, Gavin. *Lords of the Atlas*. London: Arrow Books, 1991.

"May 23, 1916 George Dewey Letter to Henry A. Wise." *New York Herald Tribune*, 27 September 1925, 9. Theodore Roosevelt Collection, Harvard University.

May, Ernest R. *American Imperialism*. New York: Atheneum, 1968.

―――. *Imperial Democracy*. New York: Harcourt, Brace and World, 1961.

McBeth, Brian S. *Gunboats, Corruption, and Claims: Foreign Investment in Venezuela, 1899–1908*. Westport, Conn.: Greenwood Press, 2001.

McCullough, David G. *Mornings on Horseback*. New York: Simon & Schuster, 1981.

―――. *The Path between the Seas: The Creation of the Panama Canal, 1870–1914*. New York: Simon & Schuster, 1977.

Merk, Frederick *Manifest Destiny and Mission in American History: A Reinterpretation.* New York: Alfred A. Knopf, 1963.

Metcalf, Clyde H. *History of the U.S. Marine Corps.* New York: G. P. Putnam's Sons, 1939.

Miller, Nathan *Theodore Roosevelt, a Life.* New York: William Morrow, 1992.

Morison, Elting E. *Admiral Sims and the Modern American Navy.* Boston: Houghton Mifflin, 1942.

Morris, Edmund. "A Few Pregnant Days." *Theodore Roosevelt Association Journal* 15, no.1 (1987): 2–13.

———. "A Matter of Extreme Urgency." *Naval War College Review* 55 (Spring 2002): 73–85.

———. *The Rise of Theodore Roosevelt.* New York: Coward, McCann and Geoghegan, 1979.

———. *Theodore Rex.* New York: Random House, 2001.

Mowry, George Edwin. *Theodore Roosevelt and the Progressive Movement.* New York: Hill and Wang, 1960.

Mulanax, Richard B. *The Boer War in American Politics and Diplomacy.* Lanham, Md.: University Press of America, 1994.

Navy Yearbook. New York: Duell, Sloan and Pearce, 1909.

Nevins, Allan. *Henry White: Thirty Years of American Diplomacy.* New York: Harper and Brothers, 1930.

Nish, Ian. *The Russo-Japanese War, 1904–5.* 8 vols. London: Global Oriental, 2003.

Nobel Peace Prize 1906 Presentation Speech by Gunnar Knudsen. http://nobelprize.org/peace/laureates/1906/press.html.

O'Gara, Gordon Carpenter. *Theodore Roosevelt and the Rise of the Modern Navy.* Princeton, N.J.: Princeton University Press, 1943.

Oyos, Matthew M. "Theodore Roosevelt and the Implements of War." *Journal of Military History* 60, no. 4 (1996): 631–655.

Parks, E. Taylor. *Colombia and the United States: 1765–1934.* Durham, N.C.: Duke University Press, 1935.

Penfield, W. L. "Anglo-German Intervention in Venezuela." *North American Review* 177 (July 1903): 86–96. Theodore Roosevelt Collection, Harvard University.

Pennell, C. R. *Morocco since 1830, a History.* New York: New York University Press, 2000.

Perdicaris, Ion. "In Raisuli's Hands: The Story of My Captivity and Deliverance, May 18th to June 26, 1904." *Leslie's Monthly Magazine* 7 (May 1906).

————. "Morocco, the Land of the Extreme West and the Story of My Captivity." *National Geographic* 17 (March 1906).

"Politics in the Panama Question." *Progress of the World, American Review of Reviews* 26 (February 1904): 141–146.

Posen, Barry R. *The Sources of Military Doctrine.* Ithaca, N.Y.: Cornell University Press, 1984.

Potter, E. B., and Chester Nimitz, eds. *Sea Power: A Naval History.* Englewood Cliffs, N.J.: Prentice-Hall, 1960.

Poundstone, Homer C. "Proposed Armament for Type Battleship of U.S. Navy, with Some Suggestions Relative to Armor Protection." *U.S. Naval Institute Proceedings* 29, no. 2 (1903): 377–411.

————. "Size of Battleships for U.S. Navy." *U.S. Naval Institute Proceedings* 29, no. 1 (1903): 161–174.

Pratt, Julius W. *A History of United States Foreign Policy.* Englewood Cliffs, N.J.: Prentice-Hall, 1958.

————. "The 'Large Policy' of 1898." *Mississippi Valley Historical Review* 19, no. 2 (1932): 219–242.

Pringle, Henry F. *Alfred E. Smith: A Critical Study.* New York: Macy-Masius, 1927.

————. *Big Frogs.* New York: Vanguard Press, 1928.

————. *Theodore Roosevelt, a Biography.* New York: Harcourt Brace, 1931.

"Progress of the World." *American Review of Reviews* (April 1902): [404]. Theodore Roosevelt Collection, Harvard University.

Puleston, Capt. W. D. *Mahan: The Life and Work of Captain Alfred T. Mahan, USN.* New Haven, Conn.: Yale University Press, 1939.

Randall, Peter E. *There Are No Victors Here.* Portsmouth, N.H.: Portsmouth Marine Society, 2002.

Renehan, Edward J. Jr. *The Lion's Pride: Theodore Roosevelt and His Family in Peace and War.* New York: Oxford University Press, 1998.

Resek, Carl. *The Progressives.* Indianapolis: Bobbs-Merrill, 1967.

Reter, Ronald. "The Real versus Rhetorical Theodore Roosevelt in Foreign Policy Making." Ph.D. diss., University of Georgia, 1973.

Reuterdahl, Henry. "The Needs of Our Navy." *McClure's Magazine* 30, no. 3 (1908): 251–263.

Review of Reviews 15, no. 5 (1897): 517–519. Theodore Roosevelt Collection, Harvard University.

Reynolds, Clark G. *Famous American Admirals.* Annapolis: Naval Institute Press, 1978.

Ricard, Serge. "Roosevelt Style Personal Diplomacy." In *Artists of Power: Theodore Roosevelt, Woodrow Wilson, and Their Enduring Impact on U.S. Foreign Policy,* ed. William N. Tilchin and Charles E. Neu. Westport, Conn.: Praeger Security International, 2006.

———. "Theodore Roosevelt et la Justification de l'Imperialisme." *Revue Française d'Etudes Americaines* 14 (May 1982): 277–289.

———. *Theodore Roosevelt et la Justification de l'Impérialisme.* Aix-en-Provence: Université de Provence, 1986.

Rippy, J. Fred. *The Caribbean Danger Zone.* New York: G. P. Putnam's Sons, 1940.

Robinson, Margaret. *Arbitration and the Hague Peace Conferences.* Philadelphia: University of Pennsylvania, 1936.

Robison, S. S., and Mary L. Robison. *A History of Naval Tactics from 1530 to 1930.* Annapolis: Naval Institute Press, 1942.

Röhl, John C. G. "The Emperor's New Clothes." In *Kaiser Wilhem II: New Interpretations: The Corfu Papers,* ed. John C. G. Röhl and Nicolaus Sombart, 23–61. Cambridge: Cambridge University Press, 1982.

Röhl, John C. G., and Nicolaus Sombart, eds. *Kaiser Wilhem II: New Interpretations: The Corfu Papers.* Cambridge: Cambridge University Press, 1982.

"Roosevelt and Venezuela." *New York Herald Tribune,* 27 September 1925, 26.

Roosevelt, Theodore. *American Ideals, the Strenuous Life.* Vol. 13 of *The Works of Theodore Roosevelt,* National Edition. New York: Scribner's, 1926.

———. *The Naval War of 1812.* Vol. 2 of *The Works of Theodore Roosevelt,* National Edition. New York: Scribner's, 1926.

———. *Thomas Hart Benton. Gouverneur Morris.* Vol. 7 of *The Works of Theodore Roosevelt,* National Edition. New York: Scribner's, 1926.

Rosen, Roman. *Forty Years of Diplomacy.* 2 vols. New York: Alfred A. Knopf, 1922.

Schelling, Thomas C. *Arms and Influence.* New Haven, Conn.: Yale University Press, 1966.

———. *The Strategy of Conflict.* New York: Oxford University Press, 1963.

Schoonover, Thomas. "Research Note: Max Farrand's Memorandum on the U.S. Role in the Panamanian Revolution of 1903." *Diplomatic History* 12 (Fall 1988): 501–506.

Seager, Robert. "Ten Years before Mahan." *Mississippi Valley Historical Review,* 40, no. 3 (1953): 491–512.

Sellen, Robert W. "The Just Man Armed: Theodore Roosevelt on War." *Military Review* 39 (May 1959): 33–44.

Seymour, Charles. *The Diplomatic Background of the War.* New Haven, Conn.: Yale University Press, 1916.

Sims, William S. "Roosevelt and the Navy, Part 1." *McClure's Magazine* 54, no. 9 (1922): 32–41.

———. "Roosevelt and the Navy, Part 2." *McClure's Magazine* 54, no. 10 (1922): 56–60, 78.

———. "Theodore Roosevelt at Work." *McClure's Magazine* 54, no. 11 (1923): 61–66, 95–101.

Smith, Elbert B. *Magnificent Missourian: Thomas Hart Benton.* Philadelphia: Lippincott, 1957.

Spector, Ronald. *Admiral of the New Empire.* Baton Rouge: Louisiana State University Press, 1974.

———. "Roosevelt, the Navy, and the Venezuela Controversy: 1902–1903." *American Neptune* 32 (October 1972): 257–263.

Sprout, Harold, and Margaret Sprout. *The Rise of American Naval Power, 1776–1918.* Princeton, N.J.: Princeton University Press, 1939.

Steiner, Zara S. *Britain and the Origins of the First World War.* New York: St. Martin's Press, 1977.

Storer, Mrs. Bellamy. "How Theodore Roosevelt Was Appointed Assistant Secretary of the Navy." *Harper's Magazine,* 1 June 1912, 8–9. Theodore Roosevelt Collection, Harvard University.

Sumida, Jon T. *In Defence of Naval Supremacy.* Boston: Unwin Hyman, 1989.

Takeuchi, Tatsuji. *War and Diplomacy in the Japanese Empire.* New York: Doubleday, 1935.

Thayer, William R. *Life and Letters of John Hay.* Boston: Houghton Mifflin, 1915.

———. *Theodore Roosevelt.* New York: Grosset and Dunlap, 1919.

Tilchin, William N. *Theodore Roosevelt and the British Empire: A Study in Presidential Statecraft.* Franklin and Eleanor Roosevelt Institute Series on Diplomatic and Economic History. New York: St. Martin's Press, 1997.

Tilchin, William, and Charles Neu, eds. *Artists of Power: Theodore Roosevelt, Woodrow Wilson, and Their Enduring Impact on U.S. Foreign Policy.* Westport, Conn.: Praeger Security International, 2006.

Titherington, T. H. "The Great Peace Conference." *Munsey's Magazine* 33, no. 6 (1905): 642.

Trani, Eugene P. "The Treaty of Portsmouth: An Adventure in Rooseveltian Diplomacy." Ph.D. diss., Indiana University, 1966.

Tuchman, Barbara W. "Perdicaris Alive or Raisuli Dead."*American Heritage* 10, no. 5 (1959): 18–21, 98–101.

Turk, Richard W. *The Ambiguous Relationship: Theodore Roosevelt and Alfred Thayer Mahan.* New York: Greenwood Press, 1987.

————."The United States Navy and the 'Taking' of Panama, 1901–1903." *Military Affairs* 38, no. 3 (1974): 92–96.

Vivian, James F. "The 'Taking' of the Panama Canal Zone: Myth and Reality." *Diplomatic History* 4 (1980): 95–100.

Wagenknecht, Edward. *The Seven Worlds of Theodore Roosevelt.* New York: Longman, Green, 1958.

Warner, Oliver. *Great Sea Battles.* New York: Macmillan, 1963.

Weibull, Jorgen W. *Evolutionary Game Theory.* Cambridge, Mass.: MIT Press, 1997

Weisberger, Bernard A. "The Strange Affair of the Taking of the Panama Canal Zone." *American Heritage* 27, no. 6 (1976): 6–11, 68–77.

West, Richard S. *Admirals of American Empire.* Indianapolis: Bobbs-Merrill, 1948.

Widenor, William C. *Henry Cabot Lodge and the Search for an American Foreign Policy.* Berkeley: University of California Press, 1980.

Wilson, H. W. *The Downfall of Spain: A Naval History of the Spanish American War.* London: Low, Marsten, 1900.

Wimmel, Kenneth. *Theodore Roosevelt and the Great White Fleet.* Washington, D.C.: Brassey's, 1998.

Wister, Owen. *Roosevelt: The Story of a Friendship.* New York: Macmillan, 1930.

Witte, Serge I. "Memoirs: My Visit to America." *World's Work* (March 1921): 484–496. Theodore Roosevelt Collection, Harvard University.

Woolman, David. "Did Theodore Roosevelt Overreact When an American Was Kidnapped in Morocco?" *Military History* (October 1997).

"World Cruise of the Great White Fleet." *U.S. Naval Institute Proceedings* 84, no. 10 (1958): 87–93. Theodore Roosevelt Collection, Harvard University.

Zimmermann, Warren. *First Great Triumph: How Five Americans Made Their Country a World Power.* New York: Farrar, Straus and Giroux, 2002.

Index

Adams, Henry, 1, 21
Adams, John Quincy, 29
Afghanistan, 171
aircraft, 151, 153, 154, 172
aircraft carriers, 172, 173
Alabama (battleship), 42, 46
Alabama (Civil War-era ship), 3
Alger, Phillip, 149–50
American Historical Association, 1
ammunition, 20–21
Antioquia (Colombia), 71
arbitration, 40, 167
Argentina, 156–57, 164
Arkansas, 150
arms limitation negotiations, 147
Asiatic Fleet, xv
Asiatic Squadron, 19
Atlanta, 42, 46, 63, 70, 71, 84, 87, 134
Atlantic Fleet: bases to support, xv; coal
    for, xiii, xv, 156, 157, 159; communica-
    tion within fleet, 155–56; Dewey as
    commander, 35–36; diplomatic benefits
    of circumnavigation, 156–58, 160–62;
    displacement weight, xiii; division of,
    xv–xvi; exercises in Caribbean, 41, 46,
    170–71; Great White Fleet, naming of,
    155; gunnery drills, 158, 159; guns on,
    xiii; itinerary and refueling require-
    ments, xvi; mine-laying exercises, 159;
    Monroe Doctrine and, 156–59; move-
    ment to the Pacific Ocean, xiii–xvi,
    147–48, 155–59; Pacific Ocean cruise,
    160–61; positioning of, 19; repaint-
    ing of, 163; return to Atlantic Coast,
    155–56, 158–59, 162–63; supplies for, xv;
    training exercise plan, xv; West Coast
    arrival, 159–60
Australia, 159, 160

Balfour, Arthur, 39, 47–48, 53
Baltimore, 84, 90
Barker, Albert S., 83, 84
Battle Efficiency, 139
Battleship Squadron, 83, 84
battleships: construction of, 16, 134, 135–36,
    143–44, 146–48, 159; construction of,
    stand down from, 144–46; cruising
    range, 135; design of, 137–38, 140–46,
    148–50, 154, 172; design process,
    135–36; division of fleet, xv–xvi, 163;
    Dreadnought-style battleships, 146–47;
    fleet strength proposal, 17, 135; fleet-
    support infrastructure, 15–16, 17; guns
    on, 134, 135, 137–38, 141–46, 149–50,
    154, 172; naval power role of, 143; strat-
    egy for using, 16; technological trans-
    formation of, 133–34; turret design,
    135–36, 137, 138, 140–41
Beaupré, Arthur M., 56, 57, 69
Bennington, 111
Benton, Thomas Hart, 6–7
Biddle, W. P., 75
Bliss, Cornelius, 82
Bonaparte, Charles J., 111–12
Boston, 63, 70–71, 134
Bowen, Herbert, 40
Bradford, Royal, 143
Brazil, xvi, 156
Brooklyn, 84, 86, 88, 99
Bulloch, Irvine, 3
Bulloch, James, 3, 4
Bunau-Varilla, Philippe, 58–59, 62, 63–64, 68
Bunz, Karl, 44
Butler, Smedley D., 37, 77

Camp Roosevelt, 33
Canada, 29, 164, 171

Canada (France), 68–69

Caribbean Sea: British possessions in, defense of, 52–53, 164; communication with fleet in, 45, 46; Culebra Island naval base, 33; exercises in, 32, 34, 35–36, 37–38, 41–47, 50–51, 170–71; exercises in, success of, 49; fleet support for ships in, 43; Marine Corps exercises in, 37–38; Navy control of, 32–33

Caribbean Squadron, 41, 42

carrier strike groups, 173

Cartagena (Colombia), 65

Castine, 84, 97, 99

Castro, Cipriano, 28–29, 32, 33, 40

Chadwick, French E.: British battleship, request for, 93, 95; career of, 87; death of, 102; Moroccan force, 95; Morocco, accolades for, 101; Morocco, arrival in, 86–87; Morocco, assessment of situation in, 88, 90, 91, 103; Morocco, military solution in, 97–100; Morocco, negotiations in, 93, 94–95; Morocco, protection of U.S. interests in, 91–92; South Atlantic Squadron command, 83, 84; Spanish-American War success of, 87; writings by, 87, 102

Chandler, Lloyd, 42, 46

Charybis (Great Britain), 47

Chicago, 42, 46, 134

Chile, 134, 156, 157

China, 32, 104, 161

Civil War: Roosevelt family division over, 2–3; ship design from, 133, 134, 135; veterans of, 18, 37, 87, 159

Cleveland, 84, 90, 97

coal, xiii, xv, 19–20, 134, 156, 157, 159

coastal defense strategies, 7, 22, 135, 172

coercive diplomacy: Colombia and, 81; definition, 168; Japan and, xiii–xvi; Roosevelt's use of, 168–70; Venezuelan Crisis, 25–26

Coghlan, Joseph B., 38, 41, 42, 46, 68–69, 71, 76

Colombia: bribes to buy canal treaty votes, 56–57; canal treaty confirmation, 55–57; Colón, Colombian troops in, 65–66; intelligence gathering in, 59–62; occupation of, preparations for, 54–55, 73–78, 80–81, 171; Panama, withdrawal of troops from, 78–79; Panama Canal treaty rejection, 61, 81; Panama's revolution against, 54–55, 67–72, 171; recall of minister to, 69; troop movement in Panama, 70–72; troop movement, interference with, 72

Concord, 63, 70

conflict. *See* war and conflict

Connecticut and *Connecticut*-class battleships, xiii, 141, 143, 144

Corbett, Julian, 144–45

Crowninshield, A. S., 41, 42, 46

C-SPAN, 1–2

Cuba: Chadwick and success at, 87; Cuban Missile Crisis, 170; fleet positioning near, 18; foreign policy toward, 14; Kettle Hill charge, 23; *Maine* sinking in Havana harbor, 19, 21, 137; Navy control of Caribbean, 32

Culebra Island, 33, 38, 50

Delaware, 146, 147, 148, 149

desertion rates, 43

destroyers, 151–52, 154, 172

Dewey, George: as Asiatic Squadron commander, 19; as Atlantic Fleet commander, 35–36; battleships, design of, 143; east coast, return to, 49; fleet expansion proposal, 141; fleet positioning message to, 21; General Board membership, xiv–xv, 32; naval exercises in Caribbean, 35–36, 39, 41–47, 50–51; naval exercises, planning for, 34; Navy control of Caribbean, 32; opinion of Germany, 38; Roosevelt's opinion of, 49; schedule of, 35; White House dinner, 38

Dewey, George, Jr., 49, 50

Dewey, Mildred, 38, 39, 50
diplomacy. *See* foreign policy and
    diplomacy
Diplomatic History (Mitchell), 27
Dixie, 63, 66, 73, 74, 75, 80
Dolphin, 36, 115, 117, 118, 134
domestic politics, 164–66, 175
Dorn, Edward, 97, 99
Dreadnought (Great Britain), 145
Dreadnought-style battleships, 133

economic interests and trade, 8, 166–67
Ehrman, Felix, 60–61
Elliott, George F., 73–78, 79, 112, 119
Empire of Liberty, 166
European Squadron, 41–42, 83, 84, 89–90
Evans, Robley "Fighting Bob": as Atlantic
    Fleet commander, xiii; Atlantic Fleet
    move to Pacific Coast, 156–59; career
    of, xiii; Chile incident, 157; commu-
    nication with fleet, 155–56; General
    Board membership, 31; guns on battle-
    ships, 142; health of, 159; naval expan-
    sion, support for, 31; port authorities,
    meetings with, xvi; retirement of, 159
expansionist movement, 5
Expeditionary Strike Groups (ESGs), 171, 175

Fisher, John "Jackie," 145, 160, 170
Florida, 148, 149
foreign policy and diplomacy: American
    interests and, 166–68; Atlantic Fleet
    circumnavigation, 156–58, 160–62;
    back-channel communications, 52,
    106–7, 108, 130; big stick aspect of,
    xvi–xvii, 53, 131, 169; domestic politics
    and, 164–66, 175; elements of, 108;
    manifest destiny, 6–7; military power
    and, 7, 175; Monroe Doctrine, 9–11,
    17, 23, 53, 156–59, 165, 169, 176; in
    Morocco, 102–3; naval power and, xvi,
    xvii, 7, 132, 169–70, 175; naval services,
    role of in, 130–31; reputation as expert
    in, 2; Root-Takahira Agreement, 161;

show-the-flag tour of Mediterranean,
    83–84; speak softly aspect of, xvi–xvii,
    131; style of Roosevelt, 129–31
Four Block War, 174
France, 30, 92–93, 95, 96–97, 151
frigates, 172

George, Alexander L., 168
Germany: China, temporary occupation
    of, 32; *Dreadnought*-style battleships,
    145; expansionist interests of, 169;
    immigrant population in Venezuela,
    33–34; imperialist plans of, 32, 34–35,
    40, 48, 51–52; Morocco, reaction to
    naval power in, 93; naval order of
    battle, 30; Panama Canal, bidding for,
    57, 59; Venezuela, arbitration offer,
    25–26, 40–41, 44, 48, 51–52, 170–71;
    Venezuela, blockade of, 38, 39, 40;
    Venezuela, temporary occupation of,
    31–32; Venezuelan Crisis, diplomatic
    negotiations over, 28; Venezuelan
    Crisis, diplomatic records about, 27;
    Venezuelan loan defaults, 28–30; war,
    profit from, 32
Glass, Henry, 67, 68, 69–73, 76, 77
Gouverneur Morris (Roosevelt), 6
Great Britain: colonial expansion in
    Venezuela, 28; defensibility of posses-
    sions of, 52–53; Empire, defense of,
    52–53, 160, 164; Morocco, battleship
    to influence, 92, 93, 95, 101; Morocco,
    negotiations with about, 96–97; naval
    order of battle, 30; naval power of, 10,
    29, 133, 143, 164; Portsmouth peace
    conference, request for involvement
    in, 120–21; seizure of territory by, 10;
    technological modernization of navy,
    145; U.S., relationship with, 29, 39,
    47–48, 53, 164; Venezuela, arbitra-
    tion offer, 40, 47–48, 52–53, 170–71;
    Venezuela, blockade of, 38, 39, 40;
    Venezuela, temporary occupation of,
    31–32; Venezuelan Crisis, diplomatic

negotiations over, 28; Venezuelan Crisis, diplomatic records about, 27; Venezuelan Crisis, participation in, 39; Venezuelan loan defaults, 10, 28–30

Great White Fleet, 155. *See also* Atlantic Fleet

Gummeré, Samuel René, 82–83, 85, 88, 93–94, 96, 99–100, 102, 103

guns and weapons: on battleships, xiii, 134, 135, 137–38, 141–46, 149–50, 154, 172; continuous aim technique, 138, 139, 140, 142; gunnery drills, 18, 20, 137–38, 158, 159; marksmanship and gunnery procedures, 138–40; naval gun development, 20; replacement of obsolete, 17

The Hague, 40, 167

Hannibal, 63

Harris, Walter, 84–85, 89, 102

Hartford, 20

Hawaii, 9, 14, 16, 17, 19, 104

Hay, John: biography of, 25, 51; death of, 111, 129; Germany and profits from war, 32; health of, 111; Monroe Doctrine and Venezuela, 30; Morocco, letter to sultan, 90; Morocco, transport of citizens out of, 89; Navy squadron, mission of, 85; Panama, defense of, 78; Panama, revolution in, 62, 67; Panama Canal concessions, 57; Panama Canal treaty, 23, 56, 68; Perdicaris, citizenship of, 91, 100; Perdicaris, thank you from, 101; Perdicaris cable, 83, 100; Raisuli's demands, 96; recall of minister to Colombia, 69; show-the-flag tour of Mediterranean, 83; Venezuela, blockade of, 39

Henderson, Archibald, 74

Herbert, Michael, 39, 47

Higginson, Francis J., 38, 41, 42, 46

Hill, Henry C., 27

Hobart, Garret, 23

Holland, John, 172

Hubbard, John, 62–63, 65–66

Hughes, John F., 79

Humphrey, Chauncey "Thomas" B., 59–62, 65, 80

Hunt, Gailand, 100

Idaho, 141

Illinois and *Illinois*-class battleships, 42, 46, 137, 141, 159

Indiana, 42, 46, 135

The Influence of Sea Power upon History: 1660—1783 (Mahan), 8

international institutions, 167–68

International Monetary Fund, 167

ironclads, 133

Italy, 28–30

Ito Hirobumi, 109

Jackson, Andrew, 6

Jamaica, 156

Japan: Atlantic Fleet cruise, 160–61; carrier strike groups to meet threat of, 173; color of fleet, 163; expansionist interests of, 169; immigration policies in U.S. and, xiii–xiv; indemnity payment demand, 120–21, 124, 125–29; mediation between Russia and, 105–7; naval buildup to counter war talk by, 161; naval order of battle, 30; peace treaty with Russia, 104–5, 129 (*see also* Portsmouth peace conference); power of, 105–6; Root-Takahira Agreement, 161; Russia, defeat of, 104; sea battles in Russo-Japanese War, 142, 144–45, 151; treatment as lesser race, xiv; war talk by, xiv

Jefferson, Thomas, 6, 7, 166

Jeune Ecole (Young School), 151

Jewell, Theodore F., 83, 84, 90, 91

Jones, John Paul, 111–12

Kaneko, Kentaro, 104, 109, 124–25, 127, 129, 130

Kansas, 141

Kearsarge (Civil War-era ship), 3

Kearsarge and *Kearsarge*-class battleships, xiii, 42, 46, 135, 137

Kentucky and *Kentucky*-class battleships, 135–36, 137, 140

Key, Albert, 148

Key West, 19

Kimball, William W., 16, 17, 19, 151

Komura, Jutaro, 110, 117, 120, 121–22, 123–24, 127, 128–29

Lamsdorff, Vladimir, 109

Langley, Samuel P., 151, 172

Lansdowne, Henry, 39, 48, 53

Large Policy, 9–10

League of Nations, 167

Lee, Arthur, 36

Lejeune, John A., 66, 73, 75, 79

Livermore, Seward, 27

Lodge, Henry Cabot: Assistant Secretary of the Navy appointment, 12; battleship construction, stand down from, 146; Congressional career of, 9; early life of, 9; Germany's opinion of U.S., 51; gunnery drills, 137; Hay treaty, opposition to, 23; Large Policy, 9–10; Republican Party platform, 82; Roosevelt, relationship with, 9; Taft presidency, 163

Long, John D.: farm, return to, 15; fleet positioning, authorization for, 22; naval exercises, planning for, 34; naval expansion, acceptance of, 17; naval expansion, skepticism of need for, 16–17, 136; opinion of Roosevelt, 12–13, 21; resignation of, 35, 50; ship design decisions, 138–39; war preparation, inaction on, 19, 22

Loomis, Francis, 85, 89

Louisiana, 54

Lucas, Louis C., 75

Luce, Stephen B., 5–6

Machias, 42, 46, 87

Madison, James, 7

Mahan, Alfred Thayer: battleship fleet, division of, xv; early life of, 8; elements of sea power, 5; fleet-support infrastructure, 15–16; General Board membership, xiv; guns on battleships, 141–42; *The Influence of Sea Power upon History: 1660—1783*, 8; naval expansion, support for, 16–17; as Naval War College president, 6; Roosevelt, relationship with, 8; sea battles in Russo-Japanese War, 145; technological improvements, appreciation of, 132–33

Mahoney. James E., 75

Maine, 19, 21, 137

Maine (battleship), 63, 67, 134

manifest destiny, 6–7

Marblehead, 63, 68

Marietta, 42, 46, 47, 84, 87, 97

Marroquín, José, 56, 67

Massachusetts, 42, 46, 135

Mayflower: Atlantic Fleet review, xiii, 155, 162–63; as Dewey's flagship, 36, 46; east coast, return to, 49; engineering plant refit, 111; marksmanship experiments, 139–40; Portsmouth peace conference, 115, 117–18

McKinley, William: Army career of, 18; death of, 23; fleet management report, 136; fleet positioning, authorization for, 22; Monroe Doctrine and Venezuela, 30; naval expansion, Roosevelt's call for, 14–15; Navy future, indifference about, 18; opinion of Roosevelt, 12; passive assent of, 18; reelection of, 23; war preparation, inaction on, 22

McLane, John, 108, 119

Mead, William W.: gala social event for delegations, 124; Marines' ceremonial presence, 119; peace conference arrangements, 112; peace conference security, 112–14; protocol for rank of delegations, 115–16, 130; telephone and telegraph capabilities, 114–15; transportation for delegations, 115–16; U.S. representatives at peace conference, 111

Mediterranean Sea: Atlantic Fleet cruise, 161–62; show-the-flag tour of, 83–84, 85–87

Meiji, Emperor, 128, 161

Metcalf, Victor, 158–59

Mexico, 158–59

Meyer, George von Lengerke, 106, 107, 125–26

Michigan, 144

military power, foreign policy and, 7, 175. *See also* naval power

Miller, William G., 77

mine-laying exercises, 159

Minnesota, 141, 163

Mississippi, 141

Missouri, 140

Mitchell, Nancy, 27

Monocacy, 21

Monroe, James, 29

Monroe Doctrine: Atlantic Fleet cruise and, 156–59; foreign policy based on, 9–11, 17, 23, 53, 156–59, 165, 169, 176; Great Britain's naval power to enforce, 10, 29; legitimacy of, 35; Panama Canal and, 23; respect for, 48–49; Roosevelt's interpretation of, 30, 52, 158; Venezuelan Crisis and, 10–11, 29–30

Moody, William H.: career of, 35; Colombia, offensive against, 77; communication with fleet, 45, 46, 47, 49, 51; desertion rates request, 43; *Missouri* accident, 140; naval expansion, 141; Panama, defensive role in, 72–74; Secretary of the Navy appointment, 35, 50; Venezuela, survey of coast of, 37

Morocco: chaos and lawlessness in, 84–85, 91–92, 173; diplomatic negotiations, 93, 96–97, 98, 102–3; government of, 94, 102; intelligence gathering resources in, 173–74; international negotiations, 96–97; kidnap victims, release of, 101; kidnapping in, 82, 102; military solution in, 96, 97–100, 101; Moroccan force, 95–96; naval power, influence on, 90; naval power, international reaction to, 92–93, 95; naval power, show of in, 82–83, 85–87, 102–3; Raisuli's demands, 88–89, 94–95, 96; release of kidnap victims, 98; South Atlantic Squadron arrival, 86–87

Morrell, Henry, 97

Morris, Gouverneur, 6

Morton, Paul, 142

Mouravioff, Michael, 109

Mr. Midshipman Easy (Marryatt), 3

Murphy, Grayson M. P., 59–62, 80

Myers, John Twiggs "Handsome Jack," 97–98, 99

Nashville, 42, 46, 62–63, 64–66, 70

national power: economic interests and trade and, 8, 166–67; Monroe Doctrine and, 9–11; naval power and, 7–11, 51–52, 86, 167; Roosevelt's establishment of, 164–65

naval forces. *See* U.S. Marine Corps; U.S. Navy

Naval Intelligence, Office of, 16, 114

naval policy: fleet-based strategy, 152–53; passive policy of Jefferson, 7; reputation as expert in, 2

naval power: battleships, role of in, 143; control of, 146–47; foreign policy and, xvi, xvii, 7, 132, 169–70, 175; of Great Britain, 10, 29, 133, 143, 164; international reaction to, 92–93, 95; limits of, 173–75; national power and, 7–11, 51–52, 86, 167; Perdicaris' citizenship and, 101; show of in Morocco, 82–83, 85–87, 102–3; show-the-flag tour of Mediterranean, 83–84; support for, 136–37; transformation of, 139

Naval War College, 5–6, 13–15, 168

The Naval War of 1812 (Roosevelt), 1, 4–6, 11

Navigation, Bureau of, 36–37, 50

Nelidoff, Alexander I., 109

New Hampshire, 142, 143

New Hampshire National Guard, 119

New York, 138

New Zealand, 160

Newberry, Truman, 147, 149–50

Newport ship design conference, 148–50

Nicholas II, 40, 105, 106–7, 122–23, 124, 125–26, 127, 129

Nicholson, Arthur, 93

Nobel Peace Prize, 105, 129

North Atlantic Squadron, 41, 42

North Dakota, 147, 148, 149

O'Laughlin, John Callan "Cal," 123, 126, 127, 128

Olympia, 42, 46, 68, 84, 90

O'Neil, Charles, 143

Oregon, 135

Orinoco (Colombia), 66

Ortiz, Daniel, 71

"over, under, or through" game, 176

Panama: Colombian troop movement, 70–72; Colombian troop withdrawal, 78–79; Colón, Colombian troops in, 65–66; defensive role of U.S. military, 71–73, 76, 80–81; intelligence gathering in, 59–62; prevention of landing in, 67, 69; revolution in, 54–55, 58–59, 60–62; revolution in, U.S. support for, 62–72, 78, 79–81, 171

Panama Canal: bidding for canal concession, 57, 59; completion of and division of fleet, 163; fortification of, 23; lease term, 57, 68; payments for, 56–57, 60, 68; Roosevelt's travel through, 54; treaty to create, 23, 54–58, 60, 68, 81; treaty to create, rejection of, 61, 81; treaty to create, signing of, 68; withdrawal of troops from, 78–79

peace, preparation for war as guarantee of, 13–14, 17, 168–70

Pearson, Edward N., 108

Peirce, Herbert H. D.: building for peace conference, 112; gala social event for delegations, 124; Nobel Peace Prize

acceptance, 129; peace conference communications, 128; peace conference location selection, 107–8; peace conference reports, 123; peace conference success, 129; reception for delegations, 116–18; U.S. representatives at peace conference, 111

Pelayo (Spain), 92

Perdicaris, Ion, 173–74; citizenship of, 91, 100, 101; health of, 94; kidnapping of, 82, 85, 86; release of, 98, 101; writings by, 84

Peru, 134, 156

Philadelphia, 20

Philippines: Atlantic Fleet cruise, 159, 160; fleet positioning near, 18, 19, 21; Germany's imperialist interest in, 34–35; Manila Bay battle, 32, 34, 38; Root-Takahira Agreement, 161; Subic Bay, coal supply in, xv; Subic Bay, fortification of, 104

Plunger, 152

Pope, Percival C., 37, 45

Portsmouth peace conference, 105; arrival of delegations, 119; authority of delegations, 110–11, 120, 126; building for, 112; communications capabilities, 114–15; communications monitoring, 114, 128; composition of delegations, 108–10; gala social event for delegations, 124; Great Britain, request for involvement in conference, 120–21; indemnity payment demand, 120–21, 124, 125–29; Marines' ceremonial presence, 119, 130; negotiations at, 119–29; negotiations at, Roosevelt's participation in, 124–29, 130; Nobel Peace Prize for, 105, 129; peace treaty signing, 129; Portsmouth Navy Yard, 108; press access to, 113–14; protocol for rank of delegations, 115–16, 119, 130; reception for delegations, 116–18; reports to Roosevelt about, 123; security for delegations, 112–14, 119; selection of site,

107–8; success of, 129; transportation for delegations, 115–18; U.S. representatives at, 111–12

Post, Augustus, 153

Poundstone, Homer C., 140–41, 143

Prairie, 37, 38, 46, 75

Prince of Wales (Great Britain), 92, 93, 95, 101

Pringle, Henry, 27

Puerto Rico, 32, 43

Qaida, al-, 174

Raisuli, Moulay Ahmad el, 82, 84–85, 87, 88–89, 94–95, 96, 102

Reagan, Ronald, 132

Reuterdahl, Henry, 148

Reyes, Rafael, 67–69, 71, 78

riverine defense strategies, 172

Roosevelt, Alice, 6

Roosevelt, Anna, 4

Roosevelt, Martha "Mittie" Bulloch, 2, 3

Roosevelt, Quentin, 153

Roosevelt, Theodore: African hunting trip, 163; Assistant Secretary of the Navy appointment, 11–13, 136; Assistant Secretary of the Navy duties, 13; Assistant Secretary of the Navy resignation, 22–23; battleship fleet, division of, xv–xvi; character of, xvii; death of, 163; devotion to duty, 13; election of, 82; family and early life of, 2–3; 1st U.S. Volunteer Regiment command, 23; *Gouverneur Morris*, 6; health of, 3; as hot weather Secretary, 15–17; imperialism of, 175–76; intellectual interests, 1–2; Lodge, relationship with, 9; Long's opinion of, 12–13; Mahan, relationship with, 8; McKinley's opinion of, 12; naval engagement strategy, xiv–xv; *The Naval War of 1812*, 1, 4–6, 11; as Navy patron, xvi; as New York governor, 23; Nobel Peace Prize for, 105, 129; opinion of Dewey, 49; physical

fitness of, 1; as president, 23–24; public service destiny, 7; response to Japan's war talk, xiii–xvi; review of Atlantic Fleet, xiii; sea, interest in, 3; social events at White House, 2; status of, xvi–xvii; strenuous life, 1, 175–76; *Thomas Hart Benton*, 6 7; urgency of actions, 21; as vice president, 23; vice president candidates, 82; war, enthusiasm for, 2; White House dinner, 38–39; Wilhelm II, relationship with, 26–27; *The Winning of the West*, 1

Roosevelt, Theodore, Sr., 2

Root, Elihu, 78, 80, 86, 111, 130, 157, 158

Root-Takahira Agreement, 161

Rosen, Roman, 109–10, 117, 118, 125

Rough Riders, 23

Russia: defeat of naval force, 104; mediation between Japan and, 105–7; peace treaty with Japan, 104–5, 129 (*see also* Portsmouth peace conference); sea battles in Russo-Japanese War, 142, 144–45, 151

Rye Beach, 114

sail-powered ships, 134

Sampson, William T., 87, 137

San Francisco, 20, 42, 46

Sargent, Nathan, 33–34, 36, 37

Scorpion, 33, 37, 42, 46

Scott, Percy, 138, 139

shipbuilding: funding for, 136; ship design process, 135–36; steel-hulled ships, 134; technological transformation of, 133–34, 154. *See also* battleships

Sicily, 162, 171

Sims, William S.: battleship design, 148–49; *Dreadnought* design, 145; guns on battleships, 140, 141, 142, 145; marksmanship and gunnery procedures, 44, 138–39; *Minnesota* command, 163; technology, Roosevelt's grasp of, 154; turret design, 135–36

soft power, 174

South Atlantic Squadron, 41–43, 84, 86–87, 97–98, 101

South Carolina, 144

Southerland, H. H., 97

Soviet Union, 173

Spain, 18, 19, 92

Spanish-American War, xiii, 16, 18–22, 87

Straus, Oscar S., 124

strenuous life, 1, 175–76

submarines, 152, 154, 172

Suez Canal, 155, 161

Sumner, George W., 41, 42–43, 46

Taft, William H., 162, 163

Takahari, Kogoro, 110, 117

Taylor, Henry C., 32, 36–37, 38, 44, 47, 50, 72, 79, 85

technology: advocacy for, 132–34, 137–38, 150–51, 153–54, 172; aircraft, 151, 153, 154, 172; balance of, 173; battleship design, 137–38, 140–46, 148–50; funding for, 173; to meet current threats, 173; progress in, 172–73; Royal Navy, technological modernization of, 145; submarines, 152, 154, 172; torpedo destroyers, 151–52, 154, 172; U.S. development of, 133

terrorism, 174–75

Texas, 46, 134

Thayer, William R., 25, 49, 51

"Theodore Roosevelt, the American Navy, and the Venezuelan Crisis of 1902—3" (Livermore), 27

Thomas Hart Benton (Roosevelt), 6–7

Togo, Heihachiro, 104, 105, 106, 144

Topaze (Great Britain), 40

torpedo destroyers, 151–52, 154, 172

Torpedo Flotilla, 42

Tracy, Benjamin, 135

Trinidad, 156

Turkey, 83, 86

Union League Club, 8

United Nations, 167

United States: anti-European attitude, 47; Asians, treatment of in, xiii–xiv; Great Britain, relationship with, 29, 39, 47–48, 53, 164; imperialism of, 175–76; interests and foreign policy development, 166–68; international conduct and fear of, 86; Japanese immigration to, xiii–xiv; Root-Takahira Agreement, 161; Venezuelan Crisis, diplomatic negotiations over, 28; Venezuelan Crisis, diplomatic records about, 27

U.S. Marine Corps: Colombia occupation, preparations for, 54–55, 73–78, 80–81; Colón position of, 66; exercises in Caribbean, 37–38; Expeditionary Strike Groups (ESGs), 171, 175; Four Block War, 174; hospital ward built by, 43; jungle warfare training, 45; Panama, outfitting of for, 75; Panama, training of for, 76–77; Panama, withdrawal from, 79; Portsmouth peace conference, ceremonial presence at, 119, 130; rescue operations training, 174; role in diplomacy, 130–31; scalability of response, 170–72

U.S. Navy: Assistant Secretary of the Navy appointment, 11–13; Assistant Secretary of the Navy duties, 13; battle group formations, 18; Benton's opposition to, 7; coastal defense strategies, 7, 22, 135, 172; exercises of, 18; expansion of, 7–11, 13–17, 49–50; expansion of, skepticism about, 16–17; Expeditionary Strike Groups (ESGs), 171, 175; fleet expansion proposal, 141; fleet management, 17–18, 85, 136; fleet positioning, 18, 19, 21–22, 136; fleet-based strategy, 152–53; fleet-support infrastructure, 15–16, 17, 19–20, 43; General Board, xiv–xv, 31, 32, 34, 141, 143; gunnery drills, 18, 20, 137–38; hot weather Secretary, 15–17; intelligence gathering resources, 173–74; intelligence reports from Navy vessels, 33–34, 37; naval engagement

strategy, xiv–xv; order of battle, 30; organization of, 36–37; ranking in world power, xiii, xvi, 134, 141, 144, 147; readiness of ships, 21; rescue operations training, 174; riverine defense strategies, 172; role in diplomacy, 130–31; Roosevelt as patron of, xvi; scalability of response, 170–72; ships, modernization of, 133–34, 154; technological transformation of, 133–34
Utah, 148, 149

Varley, Cromwell, 85, 92, 98
Venezuela: anti-American resentment, 33–34; arbitration offer, 40–41, 44, 47–48, 170–71; arbitration offer, coercion to accept, 25–26, 51–53; blockade of, 38, 39, 40; diplomatic negotiations, 25–26, 28; diplomatic records about, 27, 49; German colony in, 32, 40, 48; government of, 28; loan defaults by, 10, 28–30; military records about, 25, 28, 49–53; Monroe Doctrine to shield, 29–30; Roosevelt's recollection of, 25–27; survey of coast of, 37; temporary occupation of, 31–32
Vermont, 141
Vietnam, 169
Vineta (Germany), 47
Virginia-class battleships, 140
von Holleben, Theodor, 30, 34, 40–41, 44, 52
von Metternich, Paul, 39, 48
von Sternburg, Speck, 38

Walker, Asa, 46
Waller, L. W. T., 75, 79
war and conflict: avoidance of, 169–70, 174–75; peace, preparation for war as guarantee of, 13–14, 17, 168–70; preparation for, xvi; preparation for, naval expansion for, 7–11, 13–17; study of, 6; war contingency plans, 16, 17, 19; war of ideas, 174
War Portfolio No. I, 54–55, 73–79
"Washington's Forgotten Maxim" speech, 13–15, 168
weapons. *See* guns and weapons
Wilhelm II: German presence in South America, 34; Monroe Doctrine and, 30, 35; Roosevelt, relationship with, 26–27; Russia, mediation between Japan and, 107, 125, 127, 130; Venezuela Crisis, 30, 38, 39, 48, 52
Wilson, Woodrow, 167
The Winning of the West (Roosevelt), 1
Witte, Serge, 109, 110, 117–18, 120, 122–24, 125, 126, 127, 128–29, 130
Witzel, H., 65
Wood, Leonard, 38
World Bank, 167
World Court, 167
World War I, 27
Wright, Orville, 153
Wyoming and *Wyoming*-class battleships, 63, 71, 150, 154

Yorktown, 157
Young School (Jeune Ecole), 151

About the Author

Cdr. Henry J. Hendrix, USN, is a career naval officer currently assigned to the Office of the Under Secretary of Defense for Policy. In his twenty years of active service he has made six operational deployments, five in support of combat operations, and commanded a naval tactical air control squadron. An active writer, he has authored numerous articles in professional journals over the years and has earned advanced degrees from the Naval Postgraduate School and Harvard University, as well as a Ph.D. from King's College, London. He is married to his high school sweetheart and fellow Hooiser native, Penny Hendrix, and they have two daughters and make their home in northern Virginia.